CRY FOR JUSTICE

A TRUE STORY

DAMIR MISSBRENNER

SEVEN LOCKS PRESS
SANTA ANA, CALIFORNIA

While this is a work of non-fiction, no claim is made that all quoted conversations are derived from or based on verbatim memory. The quoted material is accurate in substance and the book recounts the private thoughts, feelings and impressions, opinions of his own and family's experiences, his opinions of others and his fair comment about issues of public concerns. All the names of minors mentioned herein have been changed with the exception of Adrian Missbrenner.

In an attempt to avoid and preempt any possible repercussions stemming from the information contained in this book, the publication thereof has purposely been postponed until the terms of the probation had been fully complied with. Individuals who are under the scrutiny of probation are easy victims of the slightest of indiscretions, whether real, suggested or fabricated.

Seven Locks Press
P.O. Box 25689
Santa Ana, CA 92799
(800) 354-5348

Individual sales: This book is available through most bookstores or can be ordered directly from Seven Locks Press at the address above.

Quantity Sales: Special discounts are available on quantity purchases by corporations, associations and others. For details, contact the "Special Sales Department" at the publisher's address above.

Cover & Interior Design Kira Fulks • www.kirafulks.com
Printed in the United States of America

Library of Congress Cataloging-in-Publication Data is available from the publisher

ISBN: 0-9801270-2-5   978-0-9801270-2-7

DEDICATION

———◆•◆◆•◆———

True love is the delicate, perennial miracle that blooms magnificently
after the harshest of winter storms.
True friendship is the shelter which offers warmth and comfort
during frenzied blizzards of adversity.
Blessed is he who finds the two in a lifetime.
I have been truly blessed.

To Dobrila.
My lover and my best friend,
who refused to accept anything but the truth and righteous vindication.
I.L.D. Forever.

ACKNOWLEDGMENTS

First and foremost, I wish to acknowledge Patrick M. Campanelli, our attorney, who has gone above and beyond all expectations and obligations during his personal involvement in my son's case. Calling it merely an involvement would be doing him injustice, for it was his personal intervention which brought about the verdict in the end. He has been our attorney, our adviser, confidant and trusted friend. I will forever be indebted to him for his dedication to our cause.

My heartfelt gratitude to Father Raymond F. Klees who has shown us the means by which to cope and to find the strength and perseverance to stay the course. At a time of our greatest need, he was the sole beacon—illuminating the path to our dormant faith that was needed for achieving our vindication.

My deepest thanks to Anita Pervan who has given me the courage and resolve to take that last leap of faith in voicing my opinions and channeling my rage. Her encouragement was invaluable and appreciated beyond mere words.

To my publisher, James C. Riordan, who believed in the integrity of my story and helped me bring it to light.

Lastly, I wish to thank all those individuals who had not formed an adverse opinion despite the constant assaults on my family's name and character. Herein again, I will forever cherish their friendship and support. Thank you, Ljubinka and Boris Corluka, Tomislav Gajovic, Zoran Stankovski, David Audino, Alice McGinley, Gina DeVeno, Robert Pervan, Vlado Milutinovic, and everyone who had kept us in their thoughts and prayers.

In the land of the blind, the one-eyed man is king.

Desiderius Erasmus

CONTENTS

CRY for JUSTICE

FOREWORD

<hr />

When the dark side of justice lashes out, it can inflict terrible wounds. In the suburbs of Chicago, Illinois, a tidal wave of law and disorder swept over a successful businessman whose son was accused of sexual crimes in 2002. Damir Missbrenner and his family suffered agony through more than three years of stunning charges, confusing legal mazes, a kidnapping leading to international intrigue, and twisted legal proceedings. The son attempted to flee from it all, but his journey turned out to be like escaping England aboard the Titanic.

This is the story of a father's desperate fight, using every fiber of his being to protect his son against overzealous actions by investigators and prosecutors.

In the American arena of criminal justice, courtroom battles aren't always what they should be. Our system is an adversarial one in which prosecutors and defenders conduct war. Both sides sometimes resort to the use of extreme measures to sway juries and win their cases.

Defense attorneys are paid to win. Verdicts of "not guilty" are their primary objectives.

Not everyone realizes that prosecutors, on the other hand, have no such mandate to win. A few have gained fame and public applause with reputations for never having lost a case. They are admired for being tough on crime and putting criminals behind bars. Yet, I have heard criticisms of these "winners" by their colleagues who say that such records smack of "cherry picking" the cases, choosing to prosecute only when the odds are on their sides.

The U. S. Supreme Court declared in 1935 that it is the prosecutor's duty not necessarily to win, but to seek justice. In Berger vs. the United States, the majority wrote, "The [prosecutor] is the representative not of an ordinary party to a controversy, but of a sovereignty whose obligation to govern impartially is as compelling as its obligation to govern at all; and whose interest, therefore, in a criminal prosecution is not that it shall win a case, but that justice shall be done. As such, he is in a peculiar and very definite sense the servant of the law, the twofold aim of which is that guilt shall not escape or innocence suffer. He may prosecute with earnestness and vigor-- indeed, he should do so. But, while he may strike hard blows, he is not at liberty to strike foul ones. It is as much his duty to refrain from improper methods calculated to produce a wrongful conviction as it is to use every legitimate means to bring about a just one."

In the real world, a great deal of pressure rests on prosecutors' shoulders. The public demands the apprehension and conviction of criminals, politicians clamor for justice, while victims' families pray that evildoers will be caught and punished. District Attorneys are elected officials and a voting constituency can be cruel regarding unpopular verdicts of "not guilty."

This quandary has sometimes led to disaster. An overzealous police investigator, combined with an ambitious prosecutor, is a dangerous combination.

Damir Missbrenner believes this is exactly what happened to him and his son.

Remarkably, a case nearly identical to Missbrenner's took place in Orange County, California at about the same time. Gregory Haidl, 18, the son of a wealthy public official, was charged with sexual assault of a 16-year-old girl in the Haidl home. He and two of his pals allegedly performed depraved sex acts on the intoxicated girl while she lay on a pool table. They compounded their problems by videotaping the encounter. News media thrived on the lurid details for months. When the trio of boys finally faced a jury, controversy raged. Their defense attorneys insisted that the young woman's life had been wrapped around parties, sex, drinking, and drugs, and that she had wanted to be a porn star. The defendants faced up to 55 years imprisonment if convicted. The jury, though, deadlocked and the judge declared a mistrial.

Unsatisfied, the District Attorney sought a second trial. In March 2005, all three defendants were found guilty of sexual assault, but acquitted of rape charges. One year later, all three were sentenced to serve six years in prison.

Of course, the most notorious of criminal cases that had mirrored this type of overzealous and unfounded prosecution in recent memory involved the Duke University Lacrosse players who had been accused of raping an exotic dancer at a rented dorm house in 2006. Motivated by a crumbling political career, the prosecutor, District Attorney Mike Nifong, needed a magic bullet to save his job in the upcoming elections. In the process he had committed a series of grievous errors in his obsessive pursuit to prove their guilt, as all supportive evidence was purely circumstantial if not speculative. Errors quickly turned to a cover-up, then fraud and finally deceit, as in the end he stood guilty of withholding evidence and obstructing justice. He was disbarred on June 16, 2007 and sentenced to one day in jail for criminal contempt of court. He was also fined $500.00. Their defense had cost the accused in excess of $3 million. A civil suit against the city of Durham had been initiated by the accused's families. Co-defendants in this suit are several members of the Durham police department for allegedly aiding and abetting Nifong during his investigation. On January 15, 2008, Nifong filed for bankruptcy, citing claims against him in excess of $180 million.

—Don Lasseter
Author and Journalist
2009

CHAPTER 1

ON THE RUN

There was nothing left to think about. He had been wracking his brain for the past two years, and the time to think had morphed into a time for action.

Adrian had mentally wrestled with every possible alternative to his predicament. An oft-used cliche from old western movies repeated itself in his mind. "There comes a time in a man's life, when a man has to do what a man has to do." When he considered what he had been taught, thought about advice he had received based on his family's intuition, and pondered the counsel by friends and even attorneys, it added up to only one conclusion. Only one course of action made sense.

He ran.

He embarked on a journey that would change his life forever; a transmigration which held no defined future and a past that no longer mattered. Uppermost in Adrian's mind, a single goal drove him: to escape from the present, away from this place, and most important of all, to find emancipation from his own mental agony.

Life during those past twenty-four months had been a dark and hazy nightmare in which his world no longer offered meaning, purpose or direction. It played out like an ongoing dream in which he saw himself as a spectator of surrealistic images symbolizing his past, present, and future, all unfolding in a formless world.

In the role of observer, he could see himself strutting on this stage of a Greek tragedy, in a matrix of morality, among a cast of vindictive prosecutors, tenacious attorneys, stoic judges and a frenzied, blood-thirsty news media. Unlike the script of a play or a movie, though, which generally contains an uplifting message, life's reality and con-sequences are seldom so well defined.

Time, he understood, moved at an immutable pace for everyone, but circumstances could accelerate the passage of hours and days into breathtaking speed, or make seconds crawl at an excruciating pace. Adrian, eager for the moment of departure, counted the hours and minutes, feeling the hands of time grasp his neck and slowly but surely choke the last breath of reality out of his body.

He thought that he had worked up the strength to accomplish this desperate voyage. Now, though, as he crouched in the rear seat of a dark sedan, listening to the staccato beat of rain, his power drained from him like water dripping off the car and swirling into a gutter. The two men sitting up front stared straight ahead into the night. Despite their presence, Adrian realized that he was suddenly all alone. For the first time in his life, he was all alone. No one to consult. No one to confide in. No one to cry with. He felt buried in an overwhelming sense of loneliness, under a shroud of utter fear, despair, and anguish.

It is not unusual for youths in their late teens to believe they have grown beyond the need for parents. An instinctive urge for independence is natural. Sometimes, though, smashing head-on into a lethal crisis brings a new understanding and appreciation of the protective shield endowed by mom and dad. Leaving that shield behind, Adrian felt an unfamiliar vulnerability. Separation from his family tore at his heart as the sedan accelerated through black pouring rain. He resisted the urge to look back toward the home that he might never see again. Instead, he slouched down in the rear seat of the car in an abject manner to make himself invisible. Invisible, not to any possible observer, but invisible to his own conscience.

Of all the emotions ripping through Adrian, one key issue was absent. He felt no sense of guilt for the criminal charges against him. The only thing bothering his conscience was his failure to say goodbye to his parents and four brothers, because in his mind he was convinced that he would never see them again. And there was so much that he wanted to tell them—that he loved them—that he was sorry for what had happened—that he was sorry for causing so much trouble and grief—that he was sorry for making promises to his father that he couldn't keep—that he was sorry for all the arguments—that he was sorry for not listening to all the advice—that he was sorry for ever being born. Trying to shake melancholia, Adrian focused on the windshield wipers' steady, wet, mesmerizing rhythm. Their soft, regular thud at the end of each arc seemed to keep time with the beat of music from the car's stereo speakers. If only life's problems could be wiped away so easily. At first, escape seemed like such a good idea, but now he wasn't sure that he had made the right decision. Hell, he wasn't sure of anything these days. His entire world was turned inside out and the only denominator common to all of his thoughts, beliefs and actions, was fear.

In his mind, he knew of only one logical outcome if he stayed and faced the crisis. The verdict would be "guilty" and he would go straight to prison for years or even decades. His defense attorney could not tell him how long, but they both knew that prosecutors would demand an unbearably long sentence.

Adrian had seen the inside of Stateville Prison during a school trip several months earlier. The stunning images still burned in his brain. He couldn't help but shiver with fear and disgust each time he envisioned the black-and-white images grotesquely illuminated by flickering fluorescent lights that exposed jagged cracks in the concrete floors. Massive steel doors and bars loomed everywhere in a maze of bare walls covered by peeling layers of paint, as if attempting to hide previous generations of pain and suffering. No book or movie could describe it; it took personal experience to fully appreciate the malignant, soulless existence in that bleak, gray world.

And yet the visual impact had been the least troublesome.

A vile odor infiltrated every corner with a nauseating stench of sweat, urine, and feces. Pungent disinfectant failed miserably to disguise the putrid fumes, creating instead an even more toxic effluvium.

Incessant noise reverberated from wall to wall, making the

environment even worse. A constant, incoherent chorus of shouts, screams, curses, and pleas echoed human despair, suggesting a descent back to the moral indifference and hopelessness of the Dark Ages.

That place was pure evil and mandated a fate worse than any punishment could possibly justify. In his mind, this clearly was a fate worse than death.

He was afraid of dying, and he knew that everyone dies at one point in time. However, in this place you died a little bit every day.

The entire, shattering experience resonated through Adrian's mind long after he had left Stateville that day. It was a place to be avoided at any cost. He vowed never to stagnate and crumble in prison, where a person's whole future is squandered and dismantled, and where he is simply left to die an agonizing death.

With this in mind, he listened to an offer by two men, and it seemed irresistible. "We'll get you to safety, and you will be a new man." They offered a clean getaway and outlined a plan in which timing and speed were essential to success. He continued to reassess his requirements. He had to wait until the home-confinement police officers completed their night check of his parents' house, then leave as soon as they were out of sight. Normally, this would give Adrian approximately eighteen hours before the next official visit, which usually took place shortly after his evening arrival at home from night classes. Eighteen hours to put as much distance as possible between himself and his past.

As usual, though, glitches turn up in plans, no matter how carefully they are constructed. The officers had failed to show up this evening. He was afraid to leave, yet could not afford to wait any longer. This had delayed his departure until after three o'clock in the morning. He reasoned that the disruption had occurred because his departure was taking place on the night after Labor Day. Apparently, the officers had extended their time off, but Adrian couldn't be certain. He worried that they might show up much later than usual.

Another recent incident had nearly upset everything. One of the other three boys facing charges with Adrian had vanished a week ago. It raised the specter of being shackled by an electronic monitor or, worse yet, kept in jail while waiting for the trial to start.

Thoughts of his friend's disappearance brought to Adrian's mind the painful memory of a recent discussion with his father, Damir. As they sat down to talk, Adrian fully expected a lecture about his buddy's decision to flee and the consequences of his misguided actions. The session didn't turn out that way at all. In a melancholy mood, his father had sipped from a glass of wine and reminisced about the past, randomly looking at old family photographs strewn across the table in front of them. That evening his father treated him like an adult for the first time. There was no lecture, no disparaging comments, no condescending advice.

Instead, there were tears, and the most devastating revelation Adrian could imagine. At first he stared at his father in disbelief, but based on the solemn expression in moist eyes, he listened and heard something for which he was completely unprepared.

That night, Adrian cried himself to sleep, haunted by the knowledge that the strongest person he had known in his entire life, the one person who could make all problems go away, the person who had not a single vindictive bone in his body and who always could make him laugh with a funny look or joke, was not invincible. Much less, he might not even be there when future problems emerged.

"If you run," his father had said, "You might not be able to attend my funeral." Adrian would never forget those words, nor would he forgive himself for knowing that he could not commit to the promise that had been asked of him.

The rain poured harder and both men in the front seat remained silent, the driver concentrating on navigating flooded streets. Adrian's thoughts raced as he forced himself to recall more pleasant memories and less tragic thoughts. Had the plan for escape not already been set in stone, and financial arrangements been made, he might have reconsidered in view of his father's plight. But he could now rationalize that the situation forced him to leave. It hadn't been easy to raise the money, and he couldn't believe that he had actually pawned some of his mother's expensive jewelry to fund his journey. But, he vowed to himself, he would somehow redeem the loss as soon as he could.

Trying to divert his mind from remorse and the gut-wrenching feeling that he would never see his family again, Adrian switched to thoughts of the immediate future. Even though the departure had been delayed, everything else seemed to be proceeding according to plan. One of the men helping him had warned, in a stern voice, "None of this can be noticed by anyone if it is to be successful." As far as Adrian knew, no one had noticed.

Two plastic trash bags lay crammed on the floor in front of him, which represented the sum total of the meager accomplishments his young life had to offer as proof of his tenuous existence. He hadn't been able to risk using real luggage, so he had stuffed minimal clothing and personal gear into the bags, with only minimal room for sentimental possessions.

Adrian commenced a new chapter in his life, a flight to freedom which would take him on a journey with no specific destination, no known direction and no defined duration. A race toward uncertainty, at a speed without velocity or acceleration. He turned his head and used his sleeve to wipe away a thin layer of condensation on the car's window in a vain effort to prolong his view of the faint flicker of his home's front door lights, which slowly disappeared into the rainy night.

This trip had only begun, and he was already drained by the remorseful thoughts bombarding his mind. He kept reassuring himself, over and over, that he had made the right decision. Time had run out, and time was of the essence.

"Time . . . time . . . time . . . ," repeatedly crossed his lips in a low whisper, as he attempted to keep his thoughts focused. Adrian's father enjoyed memorizing colorful and profound phrases, proverbs, precepts, or platitudes; any expression of wisdom. Several axioms regarding time popped into the son's memory.

"Time heals all wounds," elicited a slight and wishful smile.

"Time waits for no man," confirmed the conviction of his actions.

"Only time will tell," alluded to his predicament.

"Time is wasted on the young."

And while he settled in for his long trip ahead, he realized that time was truly the only irreplaceable commodity in life.

CHAPTER 2

———•——•+—•———

FUGITIVE OR HOSTAGE?

Iwould normally not answer my cell phone unless the caller's identity was displayed. For some reason though, which is still not clear to me, I instantly responded on a late September afternoon, 2004, while driving home from one of the countless meetings with one of my attorneys. I was stuck in Chicago rush-hour traffic on the Stevenson Expressway, outside the suburb of Burr Ridge, and I remember listening to a classic rock station playing "A Horse with No Name," by the 70's rock group, America. The song had barely started, when my cell phone rang.

The display window showed only "Call 1." As soon as I said hello, my son's voice sent my heart racing. "Dad, it's me, Adrian." He paused momentarily, then continued. "I'm okay. I'm sorry that I had to run away—but it's for the best." His attempt to sound convincing didn't quite work.

"Where are you?" I asked, a little too loudly.

"Don't worry. I'm okay. Please tell mom that I'm okay," he answered, ignoring my question. "I really can't talk—your phone is probably bugged."

"Where are you?"

"I'll call you on your cell phone again soon," he said. "I love you. Tell mom that I love her—I'm sorry." He hung up.

It all happened too fast for me to react with any logic and I was left in somewhat of a mental lapse after the call disconnected. It couldn't have been more than just a few moments, but in that fleeting window of time, memories of my son passed in a flash through my subconscious. I frantically tried to re-establish the connection, but Adrian must have taken the necessary precautions to prevent such a return call.

Needless to say, Adrian's disappearance had been a major shock to my family and had turned our entire world upside down. And even though this call gave me a tiny measure of reassurance that he was okay, it presented more questions than answers. It also tumbled my emotions like wet garments in a clothes dryer. From the initial joy of hearing his voice, and gratitude for the knowledge that he was safe, I descended into wretched gloom. And gloom quickly gave way to replete helplessness because of my inability to have sufficiently comforted him about his vindication, to sadness about his resolution of believing that he had to take matters into his own hands, and finally to scornful anger for the choices he had been forced to make and the hardship that I was certain he had to endure.

Worst of all, in the back of my mind, I realized that by running away, Adrian had already supplied the inflammatory fuel needed to incriminate him in the eyes of every onlooker. Contrary to his belief, his guilt in the public's eyes and in authorities' opinions, increased in direct proportion to the distance he was attempting to place between himself and his problems.

But, right there and then, I was willing to forego all of these thoughts, and simply cherish the most important thing—the knowledge, or at least the belief, that he was safe. His mother, Dobrila, as well as his brothers Eric, Justin, Deyan, and Evan, would also be relieved to hear it.

Nothing good has ever happened to me at 1:30 a.m. Least of all phone calls. I have family in different countries around the world, and 1:30 a.m. here in Illinois may be 10:30 a.m. at their location, and a perfectly good time to call.

My fear of phones ringing in the wee hours comes from one such event in 1987. A nurse at MacNeal Memorial Hospital called to inform me that my father had passed away unexpectedly about an hour earlier, and that we should come to the hospital immediately.

Since then, I am filled with dread every time the phone rings at that hour. So, as I was awakened by the jangling sound of my home phone at 1:30 a.m. on an October morning, nearly a month after hearing from my son, I immediately feared that this would not be good news. Of course, I hoped it might be Adrian calling again.

Instead, a harsh male voice, in a slight accent, snarled, "Don't say a word. Just listen." It instantly snapped me out of my groggy condition. His next words struck like a landslide. "We have your son, and if you ever want to see him again, then you will do exactly as I tell you." It took a second or two for the menacing threat to register. The worst fears of any parent had invaded my world. Nothing was more important, or cherished, to my wife and to me, than our five sons. Not even our own lives. And here was some greedy barbarian suddenly threatening Adrian's life; someone who could single-handedly change the meaning of our existence forever.

I had read articles and books about people facing crises, threats to their own lives or to the lives of loved ones, describing the anguish, fear, or despair. Many of these accounts suggested that these victims sometimes experienced a calm, tranquil, or serene feeling during that moment of danger in which they were lifted towards a "white light" of salvation.

For me, no such feelings surfaced. My crisis was nothing like that. I did experience the sensation of leaving my body, but instead of floating toward a "white light," I was spiraled into a desolate abyss, void of any serenity, calmness or tranquility. A bomb had exploded and created a fire storm of excruciating pain, panic, and despair. And like a fire storm, which completely consumes the very thing which feeds it, so too was I utterly consumed by this blaze of emotions. I struggled to remain conscious, but my body was suddenly shaken with waves of numbness, making me feel as if I had been anesthetized into surrendering my willpower. A year earlier, I had been diagnosed with life-threatening cancer. Yet, that announcement was a mere whisper when compared to the words from this criminal caller which pounded me with deafening thunder. My heart pounded like a drum and yet my body seemed completely paralyzed.

"Who is it? Who is it?" my wife asked as she turned on the bedroom lights. Her face paled when she saw my blank, frozen expression.

The grating voice spoke again. "Do you hear me? We have your son."

"Yes, I can hear you," I shouted quietly.

His demand was simple. Pay the money and they would return my son. If I didn't, they would do terrible things to him, which the voice described to me in gory detail. If I called the police, he said, they would make it look like a fugitive's suicide.

What choice does a parent have in this situation? The caller demanded $100,000, and said that I would soon have visitors.

They arrived the next evening.

CHAPTER 3

EXTORTION

I felt a bead of sweat trickle down the right side of my face, form a rivulet on my neck, and soak into my shirt collar. My face felt feverish, hot, but was ice cold to my touch. But my conscience, resolution and determination were even colder. Concentrating hard to prevent my hands or body from trembling, I watched the facial expressions of two men, trying to determine if they realized how nervous I was.

In my imagination, the trail left by that drop of sweat radiated a signal of my fear that might tell these intruders that I was hiding something. I was.

Under my bulky sweater I gripped my 9 millimeter Beretta handgun; clutching it like a drowning person grasping at a single straw. I could feel the carved imprints on the wooden handgrip and the resistance of the trigger against my forefinger, giving me a strange comfort and sense of power. I could feel the vindication that it offered, the solution that it provided. Like a drunk hoping that he is sober enough to know he is intoxicated, I hoped that I was rational enough to understand the enormity of a decision I was about to make.

Just two hours earlier, Adrian had called us with stunning news. He said that he had somehow managed to escape from his captors. In the brief moment he spoke, he said he had been able to meet with one of my wife's distant relatives, and would need some additional help. I wanted to know more, but he abruptly ended the call.

Now, a pair of gangsters occupied my home and demanded ransom for Adrian's release. I couldn't be certain which way to turn. My son was still in another country, and vulnerable, even if he had escaped the kidnappers. I felt like I was walking a tightrope. Whether or not their gang had Adrian, I was certain that these two weren't going to just leave peacefully without the loot they wanted.

Still, I was convinced that the outcome of this meeting would require peremptory action on my part in order to save the life of Adrian, if not the lives of my entire family.

Trying to appear casual, I used my left arm to wipe the sweat from my face. Hot flashes coursed through my body. Was it fear or a side effect of my medication for the cancer that also threatened my life? I hoped they couldn't feel the heat radiating from me. So I slumped further down in my chair in an effort to hide the uncontrollable trembling that had seized my body. I used my free hand to steady the other one, which held the gun under my sweater.

My throat was parched. Yet I was afraid to reach for the glass of water on the table in front of me, fearful that my shivering might spill it and reveal the extent of my terror. My palms were now soaked, compromising my grip on the Beretta.

I tried to convince myself that I had to do that which had to be done. And I was determined not to let my morals get in the way of doing the wrong thing correctly.

Something made me realize that both of these threatening gangsters were also agitated and nervous. The younger man, probably in his early twenties, seated himself on the couch next to me and kept his head moving, avoiding eye contact. He wore dark pants and shirt, with a knit cap. The older man, unshaven with a tangle of unruly salt and pepper hair, sat in a chair facing us and did all the talking. His mismatched clothing showed signs of rough wear and he reeked of old sweat. They informed me that a driver waited outside for them.

My wife, Dobrila, gracious as always, offered cold drinks, and went into the kitchen to pour them. From the adjacent room, I could hear the theme music from the "Tonight Show" on television.

I can't remember the exact words I used, but I let them both know that it would be impossible for me to come up with $100,000 instantaneously. The older man's face tensed in anger and he barked in furious language. His accomplice attempted to calm the situation, and seemed almost embarrassed by it. He struck me as an unwilling participant in this ransom scheme, and somewhere in the back of my mind, he seemed familiar. I could have sworn that I had met him before but couldn't recall when or where.

Then our eyes met.

I knew that my stare reflected contempt and hatred, like the eyes of a predator. His were empty, blank, and seemed fearful that he might be the prey.

A period of tense silence filled the room while they tried to sort out their next moves. My mind was free falling, trying to concentrate on what would happen if I used the gun. Would it really solve anything, or get my son back? What consequences would there be? No moral implication bothered me, just pragmatic considerations.

Still, I could not believe the macabre situation that I found myself in. Nor could I grasp the extreme remedy that I was considering. I felt like a madman who had lost everything and who was desperately hanging on to his last possession—his insane reasoning.

What must be done?

The question rumbled inside me like distant thunder warning of a pending storm. I've heard that people facing imminent death see their whole lives play like a movie in their minds. I closed my eyes and surveyed the landscape of my life. I was searching for a road to salvation, but instead had embarked on a path guided and confirmed by Gabriel. Holding the gun firmly, I screamed in silence, in order to not let the rumbling doubt convince me otherwise.

My thoughts turned to the one person responsible for this volatile mess, my son Adrian. In a flash, I was transported back in time to the day of his birth. From that moment, he had proven to be a survivor. Born with the umbilical cord wrapped around his neck, his lungs failed to properly expand and fluid siphoned into both lobes. I watched in disbelief as he showed none of the customary vital signs of a newborn baby. No cries, no movement, no relief in the doctors' eyes.

My wife looked at me in disbelief and pain when I clutched her hand and told her of the doctor's recommendation. He suggested immediate christening of the infant, and administration of last rights. Her face took on a look of utter disbelief. I was never able to erase the torment, pain, and infinite sadness I saw in her eyes. She desperately wanted the baby's survival, and through some miracle her wish was granted.

I blinked, and was brought back to the present—from a long-ago moment of despair to a time of current desperation.

Another troubling thought occurred to me. When I had hastily snatched the gun from a drawer earlier, I hadn't checked to see if it was loaded. This could be a fatal error. Using my hands as a scale, I tried to measure its weight under my sweater. It felt heavy enough to be loaded, but my confidence sagged. I touched the safety switch with my thumb, but couldn't remember the position which would indicate whether it was on or off. Nudging the trigger gently, I felt resistance that indicated the safety was off. But had I chambered a round? I couldn't remember.

The older thief spoke again, and I tried to listen to his demands. But my mind was preoccupied with images of the bloody carnage I would inflict if I opened fire. The sofa would be soaked with blood and the carpet would absorb puddles of it. With my eyes closed, I mentally played the scenario of a gun battle, like a film director planning the next scene. How would I carry this out? I imagined myself creating a ruse, shouting and pointing to an imaginary person behind the two individuals in order to divert their attention. At the instant they turned around, I would jump up, pull out my gun and shoot both of them. Maybe I would need to turn up the TV volume or use a pillow as a silencer so the driver outside couldn't hear the firing Then, I would rush to the door in order to shoot him. I had seen it so many times in movies. It seemed so easy . . . so unemotional . . . so successful. I saw it clearly in my mind.

I continued to convince myself that I had to do this, and that there was nothing wrong with my decision—at least nothing that a miracle could not fix. All it would take to ignite a bloodbath was an overt action by either of my tormentors. That would provide the justification. But I was still trembling. I was still shivering. And I was praying for salvation . . . absolution . . . forgiveness.

I pictured streams of blood gushing from their bodies, and gory holes in their chests or skulls. Every detail played in my mind like a Quentin Tarantino movie, in slow motion. Maybe I would have no choice if I refused their demands for money. That would probably cause them to react with fits of anger and violence, and I would have to shoot them to protect our lives. Every man has the right to shield his family and home. My motives were just. Surely my sins would be forgiven. I tried to convince myself that if I acted quickly and decisively, and if I eliminated all three men, I would have enough time to figure out a plan for getting Adrian back. But I needed to take care of this problem first.

But above all of this, I still could hear this tiny voice of conscience that continued to interrupt my resolve and determination. No matter how convinced I was of having to do the wrong thing correctly, so too was I convinced that I still had doubts about that which I had already decided to do. Doubt and uncertainty once again chipped away at my determination and weakened my justifications. The pendulum of my convictions was slowly swinging away from the courage that I had felt only moments ago and slowly toward utter fear. Suddenly my mind was drowning with fear. I became at once afraid to succeed, as well as to fail. I was afraid to do anything, and I was afraid to do nothing. But most of all, I was afraid to make the wrong mistake.

Yet I knew that I had to do something, as the cost of doing nothing was simply too high.

I felt the cold steel of the gun again. I could smell the gunpowder as it discharged. I imagined the thunderous explosions of gunshots and could already hear the sound of empty shells as they hit the floor. I could hear the vindication that it offered. I could feel the solution. I could feel the pendulum swing back to the other extreme. Back to courage, determination, and conviction. Back to survival.

Besides, I was a dead man walking, according to my doctors who had diagnosed my terminal cancer condition. There really would be no consequences that I should worry about. All I had to do was to make sure that all the evidence pointed to me, that only my fingerprints would be on this drama, and only my DNA would be in evidence.

Maybe something worthwhile might come of my medical

condition after all. Maybe the reason for my medical condition was to make my decision easier. To make me braver. Make me be the man that I didn't know how to be.

I had nothing to lose.

I knew that I was on a suicide mission, for no matter what the outcome, I would pay for my actions in pretty much the same way. It was a forgone conclusion. But it would be a worthwhile resolution to my problems. It would respond to my present condition and solve my future concerns. Somehow I was able to understand the dark thought process that a desperate person is resolved to take. The devastating, hopeless and bleak vision that seems to provide the answers. Answers that no one else was able to understand.

But was this really an answer? Maybe there were no answers, no manuals or directions, no signs from heaven, only clouds that seemed to always hide the solutions. Or maybe there were really no solutions, only a remedy which would stop the pain. The pain that lived in your mind and paralyzed your conscience. Maybe it was a remedy that would unlock the cage of uncertainty and set you free. Free from any consequences. Free from any further doubt. Free from having to think.

I waited for a sign from the men, an indication that they would do something, a reason to unleash the destruction I had planned and was prepared to use.

I continued to tremble. My wife didn't know any of this, as she would definitively object to any type of confrontation. Not that she had any answers to this dangerous riddle, but she believed in reasoning things out peacefully.

I could not calm myself, and any attempt to listen to the conversation was drowned out by the sound of my heartbeat and my belabored breathing. I tried to find my inner voice of reason. The thunder which was my conviction.

Was I really ready to do this? Could I really kill a person? I thought so. I believed I could kill a person under these circumstances, or even three people. I really could pull this off. I felt the force within me again. The force which did not require mass or acceleration. A force that only needed to be supported by conviction. Conviction which stared into the cold face of reality. A reality that had no sight or vision. A reality that was only filled with illusion. And I knew that my determination was based on knowledge. But my knowledge did not require wisdom or experience. It just needed to be sufficiently convinced by doubt.

I again felt like I held a hammer of justice, and everything I could see was a nail.

The only sound I could hear was my wife's voice explaining why we didn't have the ready cash to meet their demands. But her words meant nothing to them. It didn't matter anyway, because I had the hammer. I watched her with admiration and love, observing the smile on her face when all she could feel was pain. I noticed the hospitality and friendliness she exhibited, when all she felt was contempt. I cherished her beautiful face, her radiant smile, the twinkle in her eyes which defied the danger, the confidence she projected that no matter what the problem, it could be fixed. It hurt me to see the obvious pain that she was disguising. I watched her, but I could no longer hear her. My mind was pre-occupied with the things that I had to do.

I closed my eyes and let my memories wander. I could feel her, the fresh soapy smell after her morning bath, the lemony aroma when she would kiss me after getting dressed in the morning, the musky, herbal scent when she would come to bed to make love. I noticed and realized my love for her all over again. I watched as it grew at that very moment. It was the kind of love that you could not describe. That you didn't have to express. That you didn't have to explain. I closed my eyes and reveled in that feeling. It was a painful gratification deep within my center of consciousness that was weighed down by what I was about to do.

I wanted to hold her, to caress her, to tell her that I loved her and that I would never stop loving her. I wanted to tell her that I was sorry for what I was about to do. I wanted to assure her that things would be okay.

It hurt me to see the obvious pain that she was disguising.

I managed to wipe the tears from my eyes that had begun to trickle down my cheek. In a momentary lapse of reality, I covered my face.

God . . . I love this woman.

Goddammit!

God forgive me.

God help me.

I looked back at the older man with hateful contempt because of the pain he was inflicting. And our eyes met. His expression had changed. His look was empty and blank. He instantly looked away. Somehow, I felt that our roles were reversed. I was no longer the victim. In fact, I was the hammer. I realized that he was not a threat. Death no longer needed to be the solution. He too seemed to realize that his theatrics were obsolete, as he continued to look away from me while he talked. The more he babbled while avoiding eye contact, the more empowered I felt. But I was still sweating and clutching my gun, prepared to use it . . . no doubt about it.

But then the damned roller coaster of emotions took another stomach-churning dip.

While I was still evaluating their sincerity and considering my intent to take decisive action, the older man handed me his cell phone. "Listen to this," he demanded. Surprised, I took his phone and heard a welcome voice.

"Dad, Dad, it's Adrian! There are two police officers here. They want to talk to you . . . !"

A weight lifted from me. He was safe in the hands of the police. My prayers had been heard. The clouds had dissipated and revealed bright sunshine.

Before I could speak, though, another voice replaced Adrian's. Gruff and threatening, he spoke in the Serbian language, and sent my emotions tumbling into hell again.

It was the same voice I had heard two days ago! The one telling me that Adrian would be killed if I didn't pay the ransom. "Listen, motherfucker," he snarled, "Your son is dead if you don't pay the money to my brother. We'll cut him into pieces and mail them to you one chunk at a time. Pay the money now, asshole!" The phone went dead.

I was speechless and frozen in place again.

I had no hammer!

I had nothing!

Somehow, I managed to say to the man facing me, "We don't have that kind of money."

My wife interrupted. "But we have jewelry. Will you take jewelry?" Without waiting for an answer, she brought her box of precious possessions from the bedroom and opened the top, exposing the contents (minus the pieces Adrian had pawned). I naively assumed that they would take a few pieces equal to the value they demanded, $100,000.

They accepted her offer and took the entire box, which contained a variety of gold, silver and stones worth a combined value in excess of $400,000.

I never told my wife that I had a gun that evening.

I was too ashamed for what I couldn't do.

CHAPTER 4

FROM THE BEGINNING

"I don't care who I meet, I just hope that I get laid," Conny confided to her friend in a giggling whisper. They laughed and chattered in the back seat of a late model coupe headed toward our home. This would be the fourth and last party stop for the night. Adrian, in the front passenger seat, glanced at his watch. It was already two o'clock, Saturday morning, December 7, 2002, and unseasonably warm in the wee hours.

With my son's buddy, Jeremy, at the wheel, they left Downer's Grove en route to Burr Ridge, west of downtown Chicago, about a fifteen-minute drive. Conny's friend, Jenny, had called Adrian to say they needed a ride. She suggested that the night was still young and they'd like to have some more fun. Jeremy and Adrian, both 17, were only too glad to accommodate a pair of pretty teenagers. Adrian knew Jenny, but it was the first time he had met Conny. In what can only be described as an ironic twist of fate, two of Adrian's most devastating decisions of his young life, both of which would have a lasting imprint on the flimsy fabric of his life, involved the use of an automobile. First this trip, which would bring about the dire consequences which precipitated the need for his second journey—his self imposed exile.

Conny flirted with Adrian inside the car. He twisted his body around to face her. Jeremy adjusted the rear view mirror so he, too, could keep the girls in view.

"What music do you like?" Conny asked.

"I like vintage rock and roll," Adrian replied, while tuning the radio to a station featuring 70s rock. "Hip-Hop is okay, but that's what all the younger kids are listening to." He hoped his answer made him sound more mature. "What do you do for fun?"

Nodding her approval of Adrian's musical choice, Conny purred, "I usually go clubbing downtown."

Both boys found her attractive. She stood about five-six, with dark blonde hair, a pretty face, glowing smile, and piercing eyes. She didn't wear any make-up but had her eyebrow pierced with a silver stud. Her winter jacket was unbuttoned, revealing a tight, dark cotton top that amplified her curves.

Using the age-old technique of probing to see if a guy is serious about someone else, Conny said, "I think that your girlfriend Brittany is in my cosmetology class."

Adrian took the hook. "Oh, we broke up. So I'm available." He gave her a smug smile.

"What a bad boy. So, what drinks are you serving at your party?" Her role as coquette was unmistakable.

Adrian broke his concentration on her to direct Jeremy. "Slow down, it's the first driveway on your left." Turning back to Conny, he said, "My friends brought over some vodka."

She glanced out the window along a thousand-foot driveway intersecting dense forest she'd never seen before. "Wow, this is scary."

Following Adrian's advice, Jeremy shut off the engine and coasted up to a side door. Adrian put a forefinger to his lips and whispered, "Be quiet, my father is sleeping." Like burglars, they eased into the house through the side door, then tip-toed into his room, where five other male friends of Adrian were watching television and playing cards. Conny spoke first. "Let's get this party started."

They didn't have to be asked twice. Speakers blared an oldie by the Doors and Conny sang along, "C'mon baby light my fire, try to set the night on fire . . ." She gyrated in a promiscuously suggestive solo dance, teasing several of the boys by caressing their faces and stroking their necks, captivating them with her sensuous movements. To one of them, Tarek, she cooed, "You'll be my first victim."

Sexual tension grew in the room when a naughty infomercial, touted by entertainer Snoop Dogg, played on the television, offering "Girls Gone Wild" videos of young women baring it all in public. Conny watched with the guys. When one of them, Sal, asked her what she would do if Snoop propositioned her to appear on the video, she said, "I would show everything. My version would definitely be triple-X rated."

Another boy, Jimmy, blurted out, "You're all right. Maybe we should do a porn video?"

Conny gave him a mischievous smile. "This drink is great," she said, raising her glass in a salute. Still bumping and grinding like an experienced stripper, she added, "I'll bet I can handle this better than you can." Jimmy immediately filled her a glass with more vodka and Coke, and responded, "I'll slam your ass!" The contest was on.

While the rest of the group cheered them on, Jimmy and Conny chugged down three glasses of the potent cocktails. Just as he prepared to pour a forth round, Conny leaned forward and vomited. She attempted to cover her mouth with her hands, but the contents of her stomach spilled all over the front of her blouse. Adrian and Jenny ushered her to the bathroom and used towels trying to wipe the mess from her clothing.

Now, I am not young enough to know everything teenagers know, especially matters which involve today's party etiquette. I do know that when person throws up, that is pretty much a signal that the fun might be over. But this was no ordinary party, certainly not with Conny. After upchucking, she said she felt better, and wondered if she had just been drinking too fast on an empty stomach. She emerged from the bathroom refreshed, cheerful, and surprised them all by announcing, "It's time for the video."

Jimmy took the cue and grabbed a camcorder while Adrian pointed to a door and said, "Let's take this into the spare bedroom just in case my father checks my room."

Smiling again, Conny pointed to Tarek and said, "You're first, cutie." Turning to the other gaping boys, who couldn't quite believe their good fortune and wondered if this was for real, she added, "But don't worry, boys, you'll all get some of this." With that, she raised her wet blouse and exposed her breasts.

The empty bedroom, located directly across from Adrian's, had formerly belonged to our oldest son, Eric, who had moved out of the house some time ago. It didn't have an adjoining bath, and like Adrian's room, was also adjacent to our other three sons' sleeping quarters. Few furnishings had been left; only a twin bed, a night stand, a writing table with a chair, and a low dresser.

Adrian led the group in, followed by Conny, who was holding Tarek's hand. Next came Jimmy with the video camcorder, and finally Anthony and Robert, two other friends of Adrian's. As Adrian closed the drapes, he heard Conny questioning Jimmy. "Maybe we can sell this on the Internet. How much do you think we can get for this video?"

Jimmy fumbled with the camcorder, attempting to insert a tape. While adjusting the focus and light settings, he flipped the wall switch in a vain effort to illuminate the room as much as possible. In doing so, he inadvertently turned on the ceiling fan, which began a slow spin. Turning on the lights didn't help much since only one of the three bulbs had not yet burned out. So most of the room remained shadowed and dim.

Conny began a slow strip tease dance in which, piece by piece, she removed her clothing, including her underwear, and neatly folded each item on the floor next to the bed. Wearing only black socks, she positioned herself on the bed, kneeling in such way, that her elevated rear end was facing Jimmy and the video camera, while she turned her head and looked straight at him. "How is this for a start?" she asked with a provocative grin.

While Tarek, the invited one, struggled out of his pants, shirt, and shorts, Adrian slipped quietly out of the room for a quick check of his father to be certain that he hadn't been awakened and wouldn't interrupt the video session. He returned to join the attentive audience, all circled around the bed, eager to watch a porn-shoot up close.

In the dim lighting, the rotating fan blades created a flickering, strobe-like effect on the movements of Tarek and Conny, creating a surreal and sardonic atmosphere. They soon joined sexually while cheered on by the observers. Jimmy, his eyes glued to the camcorder's tiny screen, at first gave simple directions for better angles, but soon encouraged the writhing couple with explicit, obscene suggestions. As he moved in for close-ups, they obeyed and laughed at his heated commentary. The words and actions escalated to the level of a triple-X rated production, as Conny had promised.

Jenny, Jeremy and Robert exited the room, shaking their heads in disbelief. Jenny frowned with discomfort, concerned that the behavior had grown out of control. The two following boys simply wanted to impress her with their maturity by supporting her rejection of the steamy, overheated, conduct. Besides, they hoped to still get their turns with Conny.

Tarek didn't last long as Conny's co-star, and Adrian stepped in to replace him. To his credit, and Tarek's, they both used condoms during the intercourse. Jimmy continued as director, spurring on the action with expletive-laced advice. The naked girl's laughter ceased in favor of panting, moaning, and groaning in time with her pelvic thrusts and exploring hands. At one point, she manually helped Adrian re-penetrate while simultaneously caressing his back and arms. With a lustful, teasing smirk, she asked him, "Are you sure that this is okay with your girlfriend?"

"I don't care," Adrian grunted. Perhaps the question embarrassed him bringing on an attack of modesty, or maybe the revolving fan created a chill, but for some reason he pulled a cover over both of their interlocked bodies. He turned to Jimmy, laughed, and said, "Stop taping. Get out of here!"

The action came to a sudden halt. Not because of Adrian's request, but because Conny rolled over and appeared to pass out. No one was certain why, but it was either too much alcohol (possible), not enough excitement (unlikely), or that she had reached a climax (improbable). In any case, Conny fell asleep before Adrian had "finished" his task. Once Adrian realized that she was not responding, he stopped, crawled off the bed, covered Conny with the blanket, and got dressed.

Only Jimmy, Adrian, Conny and Anthony remained in the room at this time. Jimmy rushed to the adjacent room's television set and video player in order to view the tape he had made. Adrian followed, but stopped in the hallway again to listen for his father. Anthony also started out, but as soon as he reached the doorway, Conny revived, looked up and asked, "Where do you think you're going?"

Anthony stopped in his tracks and turned around with a smile, while closing the door behind him.

"I promised you a turn, didn't I?" Conny purred. Unlike the other two boys, Anthony didn't have a condom, and thought that he didn't have the time to look for one. Conny agreed. "It's Okay, it's okay," she panted. With his excitement already elevated from witnessing the prior sexual activities, Anthony climaxed within a couple of minutes. And while the rest of the group watched the video recording of the earlier activities in Adrian's bedroom, Anthony stayed behind and cuddled with Conny. She soon fell asleep again. Anthony got dressed, and rejoined the others in Adrian's bedroom.

Jeremy turned to him and asked about Conny, hoping to take his overdue turn. Anthony shook his head. "She's out. She's sleeping in the other room."

The boys who hadn't yet had their sessions in bed with Conny returned to her side. Adrian, Anthony, and Jenny stayed in Adrian's bedroom. Jimmy, anticipating more sexual action, fast-forwarded the video tape for a minute, then ejected it from the VHS machine and re-inserted it into the camcorder. He didn't want to overlap any of the recorded performance, and didn't mind a blank section between the earlier sequence and subsequent filming.

Conny lay under the blanket, still asleep. Jeremy's gentle prodding couldn't wake her. Two of the boys peeled off the cover and climbed in next to her, posing for Jimmy's camcorder. Even Tarek, who did have sex with her, joined in. One silly pose led to another, as they considered these actions to be mere pranks. In their minds, this was nothing compared to the explicit sexual recordings that had been made earlier, with Conny's approval.

What followed was the behavior of immature juveniles acting as idiotic juveniles. Not unlike hazing rituals, the acts were obscene, shameful and insulting to any normal human being. But these were foolish boys, whose tolerance for odious acts had a much higher threshold than that of a rational adult. A cigarette was inserted into Conny's vagina. One wonders if the boys were inspired by national news coverage of President Clinton's incident involving a cigar and Monica Lewinsky. Tarek's used condom was placed on the pillow next to Conny's face, and Jeremy and Robert used a felt tip marker to write obscenities all over Conny's naked body. As disgusting as this behavior was, even more provocative acts followed.

As Jimmy continued to record the action, Jeremy dropped his pants and shorts, and while standing above Conny's body, began to masturbate. Tarek also dropped his pants and shorts. He positioned his rear end above Conny, and proceeded to fart in her face. Using a lighter, he made a goofy, repulsive show of lighting the cigarette protruding from Conny's vagina. Jeremy, in turn, appeared to have climaxed and ejaculated on her skin.

Finally, all three boys ended their morbid behavior by spitting repeatedly on Conny's exposed breasts and genitals. Jimmy captured it all and narrated with obscenities while the boys added their own comments. They considered it all nothing but a drunken party prank, not much worse than acts they had seen in teen coming-of-age movies. It did not physically hurt anyone, and they had thought it hilariously funny.

No one can say what would have happened next, but as soon as Jenny and Adrian entered the room, the orgy ended. Jenny was clearly offended, and Adrian feared that his luck of not being caught by his father, might be running out. He declared the party was over.

Jenny and Adrian attempted to clean the mess from Conny's body. Using soap and water, they scrubbed at the inscriptions made by the felt-tip marker pen. No matter how hard they tried, though, they could not erase the inked obscenities. After dressing Conny, they attempted to carry her to Jeremy's car. The other boys were reluctant to help, and Jeremy said he didn't want to drive her home, fearing she might throw up again in the seat. As a result, they put Conny back in the bed, and Adrian locked the bedroom door. He did this, not worried that any of the boys would attempt more lusty pranks, but rather in fear that his father might discover her. Adrian knew that his father would probably not bother to search for a key to the locked spare room in the middle of the night if everything else seemed normal.

After all other partygoers had left, Adrian went to bed, wondering what he would tell his parents if Conny should be discovered. He breathed a sigh of relief as he pulled the covers up to his chest and thought to himself, "So far, so good."

But he couldn't shake the premonition that something ugly had happened.

He feared that there might be consequences.

He never imagined the price he would have to pay.

CHAPTER 5

CONFRONTATION

I rose late that same Saturday morning, invigorated by the winter sun of this Pearl Harbor Day, while every one of my family still slept. I waited for my sons to wake up so one of them could retrieve the *Chicago Tribune* newspaper, which had been delivered near the beginning of our driveway, some 1,000 feet away. Or, as I lazily thought, too far for me to fetch it on my own.

While waiting, I played several games of solitaire on the computer in my home office. Sipping on my second cup of coffee, I heard noises coming from one of the nearby bathrooms. A barely audible female voice said, "I called my friend, and she'll pick me up." I didn't recognize it as anyone I knew. She continued, "That's good. I had a good time. I hope you'll invite me to your next party." Then came what I perceived to be the sound of a kiss.

I got up from my chair, headed towards the origin of the voice, and saw Adrian talking to a girl. Since I was clad only in my underwear, I thought it inappropriate to confront them just then. Instead I went back to my own bathroom, washed up and got dressed. I had not really been in any particular hurry, so a little more than fifteen minutes passed before I approached Adrian's room. I saw the girl as she left through the side door and entered a car that had pulled up for her.

Face to face with my son, and using my father-knows-best manner, I asked, "Is there something you want to tell me?" My tone, I hoped, indicated that I knew more than I actually did.

His voice raspy from sleep, Adrian replied, "I'm too tired to talk. Can I tell you later?" He avoided looking at me and retreated to his bedroom.

"I'd better not get any surprises," I snapped as he closed his door. He remained out of sight for the rest of the day, pretending to be sleeping every time I went into his room to inquire about that morning's conversation and the girl's presence.

For the rest of that day, one thing or another kept me busy, preventing completion of my inquiry. I went to bed that night without the benefit of any knowledge about what had actually happened, and learned nothing more on Sunday.

On Monday, early morning appointments took me away from the house before Adrian was up. I returned that evening at about five, just as darkness settled in. As I approached the house, I was surprised to see numerous cars in my driveway. The minute I stepped out of my car, I heard loud voices in an apparent argument taking place by the side door. On the way to that entrance, I passed a green Dodge in which several people sat. Not giving it much thought, I continued my rush through the side entrance to find out what the commotion had been about. Once inside, I found a young woman whom I didn't know shouting accusations at Adrian and several of his friends..

Alarmed, I gained everyone's attention by screaming louder than any of them. The girl who had been shouting turned to me and unequivocally stated that she wanted the tape that was made of her friend, at a party early Saturday morning inside this house.

Having no knowledge of any tape or any party, I immediately questioned Adrian as to the meaning of this confrontation. Red-faced, he told me that there had been a party, and admitted the existence of a video tape. However, he assured me, the tape was no longer in his possession, and to the best of his knowledge, it had already been destroyed.

The young woman continued her steadfast demand, and made Jenny, who was there with a girlfriend, the target of her harassment. As a result, I too turned to Jenny, and asked about the tape.

Other friends of Adrian began to shout at the young woman, when she suddenly declared, "Give me the tape or we're going to the police and tell them that Conny was raped!"

Mass confusion took over. Trying to hear Jenny's response to my question, which was drowned out by the other young woman's threat, I saw a fight erupt outside. Some of my son's other friends had squared off in a fist fight with the occupants of the car I had passed. Not knowing what to do first, I decided to concentrate my attention on the origin of what appeared to be the center of all this commotion. So I grabbed the young woman by her arms and demanded that she tell me, what the hell she was talking about.

Throughout the shouting inside the house, and the screaming outside, all I could hear was her piercing threat. "Give me the tape or we'll go to the police!"

I asked, "Who is Conny ? What the hell are you talking about?"

"Ask your son," she bellowed. "He raped the girl who's in that car."

I shoved her aside as I ran outside to see who the girl in the car was. Adrian caught up with me from behind, trying to get my attention. "I'm sorry, Dad, I'm sorry!" was all I heard him say, as I rushed toward the parked car. We had passed some of the kids who were fighting, and Adrian stopped in an attempt to separate them.

I jerked open the driver's door of the Dodge coupe, and noticed a girl in the back seat. I pushed the driver's seat forward to get a better view, and so that I could question her. "Are you Conny?" Without waiting for an answer, I asked, "What the hell happened?"

She looked up at me, her face contorted in misery, and replied in a shaky voice, "Nothing happened. Nothing happened."

"Are you Conny?"

"Yes. Oh, yes. Nothing happened. I just want to leave."

Trying to keep calm, I said, "Your friend is making a serious allegation inside. Were you raped?"

"No, no, no. Nothing happened. This is all a big, big, big misunderstanding."

"But your friend in there is accusing my son of raping you. Is this true?"

Conny continued denying it. "No, no, no. Nothing happened. Really, nothing happened."

By this time, the young woman making the accusations had made her way to the car, and before she could say anything, I announced: "Wait here, I am going to call the police." I made this decision because the girl in the back seat sounded absolutely convincing in her disclaimer, and I did not want someone to convince her otherwise before I could have the police hear her admission.

"Wait here," I instructed before hurrying into the house to make my call.

While dialing 911, I watched through a window as the Dodge coupe sped away. My son's friends shouted at the passengers and the car barely missed a tree at the driveway's edge. Someone in the car yelled, "We'll be back with a gun and shoot this place up."

Waiting for the police to arrive, I again questioned my son, Jenny, and Sal, not knowing that he had also been present at the party. All of them told me that the tape had been destroyed. They insisted that nothing had happened. Each one agreed that today's incident had been nothing but a vindictive act, and vouched that nothing else would come of this. Even Brittany, my son's long-time girlfriend, joined in and assured me that nothing bad had happened.

While I listened to everyone's guarantees, a patrol car arrived. I informed the officer about the confrontation I had seen and explained the circumstances. I told him that a video tape had been mentioned but everyone thought it had been destroyed. Accusations of rape had been tossed around, but seemed to have no veracity. Finally, I told him of the threats regarding the gun, which had been made as the Dodge sped away. The officer listened patiently, then informed me that he could only write a report as to the confrontation. Since he was not called to investigate a rape, he could not include any mention of it in his report. According to him, any such statements would be mere allegation and hearsay. He explained, "The fact that we were called out, however, will give credence to your concerns, and confirm that you called the police."

I had no reason to question or doubt the officer's explanations. No mention of the allegations of rape was made in the report. And even though I knew better, as I firmly believe that it is better to know nothing than to know something that isn't so, I allowed myself to be satisfied by the officer's comments regarding the limitations of his report. I also allowed myself to be satisfied with my son's assurance that nothing had happened. I let myself believe that my son's moral fiber would not allow him to do such things. I was satisfied that the risk of not knowing what happened was minimized by the knowledge of what I think could never have happened. Not in my wildest dreams could I even imagine the magnitude of events that were about to crash down upon us.

CHAPTER 6

———◆◆◆———

THE ARREST

I was at my attorney's office in the late afternoon of Thursday, December 12, to deal with some civil litigation, when I received a call from my wife, Dobrila, on my cell phone. Busy with the meeting, I disregarded the call, assuming that she probably wanted to ask a casual question. A minute later, she called again, and I ignored it again. Finally, during a break, I used my attorney's office speaker phone to call her back.

The casual question I anticipated turned out to be a serious problem. She said, "There are two detectives at our house inquiring about Adrian's whereabouts. They are investigating the incident that happened at our house last Saturday. The girl has claimed that she had been raped."

She sounded surprisingly calm and relaxed, unlike what I would have expected under the circumstances. "The main detective has since told me that this was merely a formality. He knows that the girl involved is a tramp, and they don't believe a word she was saying. We've been talking for some time. I had no idea how often something like this happens. This detective says that he has a lot of experience with this type of situation, and usually nothing comes of it. He couldn't believe, when I told him, what time she had come over." Still speaking as if the matter was simple routine, she continued, "So I let them in the house to view the room where this incident had supposedly happened. They apologized for all the trouble, but he wanted to finish their report today, and this was the last thing they needed to do."

My attorney, Ariel Weissberg, had walked back into the conference room and heard most of my wife's comments. He signaled that he wanted to ask me about it. "Hold on," I said to her.

"Damn it, Damir," my attorney barked while slamming a fist against his desk. His face turned crimson and his pupils shrunk to the size of a pinhead. "You know better than to let your wife make any statements to the police! " He stopped to take a labored breath. "Tell the S.O.B. that you will not allow your son to be interrogated without an attorney."

His outburst took me completely by surprise. I had known Ariel since my first bankruptcy filing almost ten years earlier, and recognized that his tone of voice meant he regarded this matter as crucial. Despite having had conflicts with him in the past, primarily involving his fees, I still retained him out of respect for his abilities and expertise in litigating the various subtleties of the law. He was a well-respected attorney and a prominent member in the Jewish community. And while he had clients form all walks of life, ethnicities, and moral aptitudes, he nevertheless pursued their best interests with unprejudiced abandon and self-motivation to succeed. He could be the nicest person at any one time, and turn into the most obnoxious and arrogant asshole, whose assault I would not want to oppose in a courtroom myself.

I offered a cleaned-up version to my wife. "Tell the detective that we want an attorney present if he wants to talk to Adrian."

I heard her pass the demand on to the detective. In turn, she responded to me, "He told me not to worry. He's gonna wait a few minutes to see if Adrian comes home. I told him that he should be home by about 5:00 p.m. because he usually gets a ride home with a friend. I told him we want an attorney present if he is going to interrogate him. It's okay. He really seems to care. He told me that he is pretty sure that Adrian is innocent. He suspects that the girl got mad because Adrian doesn't want to be her boyfriend. This is usually what happens with kids who make such reports. Anyways, I told him about the attorney, and he is leaving now. He gave me his card, and told me that he is going to wait for my call, since there is nothing else he can do. He said he would go home to his daughter's birthday party and wait for my call." Even though she sounded confident, I thought I could detect worry in her voice.

Ariel, too, showed concern. He said, "Don't screw around. Stay on top of this." I listened while examining some papers relative to the matter that I had come to see him about. "You can't trust these assholes. They are on a mission and don't care about what really happened." He stopped shuffling papers and looked straight at me. "This is how people get screwed, and once it starts, it never ends well."

I arrived at my home at about 7:00 p.m., and my life has not been the same since. My cell phone batteries had gone dead so I hadn't talked to my wife during the commute in heavy traffic. Dobrila's voice now trembled in breathless panic. "I can't believe it. They picked Adrian up at Tarek's house. Adrian called me from his cell phone that he was arrested and in a police car. He didn't know where they were headed. He thinks that he was traveling on First Avenue. I've tried to call the detective numerous times, but his voice mail keeps answering. I've left numerous messages for him, but he's not calling back." She stopped momentarily to gulp air, and said, "But I'm sure he will. He told me he would call if I left a message. I don't know what could have happened. Maybe it's another detective. Maybe it's a mix-up."

I wanted to calm and reassure her, so I chose my words with care. "Let's wait and see. I'm sure that this is nothing to worry about. Let's just wait and see what happens."

Weissberg's voice kept echoing in my mind, "This is how people get fucked." Fearing the worst, but hoping for the best, I continued to encourage my wife to keep a positive attitude. Somehow I was also convinced that we would hear from the police once they straightened things out. And maybe a little fear would do no harm as far as Adrian was concerned. I never mentioned the ominous advice my attorney had given me earlier in the day.

Dobrila must have called the detective a dozen times before she decided to drive to the police station where she suspected Adrian was taken. She remembered that he had mentioned First Avenue, where the only reasonably close station was located.

As she was getting ready to leave, our phone rang. It was Adrian, who whispered, "Mom, where are you? Why aren't you getting me out of here?" He was at the police station Dobrila had guessed, and managed to take his cell phone into the bathroom, unnoticed by the attending officers.

"I'll be right there," my wife said. "And don't say anything to anyone," she added, while looking at me for affirmation. She left the house at a few minutes past midnight. I stayed behind, suffering recriminations for my failure to do anything about the many warning signs I had seen. There were my son's questionable reassurances, the threats of the young woman, the police officer's vague explanation of his report's limitations, and worst of all, my attorney's pounding forewarning. In my gut I could feel the cinders of regret turn into flames of anger and blazing into an inferno of bitter despair, rage, and worst of all, rampant guilt for not reacting to the ominous signs.

En route to the station, Dobrila received another call from Adrian. "Please get an attorney, I'm scared," he pleaded.

Again, she cautioned him, "Don't say anything. Tell them you want an attorney. I'm almost there."

She arrived at the station at about 12:30 a.m., but was not admitted beyond the reception area. Repeatedly, she tried to reach the detective by phone, but heard only his voice mail message. At last, she asked the reception officer to contact the detective. He got through, only to hear a tepid response advising my wife that the investigation was not yet completed. She could wait at the station if she wanted to.

Frightened and frustrated, she chose to wait.

She continued to call the detective.

She continued to pray.

She continued to get no response.

She was exhausted by this time. The fluorescent lighting and uncomfortable chairs offered no relief. To pass the time, she read the bulletin board, the plaques awarded to officers for their achievements, and the "wanted" posters. The officer on duty seemed completely indifferent and went about his own business.

The detective finally showed up at about 3:00 a.m. He informed Dobrila that they had pretty much wrapped things up, and continued to assure her that there was no reason to worry. He also apologized for not answering her numerous calls, explaining that he had been rushing to finish this case.

"My wife will kill me," he said, "because I have missed my daughter's birthday party. But I just wanted to finish this case. It will take a little longer to complete all the paperwork. There is no need for you to wait here. You look tired. I'll tell you what, I'll make it up to you. I'll give Adrian a ride home when we are all done, so that you don't have to wait. It must have been a long day for you. I can see that you are concerned, but don't worry. Adrian is a lucky kid to have a mother like you. You're the only parent who has come to the station and who has called so many times"

Dobrila could barely hold her composure. She was overwhelmed with gratitude and overcome with joy. Her eyes glistened with tears as she repressed an urge to hug the detective. The anger of being ignored, the despair of not knowing, and the fear of dreadful possibilities were at once transformed into gratitude and happiness.

The weight of the world had been lifted from her shoulders. The storm had passed.

She could breathe again.

She could smile again.

She could finally relax.

Reassured by his apparent sincerity, she drove home.

Even though we were both exhausted, we slept restlessly the remainder of that night.

Late the next morning, after not hearing anything from the detectives, Dobrila called Detective Davies, anticipating that Adrian would be released and she could pick him up. Instead, she heard stunning news. The officer informed her that our son was being charged with several crimes after all.

We looked at each other in speechless disbelief.

We were stunned.

Dobrila's deafening silence was the loudest cry I've ever heard her make.

CHAPTER 7

GUILTY BEFORE CONVICTED

The decision had already been made. By all appearances, the law's mind had already been made up. The detectives weren't going to allow this suspect to hide behind his father's attorneys. Their decision had been made; to strike while the iron was hot. Meddling lawyers would only delay things, make their job more difficult. They already knew he was guilty. They had seen the tape. Now, all they had to do was dig up a few supportive facts. In the words of legendary Old West Judge Roy Bean, "Bring in the guilty bastard. We'll give him a fair trial and then we'll hang him."

Even the profile was typical. A spoiled, rich kid, who thought that he was above the law. He thought that he could do as he wanted to, because his parents had the money to hire a powerful attorney who would get him out of any trouble.

But not this time. This was their watch. No one was above the law here. No amount of money could buy his salvation.

I could think of no other explanation for their prejudice and flawed reasoning, and evasive treatment of my wife and me. It certainly wouldn't have been the first time law enforcement officers tried to influence the outcome of an investigation. In fact, history seems filled with similar incidents, in which police have zeroed in on a suspect, positive of his guilt, and tailored the investigation to support their suppositions. In some cases, it has been later shown that rigid standards of the law, under which they were sworn to operate, had been abrogated. "Due process of the law" had been ignored.

Throughout history, opinions about the law have been expressed by the famous and the notorious Vladimir Ilich Ulyanov, who called himself Lenin, was of the opinion that, "In matters involving prosecution of criminals, speaking the truth is a petty bourgeois prejudice. A lie, on the other hand, is often justified in the end."

Then there was Napoleon Bonaparte, who had made the observation that "The police must sometimes invent more than they discover."

A Dallas, Texas police officer shot and killed three suspects in a period of seven months in 1989. Even though investigators found notches in his service pistol before he was fired, no charges were ever filed against him.

Los Angeles detectives were suspected of manipulating evidence in the notorious case of a famous athlete tried for murder.

All of these individuals, and countless more, seemed to have known that something had to be done to provide assistance in terms of a clearer view and more unobstructed opinion of Lady Justice's blind pursuit of truth.

On the other hand, unprejudiced citizens have spoken in favor of fair treatment. In 1788, Thomas Jefferson declared, "It is more dangerous that even a guilty person should be punished without the forms of law, than that he should escape."

Apparently, this perplexity involving methods and tactics employed by the police in prosecuting an individual has been a dilemma for quite some time. But the choices are limited and very clearly defined. In fact, the law only recognizes two standards: legal or illegal, right or wrong. Either you adhere to the idyllic path, whereby you abide by the law and act strictly within its boundaries, or you don't. And if you don't, if you incorporate your own interpretation of what you are allowed to do, then, by simple definition, you are not abiding by the law, and your actions would be illegal.

The director of the FBI (of all people) under President Clinton, Louis Freeh, comes to mind. He insisted on DNA evidence from the President, while investigating the Monica Lewinsky debacle. He simply did the job that was expected of him. Nothing more, nothing less. He didn't add, and he didn't subtract. He didn't embellish, deceive, misrepresent or say anything that wasn't the truth. To him, no one was above the law, and no one was below the law. Not even the President of the United States.

Unfortunately, there are some police officers who seem to "simply know," or believe to have a keen intuition, what actually happened, and who consequently might want to help reach the foregone conclusion by embellishing the facts and procedures a bit. They may not harbor any ill feelings for the individual that they are persecuting, and it may be entirely possible that the years of experience have taught them that they have to be flexible in the interpretation of the meaning of the law, in order to get a conviction. It would be acceptable if they would hide their real intentions to a suspect in order to gain his confidence, if it helped to uncover a crime, or gave them enough time to prevent the suspect from realizing his actual situation.

However, eighteenth century English jurist William Blackstone is still widely quoted today in his observation that, "It is better that ten guilty persons escape than one innocent suffer."

I am disappointed to have to say that I am guilty of pre-judging people. Based on preliminary and often flawed information in the news media, I have all too quickly decided that a crime suspect is probably guilty. In the interest of public safety, I want that individual removed from society. However—and in my opinion, it is a gigantic however – I am not a law enforcement officer. I am not the police officer who has sworn to uphold the law. I am just an average citizen who is influenced by his own personal beliefs, biased opinions and inaccurate interpretations.

The police are supposed to be better than that.

They have to uphold a higher standard.

Obviously, the detectives handling my son's arrest had decided to apply their own values in law enforcement. They came to our home and misrepresented their intentions. In the process, they attempted to gain information about the alleged crime. Then they told my wife something that wasn't true, namely that this was a nuisance case, and that there was nothing to it. Next they deceived her by telling her there was no need to worry, in a duplicitous effort to gain enough time to collect all the missing evidence before an attorney would be involved. In effect, this denied us the protection of our legal rights. Following that, they kept my son isolated. They knew how to deal with an inexperienced, naive, immature adolescent who had never been in trouble before. Finally, they were extremely flexible in their liberal interpretation of the law, and the method by which they interrogated our son, and by which they were finally successful in obtaining a signed confession.

With the use of these adopted tools of their trade, they were able to piece together a vivid picture, which to them, pointed to an absolute conclusion, and which required very little, if any, further investigation.

After all, if a picture is worth a thousand words, then a written confession must be worth a thousand pictures—at least. Better yet, four confessions must be worth at least, lets see, maybe a quick and easy guilty verdict?

It was clear to them. They knew that the kids were guilty. They had seen the tape.

They didn't need anything else.

CHAPTER 8

DEFENSIVE INITIATION

Over the years I have been involved in all types of civil litigation and have been both plaintiff and defendant. As such I have seen both sides of the law: the good, the bad and the ugly. During this time, I have had the opportunity to engage well over 30 attorneys, based on their expertise, reputation, negotiation, cost, and most of all, based on how much I wanted to piss off the other side. I had hired attorneys representing every shade of conscience, scruples, and morality, or lack thereof. Attorneys, who have since been elected as judges on the white end of the spectrum, to attorneys with highly specialized skills such as U.S. Customs regulations, real estate tax abatements, bankruptcy filings, and insurance litigation, as well as regular contractual and real estate closings attorneys, occupying the blander, grayish shades, all the way to unorthodox, opaque and just plain bizarre, representing the dark and bitter far end, and which would require an immediate inventory of my fingers, every time I shook their hand.

However, I had never been involved in any criminal proceedings such as we faced with my son's situation. So, I had no prior experiences with any attorney specializing in criminal law. I had no confidence in any attorney who might have been practicing both civil and criminal law, as in my mind, any attorney who needed to pursue two such disparate and distinct fields, probably wouldn't be very good at either, and probably couldn't earn enough money in either specialty alone.

As a result, I asked one of my present attorneys, in whom I did have a lot of confidence and whom I had known and consulted for nearly 25 years, for a recommendation. Because the trial would take place in Bridgeview, Illinois, she recommended that I hire someone who was conducting most of his business in that district. She gave me the name of a man who had been a former state's prosecutor. Not only did she know him to be a good lawyer, but because of his former position as a state's prosecutor, she reasoned that he probably would know many of the prosecutors engaged in my son's case, and at a minimum, would be familiar with the tactics and strategies that would be employed in this prosecution.

Of course, this had made a lot of sense, and we immediately scheduled a meeting with him. We also mobilized the parents of the other three youths to join in on the meeting in hope that they might hire him as well. I reasoned, the more clients, and of course more payment of fees, were involved, the more dedicated an attorney would be to the cause.

We met on Friday, December 13, 2002, at the office of Patrick Campanelli, the attorney who had been recommended. He was a sole practitioner, in his mid forties and, as his name implied, was of Italian descent. He had a very engaging personality, and at first glance, seemed to resemble a young Robert De Niro.

Two of the other youths' parents joined us in the meeting, including Jimmy Brown's mother and father, and the divorced mother of Anthony Roberts. The widowed mother of the fourth youth, Tarek Ibrahimovic, had her own attorney, and did not participate.

This was the first time that we met the other parents, and we made ourselves comfortable in the conference room that had been prepared for our meeting. All initial conversations, needless to say, revolved about the terrible situation that we had found ourselves in. We all immediately agreed that all our sons were innocent. And I suspect that since the incident had occurred at our house, that the other parents believed that their sons were more innocent than mine.

In the time leading up to the meeting, Patrick had contacted the appropriate police department and prosecutor's office, and had ascertained our son's whereabouts, mental disposition and physical condition. He assured us that Adrian was safe, in fairly good spirits, and that he understood that we would bail him out at the first possible opportunity. That opportunity, however, would not be until the following day, when his bond hearing had been scheduled.

Before discussing any further details, Patrick explained that he probably could not represent all three of the youths for the duration of the potential trial, as conflicts of interest could possibly arise. He could, however, represent all three boys at the initial bond hearing in an effort to get them out as soon as possible. His fee for this initial service was $500 per boy, and he could accept cash, check or even a credit card.

In a soft-spoken tone, which at times was difficult to understand unless you paid close attention to his every word, Patrick next outlined what things we should expect, what the anticipated charges might be, and what the consequences of those charges might entail. The more he elaborated, the worse the situation sounded. He did caution us that he was generally presenting a "worse case scenario," and until a ruling by a judge, all of this advice, even though based on his years of experience as a criminal lawyer, was only speculation.

Based on the tone of his voice, the expression in his eyes, and on the "cut and dried" specificity of the potential consequences, Patrick's disclaimers sounded equivalent to the possibility that the Pope might not be a Catholic every day.

Still, my wife and I grasped onto the straws of his words with the optimism of a drowning man. He reassured everyone of his qualifications and his experience in these matters, and confirmed that he, in fact, had been on the other side of this equation for countless years and even more countless trials, and that he personally did know most of the prosecutors at the Bridgeview courthouse.

My observation of body language and mannerisms over the years has taught me to draw certain conclusions about personalities and capabilities. To me, an overly assertive and excessively confident individual is usually rigid and rarely able to adapt to new conditions or situations. They often rely on their reputation and don't always work every angle in order to gain an advantage over their opponent. An overly acquiescent and attentive individual, on the other hand, is more often than not fighting for every advantage needed. They are usually scavengers who cannot take a stand on their own in order to substantiate their position.

What I recognized in Patrick's demeanor and personality was the median of the two. He appeared assertive enough to know his strengths and extent of influence. Yet he was conscientious and cautious enough to not throw his weight around or to take any situation for granted. He was the lone wolf who knew (and marked) his territory. He could make his own kill, or he could survive on the left-over remnants of a bigger predator. And he would not take anything for granted. He made his living based on adaptation.

I sensed that we had made the right choice, and that our case would be perfectly suited for his abilities. But then, I have been known to be wrong in my character evaluations before.

At the meeting's conclusion, Patrick asked if anyone had any questions.

No one responded.

I looked at my wife and realized that, like myself, she was afraid to ask. Afraid that she already knew the answers.

CHAPTER 9

ARRAIGNMENT

If there is a 50 percent chance that a predictable thing might go wrong, then nine times out of ten it will. This is one of life's experiences that I can personally attest to.

Patrick Campanelli, our attorney, cautioned us that we should be on time for the 9:00 a.m. hearing, and instructed us to bring at least $1,000 in cash for the bond. He then suggested that we might want to bring $2,000 just to be on the safe side. He also warned us that there might be extensive media interest in this case, and that we should not be surprised to find a large number of reporters and camera crews waiting for us at the courthouse.

Dobrila and I arrived at 8:45 a.m. on Saturday, December 14, 2002, and found no reporters and no camera crews anywhere. "So far, so good," we thought as we walked up the prominent steps of the venerable building.

After extensive scrutiny by security officers, we met with Patrick and the other parents. Everyone was in a subdued, yet hopeful mood, as we waited for the arrival of the sheriff's van transporting the boys from the Maywood jail. Based on Patrick's prediction of an uneventful and quick hearing, we waited patiently. Over an hour later, an officer informed us that sheriff's van had arrived, and that the boys were in the lock-up area of the courtroom.

At about 10:30 a.m. we heard that the judge assigned to this matter was still busy performing marriage rituals, which were her specialty, and which were a dominant matter on Saturdays.

So we waited. And we watched as shifting crowds of people in the hallways grew smaller with each passing minute. By now, all conversations were redundant, as everything of any meaning or importance had already been said. The sparse offerings in the cafeteria offered no diversion or relief. I felt like a man who was rushing in hopes of catching a train that I was anxious to miss. With every step taking me closer, the more reluctant I was to actually get there.

Finally, at 11:30 a.m., while we sat in room 103, a bailiff advised us that the judge was ready to adjudicate our case. As instructed, we all rose when Judge Loretta Douglas entered the courtroom. Sitting once again, we watched Patrick approach the bench as the case was called, and the boys were led into the courtroom. The prosecutor, Peg Ogarek, joined Patrick at the bench.

Contrary to our lawyer's predictions of a quick hearing, we soon learned that Ogarek had prepared for a heavy, time-consuming assault. Rather than just identify charges that the State might have planned to file, Ogarek immediately went into explicit details of the alleged assault.

Judge Douglas seemed equally surprised. This turned out to be much more than a mere bond hearing. It was elevated to a level normally expected at an actual trial involving witnesses and the introduction of evidence. Prosecutor Ogarek had no witnesses, but asserted that the main item of evidence, a video cassette that she had in her possession, would prove the charges. She promised overwhelming evidence showing that these defendants should be incarcerated and not released on bond, protocol be damned.

Patrick was stunned.

Judge Douglas seemed stunned.

Neither of them had expected the aggressive onslaught by Ogarek, nor the demands she presented.

Patrick's astonishment lay in the fact that this was not customary procedure at this juncture.

Judge Douglas's surprise lay in the fact that she had just finished wedding ceremonies and was ready to go home.

Our surprise was a little more simple: we didn't know what the hell was going on.

In the end, Judge Douglas correctly refused to listen to the evidence that was being force fed to her. And, while she refused to accept the recommendation of a mere $1,000,000 bond demanded by Ogarek, she also refused the $10,000 bond common in such cases, the amount recommended by Patrick. Instead, she ruled on a bond of $100,000. It staggered us. Each boy's family would have to post an advance of $10,000 in cash in order to get their son released. We had played it safe and, exceeding Patrick's recommendation, had brought $2,500 with us. Compounding the problem, it was Saturday and our banks were closed.

Dobrila's initial dismay quickly turned into action, as she mobilized her brother, who had attended the court proceedings, into action. Her success at borrowing money from her former mother-in-law, combined with the cash her brother carried with him, and his ability to borrow more from one of his friends, resulted in securing the required amount of bail within the hour that had been granted to us.

Adrian was finally released. He was tired and looked the part of a kid who had experienced the far-reaching consequences of tampering with the law. Dobrila hugged and kissed him. She kept squeezing his hand as she walked down the hallway toward the exit. On the steps leaving the courthouse, Adrian suddenly stopped and asked his mother whether she had any money left.

Thinking that he might be hungry, and that his inquiry was directed towards the possibility of buying a meal at Burger King, she quickly acknowledged that she had $100 left. With her reluctant approval, he took that $100 bill and handed it to a reclusive looking individual who was also exiting the building. Adrian explained, "I met him in jail and he needs the money much more than I could ever need it." At once joyous, and equally dismayed by his unselfish generosity with money that was not his own, I still realized that we must have taught him some admirable values.

All things considered, I thought that we had been successful in deflecting the opening gambit in this human game of chess.

We would try to be more prepared for the next move.

CHAPTER 10

POLICE TACTICS

It wasn't until Monday evening, December 9, 2002, that the Cook County Sheriff's Police had been contacted about the allegations of a possible rape. This had been done by the hospital, to which Conny, the alleged victim, had finally gone for evaluation. She had waited for two days after the incident had occurred before seeking any type of help.

Experts in the field of human behavior may interpret this delay as a result of psychological shock, unconscious denial, fear, or simply the inability of a purported victim to deal with this type of matter at all.

That may very well be the case. And it would probably be even more convincing if this alleged victim had been relatively chaste with limited sexual experience. If, on the other hand, she had been voluntarily involved in similar sexual activities in the past, then the explanation for the delay, based on shock, denial, fear and the inability to deal with such a situation, probably would lose some merit and reasonableness. The question, then, as to why she had not gone immediately to the hospital for treatment, may in fact shed some light onto the true circumstances of the alleged crime.

Such prior voluntary involvement and sexual experiences would probably prohibit claiming shock and outrage. Instead, she might claim to have been surprised or insulted. But these are not values recognized by psychologists, and could not justify such a delay, or at a minimum, might cast doubt on her motives for the delay.

Of course, prior involvement in various sexual acts would still not justify rape. No matter how promiscuous a lifestyle she might have led, any involuntary sexual attack should be considered as rape and should be prosecuted as such. In fact, a prostitute may have entertained twenty customers on Monday, accuse someone of rape on Tuesday, and have sex again twenty times on Wednesday, and still be entitled to the remedies of the law. However, if it were so simple to determine a rape case, then the courtrooms would be filled with prostitutes seeking monetary awards for the crimes committed against them.

Obviously, a lot more must be taken into consideration before casting judgment, and one should listen and evaluate all the evidence from both sides of an argument before believing either. And it is this advice which I believe to have been lost on the detectives investigating this matter. With this in mind, the actual behavior of all the participants would have to be evaluated, before any conclusions should have been reached. All evidence would have to be obtained, examined, and scrutinized before any accusations regarding a crime should have been levied.

Everyone knows this, if for no other reason than watching the countless TV crime dramas that occupy prime-time slots every day. Every such drama ultimately seems to revolve around the interpretation of testimony, the investigation of evidence, and the admissibility and presentation of both in a manner required by law. And certainly every seasoned, experienced detective knows this.

If one only accepts the evidence presented by one side, then a person's accusation of rape may turn out to be something altogether different. In the case of a prostitute, it might even be nothing but a dispute about payment for services rendered.

In the rape accusation against my son, it may really be about any number of other things. Maybe it was anger over something that was possibly not done. Maybe it was embarrassment over something that had been done. Perhaps the alleged victim wanted revenge for promises not fulfilled. Could there have been a boyfriend who needed to be placated about her having sex with others? Was there attempted extortion involved?

In fact, many of the incidents that happened after the alleged incident should raise questions in the investigators' minds about her motives.

Even more than needing to examine the alleged victim's intentions, I wondered about the tactics and strategies of these detectives assigned to this case. In my opinion, their behavior casts an ominous and deceitful shadow on their legitimate interpretation of the law, and I suggest that it needs intensive scrutiny.

You might remember Conny's arrival at Adrian's house, a little after 2:00 a.m. on Saturday, December 7, 2002, and her leaving long after daybreak that same morning. Next, the confrontation during which I had called the police occurred on Monday evening, December 9, 2002. By then, she had spent the remainder of Saturday, all day Sunday, and most of Monday with friends, family and teachers, and probably was engaged in all sorts of activities. Activities which did not include contacting the police and reporting that she had been raped. In fact, she had come back to our house on that Monday evening for the sole purpose of retrieving that video tape which, according to rumor, had been publicized by students at her high school. This type of scandal is surely not a pleasant thing for anyone to face, and it must have been extremely embarrassing to her. Yet she still did not make any reports to the police. Even when I confronted her that Monday evening, and she denied that any rape had happened, she chose again not to talk to anyone in law enforcement. I had told her to stay in the car while I went back into the house to call the police. Here was a golden opportunity to make that report. She instead elected to run away.

Next, at 7:00 p.m. on that same Monday evening, after having appeared perfectly fine to me while she sat in the Dodge, she had suddenly and unexplainably felt ill, and had been taken to the hospital. There, she claimed that the reason for her illness was the alleged rape two days earlier. Despite the fact that no physical evidence was found, had been presented or had been uncovered, someone at the hospital, based on what probably was a routine practice, contacted the police department to report her allegations. At approximately 10:00 p.m., detective Gleason of the Cook County Sheriff's police responded to the call and made his initial report of her statements, as they had been told at the hospital. On Tuesday, Conny went back to school, and did not give her full, written report to the detectives until 7:00 p.m. that evening.

On Thursday, the detectives visited my house and spoke to my wife, who promptly had called me to tell me of the unfolding events. The detectives had left, with instructions that she should call them when Adrian came home from school.

Notwithstanding the false security and assurances that they had given my wife, they proceeded to the house of Tarek Ibrahimovic, one of the other youths implicated.

At about 5:00 p.m., my son, Adrian, after having spoken to my wife relative to the detective's visit, went to Tarek's house, where the two detectives had been waiting. Jimmy Brown, one of the other youths who had been at the party and operated the camcorder, was with Adrian at the time. As soon as they arrived, the detectives immediately notified them that they had to accompany them to the police station in order to give their statements. And it is at this time that this investigation takes a dark turn into the legal absurdity which seems to be complacently tolerated—if not suggested, encouraged, and even promoted by the police, specifically, and in the legal system, in general.

This, in fact, seemed to be the "Tipping Point," as defined by Malcolm Gladwell, the author of a best selling book of the same title, in which he reports how little things can make a big difference in law-enforcement investigations. Without a doubt the tactics of these detectives could be interpreted as unconventional, and generally remain unknown to the general population.

But this is not about being guilty or innocent, at this point. And it's not about being accused and facing the consequences. It is about the abuse and purposeful disregard of the law by experienced detectives at their sole discretion. And it is my belief that not only did they proceed in a manner which was illegal and even unconstitutional, but they also covered up their actions with mutually supportive proof and reciprocal alibis. In doing so, they were careful to hide their manipulations and rationalize their indiscretions.

You decide. How often does a judge believe the testimony of a suspect over that of a police officer?

The suspected boys were told, in no uncertain terms, that they had to come down to the station in order to give a statement. However, in the written police report filed later on, this direct order was reduced to a mere request that the boys accompany the officers to the police station in order to "assist" in the investigation.

The youths believed that they had been arrested, and that they had no choice but to listen to the orders of the detectives. If they didn't, they might have been charged with obstruction, and who knows what else. They didn't dare ask any questions.

They certainly had some idea regarding the purpose and reason for the interrogations. Rumors had already spread about the party and what went on well before the detectives initiated action. But, in the youths' minds they were innocent, since the girl had been a more-than-willing participant. And in their minds, they were all witnesses to that fact.

The boys didn't ask if they were arrested, or if they could just disregard the orders of the detectives and simply walk away. The officers' angry demeanor, firm tone, and ready display of their badges petrified the young suspects, and wiped away any notion of legal liberties. They were teenagers who had never faced an arrest or confrontation with the police. They were surprised by the allegations, intimidated by the detectives' behavior, overwhelmed by the apparent severity of this matter, and most of all, afraid as to the implications and consequences. For their entire lives they had been taught to follow the law and obey the police.

These detectives were seasoned police officers with hundreds of arrests. And this was just another one of those pesky incidents that would be best served with a shortcut.

However, all too often a shortcut turns out to be the longest distance between two points.

At 5:34 p.m. on Thursday, December 12, 2002, Adrian was read the Miranda advisory and was asked to sign a document attesting to his understanding of that disclaimer. He reluctantly signed it, which would indicate that there could no longer be any doubt that he had been arrested.

The time of his arrest would be important for two reasons. First, the language in the disclaimer stated that he understood his rights, specifically that he had the right to remain silent, and that anything that he said could be used against him in a court of law. However, it didn't mention anything about giving up those rights. Maybe it's simply a matter of word play, but by no interpretation did he give up his rights. Even though he had signed that document, and understood his rights, he never gave them up. Some might argue that it was only a subtle differentiation, but in legal terms, it was a differentiation none the less.

Secondly, at the time of his arrest, there was not sufficient "Probable Cause" for his arrest. "Probable Cause" is one of the conditions that must be met in order to validate the legality of an arrest. And a simple accusation is not sufficient to satisfy this requirement. There has to be some kind of evidence that supports that accusation in order for an arrest to be legal. However, more importantly, if a person were arrested without "Probable Cause," then any evidence uncovered after his arrest would not be admissible. In this case, if the arrest was done without "Probable Cause," then any new evidence that was uncovered after 5:34 p.m. could not be used. And in fact, the detectives did not have any evidence in their possession at the time of the arrest. The location of the video tape, which they claimed to be the irrefutable evidence, had not been delivered to them until 7:45 p.m. that evening. Clearly that tape could not be used as evidence for his arrest. It's what attorneys like to refer to as "the fruit of the poisonous tree," whereby the tape was the "fruit" and the improper arrest the "poisonous tree."

And there was yet another reason which supports the fact that the conduct of the detectives had been illegal. The Constitution of the United States of America clearly demands that any suspect be granted the right to an attorney. Yet despite repeated requests for an attorney by Adrian as well as the other boys while they were at the police station, no attorney had ever been provided.

The interrogation lasted nearly all night. The detectives used techniques designed to break down hardened criminals. They would alternatively change the room climate, overheating it to a scorching temperature, then dramatically reducing it to bone-chilling frigidity. They would lower the lighting to near darkness, and once the eyes of the youths had adjusted, they would turn the lights up to glaring intensity. In the constricting space, they smoked incessantly, both cigars and cigarettes, until the stench had the boys choking.

Worse yet was the psychological assault. At each and every opportunity, they would explain to the youths that no one had any knowledge as to their location, and that it would be a considerable amount of time, probably days, before anyone would find out. And during that time, the interrogation would not only continue, but worse things might actually happen. Severe accidents could take place, which every one of the detectives could attest to and be very sorry for.

At 3:00 a.m., weary, demoralized, and frightened, the boys capitulated and accepted their fate. So they signed the incriminating admissions that could, and would, be used against them later on in court.

Needless to say, after nearly ten hours of such incarceration, the familiar, short attention span of all teenagers had become apparent, and as a result, the will and resolve of these inexperienced, impressionable, and scared boys was reduced to a level of total obedience.

Only Anthony Roberts, who was not brought to the station until 10:50 PM on Thursday evening, and who had not endured the entire arsenal of tactics the detectives implemented against the other three boys, had not signed the confessions.

It gave none of us any reassurance that Assistant States Attorney Barrett supervised and approved these activities, other than lending credence to the possibility that a cozy arrangement existed among these individuals who had sworn to serve and protect the rights of suspects. It would appear that in matters of the law, some people just cannot tell the whole truth—and nothing but the truth—unless they can lie about it a little.

CHAPTER 11

THE GRAND JURY'S OPINION

We had just left the Bridgeview courthouse after Judge Loretta Douglas had imposed a $100,000 bond, relieved by the fact that we had been able to collect the necessary amount of money to bail out our son. As we descended the courthouse steps, and while Adrian chatted with his new "inmate" friend, our attorney, Patrick Campanelli, cautioned us that this matter regarding the bond was probably not yet over.

"Expect them to bring this in front of the Grand Jury and ask for further resolution of the charges," he warned. And of course, his premonition proved to be correct.

While we tried to make our lives normal again and address our financial security, the prosecution turned to the Grand Jury in an effort to increase the likelihood of a conviction, by asking to broaden the charges. The jurists struck a devastating blow by incredibly approving a total of 140 felony counts! This included 60 counts of aggravated criminal sexual assault, 40 counts of criminal sexual assault, and 40 counts of child pornography. Due to the nature of these charges, the law proscribed prison terms to be served consecutively. Based on mandatory and minimum sentences for each of the counts, the youths faced a possible 60 years in prison if they were convicted!

These counts were conjured up through extensive duplication of charges in each of the three categories. This essentially meant that one act committed by any of the youths could be charged as three counts. For example, the act of touching and kissing a breast would result in one count for touching under the criminal sexual assault, one count for touching under the aggravated sexual assault, and because it had been recorded on videotape, one count for child pornography. The same duplications would then be repeated for the act of kissing.

One might ask, who is this Grand Jury and exactly what is it they do? The answer is simple. They are sixteen regular citizens from every walk of life who have been chosen, according to law, to determine if a suspect should be charged or prosecuted for a criminal act when there is probable cause to believe that the individual had committed an offense. The jury has another responsibility: to protect the innocent from unfounded accusations of criminal conduct, and spare them the trouble and expense of a trial when there is insufficient evidence to believe that the accused is guilty of these allegations.

In other words, the Grand Jury is made up of normal people chosen to protect the innocent citizen from wrongful accusations brought about by the prosecutors (i.e., the government). Clearly noble, and as the name would imply, grand intentions.

Now, the next question one might ask how this is accomplished. It is through an ostensibly straightforward process. The rules of conduct and expectations are explained to them, after which they hear the facts of the case as presented by the prosecution. They examine the evidence as put forth by the prosecution, and listen to the witnesses presented by the prosecution. When this is completed, they retire for consideration, and make a determination whether or not the accused should go to trial.

That's all there is to it.

And in case that you were wondering as to what role the defense plays, the answer is a simple one.

None!

They are not even allowed to show up. They are not able to offer any arguments or explanations. It's a remarkable process, one that might raise more questions than it answers. And usually, the person who does not show up for an argument, in all probability, will lose that argument. Furthermore, the person who referees an argument, and who is in charge of making the rules and choosing the terms and conditions of an argument, would usually win that argument.

But those are the rules, and one can only work within those parameters.

But just as one has gotten used to the unbelievable, one has to deal with the incredible.

The prosecution, in order to re-enforce the strength of their case, can randomly grant complete immunity to anyone involved in a crime in exchange for their assistance in convicting another person involved in the same crime. And while that in itself may not be all that shocking, as one would assume that in electing this option, the prosecution would select the least guilty person to be a witness against the most guilty individual. However, there are no guidelines that require the verification relative to the "least" and "most" part, as that decision is completely left to the discretion of the prosecution. In other words, if the prosecutors had made a decision that they already knew which individual they wanted to prosecute, then they could choose any other suspect to incriminate that guilty individual.

In fact, the prosecutors did bring Jenny Weller, the friend of Conny, and promised her complete immunity in exchange for her testimony to the Grand Jury. They also summoned Jeremy Culp, one of the boys who had not been immediately arrested, and gave him what would turn out to be extremely lenient terms in return for his testimony.

Neither we, nor our attorneys, were allowed to participate in this process. So we didn't know what had been said or what had been promised at the time that the testimonies were given. We would, of course, receive transcripts later on, but that would be the equivalent to closing the proverbial barn door after the horse had already escaped.

Prosecutors showed the video tape, and presented their version of what they claimed to have happened. The defense, prohibited from participation, presented nothing in this exercise of futility. We, like virtually everyone else in America, had never undergone any experience with the Grand Jury. The procedures they followed seemed unconstitutional, biased, and simply unfair. They seemed to rival those of the most antiquated legal systems, and I was wondering whether they still relied on the "oracle" method of judgment, and whether burning at the stake might still be a remedy they might exercise.

Patrick simply shrugged his shoulders and explained that nothing in our legal system provided redress to the actions of a Grand Jury.

End of argument.

In fact, an inside joke among criminal attorneys tells of the certainty that even a ham sandwich would get indicted by the Grand Jury.

Somehow, our government thought it wise to establish and define a group of individuals to pass judgment solely on the merits of hearing only one side of the argument. And with no one to scrutinize or contest the accuracy of that one-sided information, might the purveyors of it employ bias, tailoring the evidence as they deemed necessary, in order to win a favorable ruling?

It would appear that the blindfold of justice was preventing the truth to be seen, as someone was clearly tipping the scales. I had no idea that this was possible. Not only does that seem unconstitutional and unfair, but it appeared to me to border on the very deterioration of every rational interpretation of the law, a wanton regression into the Dark Ages, and the re-invention of nothing less than a tyranny, adopted and exercised by our elected government.

Ignorance is clearly no excuse in the eyes of the law, and my ignorance as it might apply to the criminal legal system involving the likes of a Grand Jury, made me feel extremely pessimistic about the probability of a successful defense. Clearly, the cards were stacked in favor of the prosecution (a.k.a. the government) as they looked to the Grand Jury (controlled by the government) for approval, supportm and testament of their venomous and uncontested accusations.

And I thought that the purpose of this investigation had been to uncover the truth.

CHAPTER 12

SELECTIVE PROSECUTION

The initial sweep conducted by Detectives Gleason and Davies resulted in the arrests of four teenagers. The two other youths, Robert Peterson and Jeremy Culp, who had also been at the party on December 7, 2002, and had arguably done the most insulting things to the alleged victim, had not been charged in the same manner or to the same extent.

Unlike Adrian, Tarek or Anthony, they were not involved in any actual intercourse activities. Instead, they wrote obscenities on Conny's chest, stomach, and legs while she was passed out. They also placed a used condom on her forehead, masturbated onto her, and spat on her. In addition, they assisted Tarek in placing a cigarette into her vagina and even helped light the cigarette. Most of this had been videotaped by Jimmy.

Robert and Jeremy were arrested on December 16, 2002, and were each charged with one count of misdemeanor battery. They were released on a $1,000 bond. In March 2003, they finalized a plea bargain that had been offered by the State Attorney's office. This arrangement consisted of two years' probation and 30 days in the sheriff's work release program.

When I heard of the outcome of the case involving these two boys, I was overcome with mixed emotions. I was at once glad for their vindication through relatively easy and acceptable terms. I was also distressed for the exact same reason. More specifically, I was upset over the disparity and inequity with which these two boys had been treated compared to the other four boys. Not that they had received such easy terms, but instead, that such disparate and recondite demands had been made of the other four youths.

Let me explain. According to existing law, the get-away driver in a bank robbery is as guilty of murder as the accomplice who shot the guard in a bank robbery. This suggests that everyone accused of having participated in a crime may be equally culpable.

In this case, of all the boys implicated, only Tarek and Adrian had sexual intercourse with the girl, which could be seen on the videotape. Both of them had been charged with 140 felony counts! Anthony, who had not appeared in the video, and who up to that point in time had neither admitted nor denied having had sex with Conny, also received 140 counts. Jimmy, the boy who handled the camera, and who never had any contact with the alleged victim, received 140 counts.

All of this happened while the girl appeared to be a willing participant in these activities.

All four of these boys had been rounded up on the first day of the investigation.

But Robert and Jeremy were charged with only one count of misdemeanor battery, even though they had fondled the girl, ejaculated on her, spat on her, inscribed obscenities on her, and placed a used condom on her face. They did this while she was passed out, and most of it was captured on the video.

These two boys had not been immediately located, and in fact, were not arrested until nine days later.

I found the entire scenario extremely confusing, and no matter how hard I tried, I could find no logic or reasoning to it. It didn't make sense. Why were the boys who participated in consensual sex with her subjected to such heavy-handed charges while the others, who performed sexual acts while she was unconscious, were dealt with in relatively light terms? A possible sixty years in prison compared to probation?

Let's look at the evidence and try to determine what factors might have influenced the prosecutors.

First of all, the video tape had been prominently described as incontestable evidence to prove the alleged crimes. What did it show? It depicted two separate and distinct activities, and could best be separated into two chapters. Chapter one shows a willing female engaged in two consecutive, consensual sex acts with two males. These activities involved straight and simple intercourse, and aside from the verbal directions of the camcorder operator, showed nothing more than what one might see on late-night, or cable TV, on every night of the week. It contained dimly lit sexual scenes that could not really be described as explicit, but instead only offered the insinuation that the individuals had been engaged in intercourse.

Chapter two showed an unconscious female being subjected to vulgar behavior by two boys, all relative to instructions from the videographer.

So what should be the deciding factor involving the video tape? Should it turn on the female's state of consciousness, and what sexual acts she had been aware of?

Obviously, this factor had made little impact on the people making legal decisions, since the youths involved while the girl was fully conscious had been charged with crimes that could lock them up for 60 years, while the boys who had acted while she was passed out would be punished only by probation.

Should the deciding factor involve consent by the alleged victim? Again, the video showed her to be responsive and giving vocal approval and directions, during chapter one. This would probably indicate to a reasonable individual that she had given her consent during this period. Chapter two, on the other hand, clearly showed that she was not responsive and that she had, in fact, passed out during this entire period. To a reasonable individual, this would probably indicate that she had not given her consent.

Perhaps the distinction lies in the definition of sex. Maybe the acts in chapter two would not be considered sexual behavior. I would find it hard to believe that any individual, reasonable or not, would construe that to be a possibility

Maybe the key element was the assault portion of the "aggravated sexual assault" charges. But here again, I would find the acts committed in chapter two to be much more assaultive than those in chapter one.

The only other available items of evidence were the written statements coerced from the four youths on the night that they were arrested. In those "confessions," they admitted to the activities depicted in the video, but none of their statements admitted to any wrongdoing. In fact, they elaborated at length as to the girl's willing participation in the activities of chapter one. These statements, which do nothing but corroborate what can be seen on the video, would appear to have negligible weight as evidence of criminal conduct.

So far, we have considered only those individuals who had been seen on the video. However, two of the boys who were charged with the mind-bending 140 counts were never seen in the video. Jimmy, of course, could only be heard giving instructions. Anthony was neither seen nor heard. Yet both of these boys faced a possible 60 years' imprisonment.

The last issue involves the 40 counts of child pornography. But here too, lies a tremendous disparity. If Jimmy, who did not appear in the video, was guilty of child pornography, as he had been charged, then equal treatment under the law should demand that anyone appearing in the video be charged as well. This would include Robert and Jeremy, the two boys facing only one count, and that count was not for child pornography.

The bottom line is, none of the evidence can explain the reason for charging four of the youths with 140 felony counts, while charging the other pair with only one misdemeanor count.

Don't get me wrong. I'm not arguing to increase the charges against Robert and Jeremy, but conversely, to drastically reduce the over-wrought, disproportionate charges against Adrian, Jimmy, Tarek, and Anthony.

And regardless of how much thought I had given in attempting to ascertain the reasoning behind such disparity, the only reasonable explanation to me seemed to have involved the length of time that it had taken for the detectives to locate and arrest one set of teenagers versus the other. After having arrested the first four youths, they appeared to have been satisfied with their task, and the arrest of the last two individuals was more of an afterthought than a sincere attempt to continue their investigation. Clearly, the detectives wanted to take their investigation to the next level, and any delay in pursuing any other participants might only have compromised the speed of accomplishing their efforts.

However, someone suggested to me that perhaps there had been political influences on the prosecutors to go after these kids and punish them to the fullest extent possible. This might have involved any number of reasons of which we would have had no knowledge about and which might, in fact, have served only to spearhead someone's political ambitions. If, in fact, politics had invaded the ranks of law enforcement, then any actions and decisions could certainly be made without regard for the law or the equity that is afforded the average individual thereunder.

It would appear that there had been some truth to the suggestion. In fact, English publisher Sir Ernest Benn might have said it right when he declared that "Politics is the art of looking for trouble, finding it whether it exists or not, diagnosing it incorrectly, and applying the wrong remedy.

CHAPTER 13

STRATEGIES

Since the initial bond hearing of December 14, 2002, which had set the bond amount at $100,000, the prosecution had been busy nurturing their cause. They were successful in arresting the two additional boys on December 16, at which time they began to structure their assault. Based on their promises of leniency, they persuaded several witnesses, including Jenny Weller, Robert Peterson, and Jeremy Culp, to join their side and testify in front of the Grand Jury.

They also supplied the media with information slanted against the defendants. And they succeeded in convincing the Grand Jury to expand criminal charges, based on the testimony of the two boys arrested on December 16.

The various parts of their strategy all seemed to fit: the square pieces went into the square holes, and the round pieces went into the other square holes—with only a little use of a chisel and hammer.

I don't know when it dawned on them that the remaining piece, a thorough investigation, should be started. Up until this moment, it certainly hadn't taken place. Investigators had never examined the alleged crime scene, nor collected any evidence that might actually be important to their case.

My God! Even my eight-year-old son knows that you have to investigate the "crime" scene in order to present, support, and substantiate your case. God forbid, there might actually be evidence that could support the defense.

Finally, the government investigators, after having convinced the media, Judge Loretta Douglas, and the Grand Jury of their "righteous" pursuit of justice, descended upon our home at approximately 7:00 p.m. on December 30, 2002, to examine the site of these allegations. This would be 23 days after the incident had taken place.

We were in the middle of dinner with my wife's parents, when six unmarked cars pulled into our driveway, and in what could only be described as a SWAT operation, ten investigators descended upon our home in an unmistakable effort to discover evidence as quickly as possible. Well, as quickly as possible after 23 elapsed days, that is.

They presented a search warrant that had been secured from an unknown judge only the night before, and herded my family into the living room, in an apparent effort to prevent our interference in their task of securing the evidence. They had recruited a local police officer to stand guard while the investigative team rummaged through our home.

These law enforcement officers were strict, to the point, and even rude. The local cop, evidently embarrassed by their behavior, apologized for their conduct. There weren't enough chairs in the room, and I remained standing, as the investigators had refused to allow anyone to bring in more chairs. Luckily, my wife had her cell phone by her side, and immediately called our attorney. He advised us to abide by the instructions of the officers, and said that he was on his way to our house. As we waited, we watched as several boxes of God knows what were being removed and loaded into their vehicles.

And, at every opportunity, they made comments deliberately loud enough for us to hear. "This is exactly what we were looking for," or, "This is good stuff that we are getting." At last one of them said, "I think we have everything that we need." I can't help but feel that they intentionally wanted to inflict fear, concern, and worry. On the contrary, we were not frightened teenagers, like the arrested boys, who could be so easily manipulated.

Patrick arrived about 15 minutes later, armed with a camera. He followed the investigators into every room and repeatedly clicked his camera during the searches. Later, he confided to us that, in hurrying over, there hadn't been enough time to stop and buy any film. However, the mere impression that he was taking photographs of the "after" condition of our property might have made the investigators more conscientious. They certainly would be concerned about liability for excessive force or unusual harm to our property. Perhaps that is why no damage was sustained and the police search left the rooms in quite orderly condition

Only now were we able to take an inventory of what items had been taken as evidence from Adrian's bedroom and the spare bedroom. These included mattresses, bed sheets, towels, pillows, drinking glasses, the camcorder that was suspected to have been used in the recording, and even the TV set that might have been used in viewing the alleged crime. They had dusted for fingerprints and had vacuumed carpets and furniture in their search for microscopic evidence that might lay hidden in the fibers.

Patrick stayed with us after the investigators left. He agreed that their actions seemed quite extraordinary even to him. He cautioned us not be surprised if they returned to search the rest of the house, if for no other reason than to simply make our lives more difficult. "Get rid of all illegal and risqué belongings such as any pornographic paraphernalia," he cautioned, and then added with a half serious smirk, "also all drugs, whips, and chains."

Patrick told us of persistent rumors at the courthouse that prosecutors intended to pursue this matter to the maximum extent of the law, and maybe even beyond. He advised us of hearing that Peter Troy and the chief prosecutor at the Bridgeview courthouse, had personally taken it upon himself to pursue a conviction in this case.

I was quite sure that spreading such rumors was common practice and just another attempt at intimidation, as deliberate rumors are clearly intended to travel fastest to the place where they will do the most harm and cause the most panic.

As a precaution, Patrick said he would prepare a written statement, which would identify his representation of us in case we were harassed or intimidated. He instructed us to carry that letter with us at all times to deter any overzealous detective or investigator tempted to cross the line of normal procedures. In essence, it would put them on notice that they could not use the same tactics they had used with the boys on the day of their arrest. Our attorney seemed genuinely concerned, and I wondered whether this investigation, based on the numerous twists, turns, and detours, might be new territory for which he had not bargained.

Furthermore, his continued dialogue regarding other possible activities by the prosecution made me now second-guess the strength of my resolve and convictions. My level of concern increased in proportion to his warnings, and I began to wonder whether we were capable of surviving this onslaught after all. I wondered if the prosecutors actually considered us as prey who could be easily intimidated and outsmarted—just like the teenagers who had been previously accused.

My confidence in our justice system was rapidly eroding. Especially when we were notified that a new bond hearing, based on the Grand Jury's decision, was scheduled for January 10, 2003, it crumbled even more. All at once, the fortified gateway which had kept at bay all of my nightmares about Big Brother, witch hunts, tyrannies, and other such storied legends, was not only smashed wide open, but was actually ripped off its hinges.

To further discuss defense strategies, we arranged a meeting at Patrick's office on January 3, 2003. Dobrila, Adrian, and I arrived promptly at 1:30 p.m. at his Palos Hills office, in a suburb adjacent to Bridgeview. We sat at a large oval desk to address our situation. He immediately confirmed to us that our case had caused a relatively major commotion with the state attorney's office, and that it had been indicated to him that they would pursue this matter vigorously and persistently. In fact, he reaffirmed that the prosecution was looking for additional indictments, and would attempt to have the amount of the bond increased. "But we are getting ahead of ourselves," he said. "We'll have to wait until we are notified of their intentions." Turning to Adrian, he cautioned, "In the meantime, you have to stay out of trouble. Go to school, get good grades, maybe get a part-time job."

He presented us with a copy of the letter he had promised, a formally written proclamation of our rights under the law. We assured him that we would keep a copy of this letter at our home and in every car, and that we would carry a copy with us at all times.

Next, he turned his attention to the news media and the probability that there might be extensive coverage. Cautioning us to be prepared for this, he urged us to refrain from making any statements. There was nothing we could say that would not be interpreted and reported in exactly the manner that reporters deemed necessary for a good story. And a "good" story always would report "bad" things. By making any statement, we could be quoted according to what they thought that they heard us say. "A good reporter," he said, "can and will give all kinds of details, without knowing any of the actual facts, as long as he can claim that he was quoting you." We nodded our understanding and assured him of our compliance.

Patrick turned to something we hadn't given much thought to, namely the need for damage control. In his view, we should make it appear that we knew something might not have been in order, and that we had taken steps to address any problems that might have caused Adrian to behave the way that he did. Of course, it should be seen as a positive step without admitting any wrongdoing.

"This is done every day" Patrick explained. "Just open any magazine, and you will find one celebrity after another admitting themselves to some kind of rehab facility. Not because they might be guilty of something, but instead, because they acknowledged that something was not in order. Half is forgiven if you acknowledge that you need help, and then take the necessary steps to get that help," he reasoned. "Because this was a party involving minors, and because the media has already reported that alcohol had been involved, we need to make the use of alcohol the real culprit. Everyone knows that teenagers drink and everyone knows that this is a major problem. Especially every parent knows this."

He kept making eye contact with all of us, in an effort to evaluate our unspoken response. We in turn kept nodding in approval, relying on his experience in dealing with such matters. "I strongly recommend that Adrian enroll in a substance abuse program because of this alcohol issue. And if we are lucky, the alleged victim, who had also been drinking, will not undergo such measures of self-improvement." Patrick sounded authoritative on the matter. "And if the other boys don't do something similar, then Adrian will look all the better."

This idea made sense to us and we agreed to look into it immediately. In fact we did enroll Adrian in an alcohol abuse program operated by a local hospital in which he began attendance a week later.

Patrick asked if we understood everything he had said, and if we had any questions. We replied that we had understood, that we agreed, and didn't have any questions just then. We would feel free to call him later, should we come up with any questions. As we started to rise from our chairs, he slightly raised his hand, gesturing us to remain seated just a while longer. "There is just one more thing," he announced. "When I originally agreed to represent Adrian, and when I quoted you the fees for my services, I had no idea that this would become this big. In fact, I've since had to turn down some new cases because of the amount of time that this case has and will demand of me," he stated. "I'm going to have to ask for an additional $10,000 because of this."

And this time he was not making eye contact.

Later that evening, we had just returned from Patrick's office and had not even taken off our coats yet, when he called with bad news. He had just been advised that the prosecution had filed the motion for an increase in the bond amount, and that arguments would be heard on January 10, 2003 by Judge David P. Sterba. We had expected it, and yet we were still caught off guard. He said, "The judge will probably only set a hearing date at which time he will make a ruling."

With that information in mind, we had a full week to painstakingly prepare for nothing that we could do. And while Adrian's case was uneventful during that week, another legal matter involving two of my businesses flared up with the brilliance of a guiding flare in the darkest of nights. We had been involved for some time in several substantial lawsuits. These involved one of my main partners, and a bank holding a mortgage on three commercial properties. This partner, believing that we could not possibly beat the bank's foreclosure, had suddenly and unexpectedly joined forces with the bank. As a result, sensitive information regarding our strategy had been revealed to the bank and we had to seek alternative means of litigating our rights. Our adversary had been strengthened by the defection of this wealthy individual, while our side suffered a potentially lethal blow. With millions of dollars at stake, any resolution seemed still in the distant future, and our monetary resources were nearly drained. Their strategy had been to force us to overextend ourselves, which they reasoned would result in our defeat.

But precisely during the week that we waited for the new bond hearing for Adrian, the most unexpected event regarding my former partner and the bank occurred. My fight with the bank might not have carried a lot of weight by itself, but combined with other problems that they seemed to have experienced, my fight proved to be the straw that broke their back (as I would like to interpret it, anyway). In fact, a "cease and desist" order had been issued by the FDIC, and the bank was thrust into a rapid and violent downward spiral of insolvency.

The once invincible bank fortress was ablaze, and we gleefully bathed our tired and weary ambitions, justifications, and anticipations in the comforting warmth of this vengeful bonfire.

With that, our defensive maneuvers were modified into a well-planned attack (as I would like to believe once again). The only drawback was that I had to use all of my financial reserves, and even mortgage the very property that I was acquiring in this process. With the stress of my business added to the problems stemming from Adrian's legal pitfalls, I felt like a pickup truck carrying the load of an eighteen-wheeler.

When we left home for the bond hearing on the freezing morning of January 10, 2003, it was with little concern or anticipation. Patrick's warning of excessive media coverage appeared to have been mistaken, as everything seemed normal and uneventful. We met Patrick in the corridor outside the courtroom. He seemed somewhat disturbed and told us that this matter was quickly turning into some kind of vendetta by the prosecution.

I heard what Patrick was saying, and it certainly sounded like bad news. At least, I rationalized, no verdict would be made today. And I am ashamed to admit that my mind was heavily occupied with the anticipation of hearing news about the negotiations with the bank.

We sat down in the front row of an unusually empty courtroom. The other youths and their families had already been seated, and we acknowledged each others' presence.

Judge Sterba's entrance was punctual, and he immediately started to call his cases. Most of them involved minor infractions of the law, drug counseling issues, probation problems, and speeders fighting traffic citations. After about forty minutes, our case was called. All of the youths and their respective attorneys approached the defense's podium, while the prosecution stood by the plaintiff's stand.

The judge seemed familiar with the facts and didn't need to review any information contained in the files. He acknowledged all of the parties present and proceeded to explain that he had received the motions filed by the prosecution. He then set a date of January 15, 2003 to make a ruling. Short, sweet, and simple. Exactly the way that Patrick had predicted.

We walked out of the courtroom at about 10:30 a.m., and while my wife chatted with Patrick, I answered my cell phone. It was my attorney handling the negotiations with the bank, who advised me that they had accepted our offer, and that I needed to be at his office at 2:00 p.m. in order to sign off on the contracts. I remember thinking, while walking toward our car, that our situation seemed to mirror the classic Charles Dickens opening of A Tale of Two Cities, "It was the best of times, it was the worst of times."

Even though Judge Sterba's ruling had no direct affect on the immediate fate of the four boys accused of 140 felony counts, the media began to raise their ugly, Medusa head with newspaper reports regarding this incident. At first, articles appeared somewhere in the middle pages filling only short paragraphs with soft allusions to group-sex encounters. As it grew, "investigative" reporters found kids from the local high school who were willing to pass along salacious gossip.

Adrian and Jimmy attended the same school, and Jimmy chose to drop out once the gossip gathered full momentum. Adrian persevered, based on the continuous encouragements (and by that I mean threats) of his parents. But he realized that schoolmates were shunning him in their perception that he had violated their moral code of conduct. I could understand how other parents might take a sanctimonious stance, but as the father of one of the accused, I wished that everyone's uninformed opinion would not automatically convict him without understanding the true circumstances. Adrian seemed to take these accusations in stride, and continuously assured us that he was dealing with the mounting pressures at school. We were proud of his decisions and his ability to withstand the negative presumptions and insinuations hounding him on a daily basis.

However, the very first Monday of that week, during an "advisory class" involving discussion of current events in the community, both Adrian, a senior at his high school, and his brother Justin, a sophomore, were instructed to go to the principal's office in order to spare them embarrassment. This proved to me that news of the incident had reached all levels of the curricular environment, involving not just the students, but also the teachers.

The atmosphere at home was equally sensitive, including feelings of anger over Adrian's misconceived activities, concern over the financial goals we were attempting to achieve, and worry about a multitude of lawsuits we were litigating. We had a full plate, and any non-eventful day was considered a success.

My relationship and attitude toward Adrian at that point had deteriorated to a new low level of mistrust about his judgment, anger over his choice of friends, and hostility over the position he had put us in. I made my feelings known at every opportunity.

Few parents can deny loving their children, as even mass murderers were nurtured by their mothers' milk. Regardless of my wrath and resentment, my deep affection for Adrian remained intact, along with a determination to protect him from any harm. Still, a wall of cool detente developed between us.

Dobrila, on the other hand, was prepared to defend him unconditionally.

I remember delegating several chores to Adrian with instructions that they needed to be completed that same day. And I remember being surprised by his unusual and non-confrontational acceptance.

And I'll never forget the panic-stricken call from Dobrila, who had been involved in some errands away from home. She pleaded, "Where is Adrian? I want to talk to Adrian. Please, see where Adrian is!"

Having monitored his procrastination of the assigned chores, I replied that I thought he was taking a shower. "Relax, I can hear the noise of the water."

"I want to talk to him now," she insisted. At once surprised by her demeanor and her refusal to accept my explanation, I questioned her about the urgency. She persisted, "Get Adrian, please see where he is, see what he is doing." I couldn't remember a previous incident that made her so anxious, and it shocked me to realize that she was crying. She explained, "I just heard the voice mail that he left. He said that he was sorry. He said that he loved me and he said that none of this was my fault and that he would always love me." I could hear her gasping for air.

I dropped the phone and sprinted to Adrian's bedroom. Finding his door locked, I pounded on it with my fist, hoping he could hear me over the shower's noise. A great sense of relief, mixed with confused anger, rushed over me when I heard him respond, not from the shower but just inside the room. I yelled, "Open the door!"

"Go away," he replied. "I'm taking a shower."

The pained tone of my wife's voice resonated in my head. I felt a new rush of temper over Adrian's stupid actions. And his nonchalant, defiant attitude was all it took to shatter my already fragile state of mind. I flew into a rage. "Open the goddamn door!" I screamed at the top of my lungs, while pounding on it with my fist. I couldn't hear any response. His indifferent attitude took me by surprise and re-ignited my fury. I slammed against the door with my full weight and broke the lock. But since Adrian was bracing himself against the other side, I was able to push it open only a few inches, enough to see him. He appeared to have been crying. I pushed harder; a non-athletic man near fifty against an athletic youth of seventeen.

Sometimes, determination and perseverance, regardless of age, can overcome the stamina of youth. I managed to force the door fully open, and enter his bedroom.

Adrian stepped back, amazed that I had been able to defeat his attempts to keep me out. Glancing around the room, I asked why he had been crying. He denied it and attempted to usher me out as quickly as possible, while avoiding any meaningful answers to my questions. Not finding any disrepair or reasons to be doubtful, I reluctantly started to leave, but instinctively glanced into his closet on my way out.

Within a split second everything became clear to me: my wife's desperate attempt to contact him and my son's evasive behavior. I couldn't believe my eyes, and while my mind was confused by the undeniable evidence of what I saw, I gasped for air, feeling a sudden sharp pain of despair numb my mind and paralyze my body.

There were no words which could possibly explain or justify the feelings that had overcome me. I felt my tears stream uncontrollably down my cheeks as I stared in total denial at the very thing that I was attempting not to see.

All I could see were a child's vain attempt to find seclusion in his own reasoning.

All I could see were the desperate attempts of a child to find answers to questions that he did not understand.

All I could see was a boy's sad attempt to escape both his past and his future.

He had fashioned a noose from several belts, and had positioned a stool underneath it, in a clear plan to deal with the problem in his own way.

Adrian stepped back, crushed, and sat on his bed while covering his face with the palms of his hands to muffle his sobbing.

I stood motionless, as my parental instincts overcame my boiling anger and rampant disbelief. The shock of witnessing the contraption fashioned by Adrian instantly defused my feelings.

There was still anger.

There was still disbelief.

There was still disappointment.

But above all, there was love and forgiveness.

They were all there, somewhere in the pit of my stomach. But most of all, I felt an overwhelming feeling which simply strangled my consciousness. Feelings of utter helplessness . . . yet saturated with monumental relief. Helplessness for realizing how powerless I had actually been in preventing a near tragedy; relief for realizing, that which I had been powerless to prevent, would nevertheless now be prevented.

Standing on the edge of a bottomless abyss, I could feel its bitter, cold reality. I could feel the blood rushing from by brain, and starve all of my reasoning, judgment and understanding. I could feel my strength and resistance be siphoned from my body.

I had to remember to breathe.

I closed my eyes in an attempt to make the spectacle go away.

To disappear.

As if it never happened.

I don't know how long it was before I could react to the stark reality which I simply could not accept. And even then, all I could do was observe my arms and hands reach out to dismantle the noose.

CHAPTER 14

NOTORIETY

Our sleepless nights and remorseful days were filled with constant anxiety while we waited for January 15, the day of Adrian's second bond hearing.

We hadn't yet recovered from the shock of our son's suicide attempt and feared that he might be desperate enough to try it again. Searching for spiritual guidance, we turned to Father Raymond Klees, the priest at our youngest boy's school. We also consulted a psychologist to support Adrian.

My wife and I would rise early these days to escape the nightmares terrorizing our sleep, only to trade them for the empty relief of a new day which would only bring on new concerns and new problems. By this point, our morale had been down for so long, that it almost seemed that we had settled into an unquestioned acceptance of constantly having to face new challenges and unexpected difficulties. Our victories and accomplishments lay simply in getting through another day and night. All thoughts of financial gratification involving my recent successful financial transaction helped relieve some of the stress, but now took a back seat to the problems ahead.

On the morning of the January 15, we sat at the kitchen table over our first cups of coffee, discussing and pondering the obligations that we would face this day, while routinely glancing at television news and weather reports. Without warning, it grabbed our throats and threatened to strangle both of us.

Our son's picture appeared on the screen, followed in quick succession by the photos of the other three boys who had been arrested with him. Patrick had warned of shocking news coverage, but it still struck like a hammer blow between the eyes. The blatant inaccuracy of reporters' coverage froze us in disbelief.

On one channel, the newscaster said, "Today's headline story is about the four men charged with brutally raping an unconscious girl and will face trial for that crime."

We switched channels, only to hear, "We are live at the Bridgeview courthouse where a judge will rule on the brutal rape of an unconscious young girl by four men last December. . . ."

On yet another newscast, we listened in horror to an anchorperson report, "Prosecutors say that they have recovered the video tape and other valuable evidence which they will offer as proof of the brutal gang rape of an innocent young girl by four men last December."

Every fifteen minutes, they had more. "Today, the four men accused of a brutal gang rape of an unconscious young victim will face their fate . . .", "Videotaped gang rape of innocent teen jolts the suburbs . . ."

"Oh my God," Dobrina gasped. Her initial anger wilted into despair as tears rolled down her cheeks. I kept a stern appearance, but inside I also cried. My conflicting emotions bounced uncontrollably like a pinball between biased treatment by the media, anger at Adrian for putting us in this situation, sadness for my wife, and outright fear. But most of all, I was terribly afraid of the uncertainties that lay ahead.

The reports incorrectly stated that a ruling on the accusations of rape was expected today. Actually, the hearing was scheduled only to adjudicate the prosecutors' request to increase bail from $100,000 to $400,000, rather than address the guilt or innocence of the youths. Not only was our faith in the justice system crashing, so was any credibility we had previously assigned to the news media. We switched the television off before Adrian came in to prevent escalating his fearful premonitions.

Dobrila is normally a feely-touchy-huggy person, and her usual embraces of Adrian were short and sweet. This morning, though, she wrapped her arms around him much harder and longer. He sensed the difference in her melancholy mood and attempted to calm her, saying, "Don't worry, Mom, it'll be okay." It had the reverse effect, causing more tears and tighter squeezes, as the uncontrolled emotions of the recent events surged through her body.

Dressing for his court appearance, Adrian put on his dark blue suit, light blue shirt and matching tie, in his best effort to look like a clean-cut young man, hoping the judge would be impressed.

At the exit to our long driveway, we deliberately avoided picking up the delivered *Chicago Tribune*. We just didn't need any more sensational and distorted information which would only insult and assault us.

Based on the media coverage on TV that morning, we had mentally prepared ourselves for the probability that the media might greet us at the courthouse.

And the atomic bomb detonated in Hiroshima was just another explosion . . .

As we exited the expressway overpass, we could actually see the raised satellite dishes that the mobile news teams were using to transmit their live newscasts. They hovered above the rooftops of all the surrounding buildings, and reminded me of medieval banners of warring armies which had laid siege to their enemies' territory.

A herd of perhaps one hundred men and women—carrying microphones and recorders, dragging cables, clamoring like seals— blocked the stairway we had to climb. A venomous swarm of reporters hungered for their prey, us. They literally shoved each other out of the way as we approached, and truth be told, we could not even understand any of the questions because of the noise generated by their overlapping voices.

After declining countless requests and demands for comments, we made it through the horde, past security, through another gaggle of reporters waving digital recorders in our faces, and finally into courtroom 102. Every seat was filled except the front two rows, which were reserved for members of the defendants' team, and standing-room-only observers lined the walls. Father Klees must have convinced the bailiff that he was a member of the defense's team, as he was already seated in the front row.

Judge David P. Sterba was expected to make a ruling on the motions raised by the prosecutors, and then assign the trial to a different judge, in a biblically symbolic gesture involving Pontius Pilate, who had "washed his hands clean" of any consequences of his initial ruling. We, and the other three families, sighed when Sterba announced he would hear all the other cases first since ours would take extensive time. Based on that decision, I exited the courtroom to make some phone calls. Passing several sheriff deputies, who had congregated around the entrance of the courtroom, and who had no idea who I was, I heard them make comments. "The boy in the blue suit is one of the rapists," was one comment. "They all look guilty," and "Why is the priest there . . . was he involved?" were other comments. These individuals, who should have known better, had prejudged and delivered verdicts before one shred of evidence could be introduced. Obviously, the media had done a good job.

When our case was finally called, each of the four boys obeyed instructions to approach the bench and stand next to their attorneys. The prosecution, led by the indefatigable Peg Ogarek, formalized the request for a new bond hearing, citing additional evidence uncovered since the arrests, but offering no details. Instead, she leaped immediately to the video recording, and proclaimed that the judge hearing this case in December did not have an opportunity to view the contents of this tape, so the matter was not properly evaluated or weighed. No one had left the courtroom, and the gallery seemed riveted by her words.

"Because of the severity and the brutality depicted in the video tape, we are now requesting that a significantly higher bond be imposed. Or in the alternative, we are asking this court to impose an immediate incarceration of the four suspects, as they pose a risk to society," were the dreadful recommendations that I remembered her making.

Reporters scribbled the words and sketch artists used colored pencils to feverishly capture the disdainful look of the prosecutors as well as the look of disbelief and abstinent denial of the defense attorneys.

One by one, defense attorneys spoke of their clients' good qualities, family values, financial hardships, school habits, and achievements.

Jimmy's family lived in Brookfield, a blue-collar community. He went to high school and helped his father with his trucking job, helping the family make ends meet.

Anthony lived in a single-parent home, also in Brookfield. He had joined the U.S. Army Reserve, attended high school, and worked weekends delivering pizzas, helping the family make ends meet.

Tarek lived in Lyons, also a blue-collar area. His father had died in a work-related accident. He was studying for his high school equivalency exams and was doing odd jobs, helping the family make ends meet.

Adrian, if truth be told, lived on an estate in upscale Burr Ridge. His only obligations were to achieve good grades in high school in preparation for a good university. He helped around the house, primarily when he needed some kind of favor or reward, and spent most of his spare time with his girlfriend. On rare occasions, he would do projects in his parents' businesses. Patrick, though, put a little different spin on his situation. In the lawyer's legally modified version, Adrian lived with four siblings and helped them on a daily basis. He was a good student in high school with aspirations for a university education. In his spare time he aided his parents in their business, in an effort to help support the family.

Obviously, Patrick could not deviate from the other lawyers' description of their client, as any good attorney knows how not to tell anything but the truth, the whole truth, and only the truth— as he is compelled to see it.

Judge Sterba listened patiently, as he must have never heard such convincing, irrefutable, true, and correct statements before. He then called a thirty-minute recess to view the video tape in his chambers, with the lawyers present. When they returned, Sterba delivered his ruling. "Now that I have had the opportunity to view the evidence presented in the form of the video recording, and after evaluating its contents, I find that the defendants pose no risk to society, pose no flight risk, and the request for a higher bond, or incarceration, is herewith denied."

Spectators and reporters appeared stunned that the judge was letting these evil rapists off the hook. But he hadn't finished. Sterba added, "I also order that all of the defendants submit to the jurisdiction of Cook County under their program of home confinement for the duration of this trial. I order them to submit to periodic tests for drugs and alcohol. Basically, I want to know where these people are at all times. I want them in school, in court, or at home, and nowhere else."

It would appear that both sides had won skirmishes in advance of the pending battle.

Additionally, the judge declined to impose a gag order, which according to the defense attorneys, based on the media exposure, extremely prejudiced their ability to receive a fair trial. However, the judge did order that no one may have any communication with the alleged victim.

The session had given us room for optimism and hope. We all wondered where the prosecution's convincing evidence had disappeared to. However, the most significant event to date was not the fact that the bond amount was not increased, or that the defendants were not incarcerated. Instead, it was the simple fact that a judge had finally watched the crucial video, and despite the promises by prosecutors of the overpowering, brutal, and disgusting evidence it supposedly offered, made a ruling not in favor of the prosecutors.

This was finally a bit of good news. It was finally proof of the exaggerations of the prosecution's evidence and the media's reports. It was finally proof that the prosecutors were full of shit, and that their motives were equally vile and rancid, and their intentions loathsome and infested with self-serving objectives.

The judge's ruling finally offered some measure of hope. It might have only been the proverbial, lonesome blade of grass, but so far, it was the only sliver of hope to which we could hold on to.

We were hoping that this would be the first step toward reaching our goal of vindication. After all, even a journey of a thousand miles requires a single first step, however small, in order to be accomplished. We hoped that this might be that first step.

It was only a somber afterthought that Judge Sterba did modify the conditions of the prior ruling by imposing home confinement for each of the boys. But we were too jubilant to really notice. In the end, I suspect that his decision was somewhat politically motivated (courthouse politics), whereby he did not wish to totally offend and humiliate the prosecutors, which would only serve to offend the States Attorney's Office.

But just as quickly as we had made the determination about the viewing of the tape, so too did we realize that a new judge would try the case, and his interpretation of what had been recorded on the tape might be completely opposite of that of Judge Sterba. But we dared to hope nonetheless.

Sterba assigned the pending trial to Judge Robert M. Smierciak, to commence in fifteen days, on January 30, 2003.

CHAPTER 15

WHO LET THE MEDIA OUT?

Justice in Illinois had suffered several serious blows in recent years. In 1999, Anthony Porter, a death-row inmate, came within twenty-four hours of being executed before Northwestern University students conducted an in-depth investigation and uncovered evidence to exonerate him. DNA evidence helped reverse convictions of a dozen other men, leading Governor George Homer Ryan to declare a moratorium on capital punishment and pardon four other men. Widespread news reports declared that they had been tortured by police investigators into confessing, and those admissions were used in their trials. Unfortunately, Ryan smeared his good-guy image with scandal. He was being accused of accepting bribes for various favors, the most serious having been the sale of commercial driver's licenses to unqualified drivers. Several motorists died in crashes with those people, the most notorious having been an accident in Wisconsin that killed six young children of one family. Ryan was later convicted on all charges of racketeering and bribery. In one of his lasts act as governor, only four days before Judge Sterba's bond hearing, Ryan commuted the sentences of 167 death-row inmates to life in prison.

Now, that sounds like important news. But guess what made headlines around Chicago and eastern Illinois during all of these events? From December 16, 2002, the day my son and the other youths were arrested, they were the big story. The media decided that sensational accounts of teen sex outweighed the deaths of numerous innocent motorists due to what appeared to be the unscrupulous greed of elected officials. It was of greater importance than the revelation that innocent convicts had been set free after years of confinement on death row. It was more newsworthy than the monumental precedent set by granting clemency to all remaining death row inmates.

The story of four boys accused of sexual assault remained a hot topic, and exponentially gained momentum with each new court hearing. Our attorney's premonition regarding the media was less than the tip of the iceberg that lay hidden beneath the actual truth. It rose with the ferocity of an erupting volcano, spewing out corrosive, malignant boulders of speculation, hearsay, and lies onto the landscape of reality, burning holes into the credibility and innocence of the accused. Eye-grabbing phrases appeared in print: "Unconscious young girl dragged into spare bedroom and brutally raped by four men" . . . "Video recording obtained by police of brutal gang rape." Even our son's high school newspaper got in on the action with "Obscene incident taints high school with evil."

And while the headlines piqued everyone's curiosity, the narrative explained in graphic detail how a young girl had arrived at a party, not unlike an innocent virgin who entered the dragon's den, and then was brutally raped by four men while she was unconscious and unaware of what happened. The stories kept flowing on a daily basis, reporting any possible interpretation, making any imaginable correlation to any hypothetical event which may or may not have actually happened.

What was the source of this tainted information? In most cases, it was credited to a spokesperson from the State Attorney's Office. A few were even attributed to Assistant State's Attorney Peter Troy.

Our house, generously described by these reporters as a sprawling estate in upscale Burr Ridge, which I interpreted as being a biased attempt to present a picture of the " rich, immoral, and guilty" vs. the "normal, innocent, everyday people," was besieged by these same newshounds on a daily basis. Even after we made a practice of locking the wrought-iron gate to our property, we would still see close-up pictures of our home on the evening news that had been taken with long-range cameras.

This remarkable imbalance in the importance of news stories is troubling. Shouldn't events that affect large segments of the population receive more press coverage than titillating accusations of sexual misconduct? I have no answers. But I do worry that we are not privileged in receiving all of the details of political events, and many important things are not being said. Someone is pushing the buttons to divert our attention from powerful, vested interests in effort to re-address the importance and redistribute the weight of matters that should concern all of us.

CHAPTER 16

THE GRINDSTONE

Home confinement, we thought, might not be as bad as it sounded. The wings and free spirit of our teenage son might be curbed a bit; and the restrictions normally imposed upon him by his parents might take a more serious meaning for him. If you are a parent of a teenager, you know exactly what I mean. As I mentioned before, unlike the average teenager, I am not young enough to know the true purpose of life. And at my age, I doubt that I ever will. But then, my father might have had a similar story to tell.

We were told that there would be routine verifications as to Adrian's detention at home throughout the day and night, that he would be subjected to routine drug and alcohol testing. Also, he would be required to check in with his parole officer at least once a week. All of that would be acceptable considering the alternative that had been proposed.

After the hearing with Judge Sterba, we arrived back at our house without having stopped anywhere. We didn't even dare to go to a drive-through restaurant, which would require us to slightly detour from our route, in fear of being followed. Furthermore, stopping anywhere might cause a delay, and we could possibly miss the very first home check, which we were convinced would happen immediately.

"Once bitten by a snake," an old Serbian proverb states, "will make you afraid of even a worm."

It surprised us that nothing happened the balance of the first day and night, nor did we see any signs of anyone checking on Adrian's movements. The following day passed uneventfully, with still no sign of home checks. We tried to settled back into our routine of everyday activities. Adrian and his brothers returned to school, and didn't allow any of the rumors to bother them. I went back to my meetings with attorneys in order to wrap up the acquisition of the mortgage and associated property. Dobrila managed all of our finances, including business affairs involving lines of credit with various banks relative to spec homes we were building.

Finally, on the third evening, the first home confinement verification occurred. At approximately 8:00 p.m. we received a phone call advising us that Adrian needed to come to the front door, as the officers would be there within a few minutes. We watched as an unmarked, white sedan approached. It rolled to a stop at our front door, and a tall African-American officer exited the vehicle. I opened the front door to invite him inside. Adrian stood behind me, and intrigued by the novelty, the rest of my family had lined up behind Adrian in anticipation of the officer's arrival. He declined our invitation to come in, and instead asked to see Adrian's identification. After marking what appeared to be an attendance record, accordingly, he pivoted without saying anything else, climbed back into the car, and drove away.

Not bad at all, we thought. If this was the routine, we could deal with it.

We changed our minds a few hours later when we received similar phone calls at 2:15 a.m. and at 4:35 a.m. In both instances, I answered, and in a mad rush to get Adrian to the door, Dobrila raced to his room, while I stood at the front door to let the officers know that he would be out shortly. The commotion also woke up Adrian's other three brothers, and everyone was groggy and struggling through the next day with barely any sleep.

It took us another three nights with similar calls, before we had this brilliant idea of putting a phone in Adrian's room, and muting all other phones in the house during the night. However, anticipating a particular event to happen will always cause anxiety and concern, until it actually happens. We constantly waited for the pot to boil, and while we tried not to watch it, we were still preoccupied by its anticipated occurrence. In addition, we were also concerned about Adrian's timely response and compliance, which only added to our anxiety.

Several different teams of officers would come to verify Adrian's presence. For the most part, they were friendly, and after getting to know us, some would even enter into fairly extensive conversations. Surprisingly, these chats seemed to always end with some kind of reassurance on the officers' part, that things would soon get better for us.

Of course, there were some officers who were so impressed by their own importance that they would pound on our door, activate their siren, or sound their car horn, regardless of the hour, especially if Adrian was not at the door the second that they pulled up.

Once we became accustomed to these home checks, and we soon did, we would relax and be content for things to remain the same, while deceiving ourselves that by remaining the same, they were actually getting better.

CHAPTER 17

INTERVENTIONS

Saint Thomas Aquinas in the 13th century postulated that, "To one who has faith, no explanation is necessary. To one without faith, no explanation is possible."

Faith, I surmised, clearly seemed to be an extremely subjective practice and, as I have learned since, an even more elusive phenomenon.

During this period, my family and I had a number of comforting sessions with Father Raymond Klees, the priest at the private Catholic school which all my sons had attended over the years. He visited our home regularly after Adrian's suicide attempt.

He was an imposing individual, in his early fifties, well over six feet tall, with white, thinning hair, and a well-rounded physique. He possessed an extremely confident attitude, which many people confused with self-motivated arrogance. However, once a person got over the initial presumptions, one would immediately recognize that he was really a very charismatic individual with a very engaging and intuitive personality, which quickly transcended the rigid expectations associated with a priest. And yet, despite his actually easygoing nature, he did posses a firm temperament. Simply put, when Father Klees would speak, people would start to pray. But our conversations were not just simple lectures. Instead, they were engaging discussions about antiquities, current events, and the philosophies and remedies of faith.

During his weekly visits, Father Klees had spent several hours at a time with Adrian. He excluded us from these discussions, but confided that he was listening more than talking. However, he could not help himself from imparting his advice on Christian values, giving spiritual guidance, compassionate understanding, and open-minded support, on all of us. And over time, he clearly instilled a glimmer of faith in my otherwise fatalistic approach to life, and he enlightened me on the wonders of faith, which I seemed to have somehow misplaced over time. He reaffirmed that success in life did not consist of holding good cards, but rather playing the cards that you had been dealt, and playing them to the best of our ability.

Having found some new meaning in the interpretation and meaning of religion, I had nevertheless been reminded of human reality and expectations by the simplistic proverb, "God helps those who help themselves."

I gratefully accepted the advice offered by Father Klees, and valued his opinions. But just to be on the safe side, I decided to also consult the advice of a mortally destined professional in order to address Adrian's search for answers as well as his ill-advised choices of a remedy. A friend of ours recommended that we talk to a psychologist named Trudy Kessler, whose son had committed suicide at the age of 13. Our common bond with Trudy allowed open discussion of our near-tragedy and of her painful experiences, along with plenty of tears.

She agreed to see Adrian twice a week at our home to accommodate the court-imposed restrictions. I hate to admit this, but it entered my mind that her involvement might also speak volumes in terms of Patrick's damage-control suggestion that we demonstrate to the courts our positive action in acknowledging a problem and dealing with it. We knew that securing Trudy's services was the right thing to do, but we also counted on recognition by those who might ultimately stand in judgment of our actions and decisions.

It is said that a knowledgeable person travels along the path of life, whereas an ignorant person wanders along aimlessly. And while it is a given fact that the path to truth and vindication is always a twisting and uphill road, our situation was further complicated and compromised by the fact that we seemed to only have an incomplete and illegible road map to guide us, which neither showed the means nor the outcome of our sojourn.

And whenever you are unsure of your destination, every road may look like the right one.

As a result, we attempted to cover as much ground as we could. And while we were determined that we would ultimately reach our destination, we were equally hopeful that our relentless efforts might allow us to possibly stumble upon the right path through the process of elimination. After all, one's chances of success are generally increased based on the number of times one attempts.

We embraced our newfound vitality in our Christian faith. It had always been there . . . somewhere. Father Klees, however, had suddenly renewed our faith, which he had suddenly stirred up from our stagnant sediment of indifference and ignorance. We welcomed his involvement with Adrian and sincerely appreciated the spiritual perspectives he offered. Our God is a loving God, with the capacity and reputation of forgiving even the most obscene and vile sinners, and it was our determination to ensure that Adrian be reminded of this spiritual tolerance.

We enrolled Adrian in a highly accredited substance-abuse program, not only because of our attorney's repeated recommendations, but primarily because of our concerns of the influences that alcohol might already have had on his life. We hoped that giving him advice now would not be the equivalent of giving medicine to a person who had already died.

We rushed to repair the cracks in his conscience and psychological self-esteem with the services of a professional counselor who had experienced the devastation of a son's suicide herself, in hopes of strengthening and re-supporting the foundation of his fragile self-esteem. We realized that we needed professional-grade cement that was not available in a do-it-yourself home-repair kit.

We dug deep within our own well of parental wisdom, and lavishly showered him with love and forgiveness, in an effort to assure him that, no matter what, he could always rely on his family.

Fearing that this legal nightmare might be too difficult for Patrick to handle by himself, we consulted with one of the most highly profiled law firms in the Midwest, reasoning that they had more manpower and were not attached to the income stream from the Bridgeview Courthouse. Based thereupon, it was our belief that they could oppose the state prosecutors in ways that Patrick might hesitate, in fear of any potential retributions with his other cases. It was our version of the "Dream Team," which would have surely caused more widespread speculations in the media. However, in the end, Dobrila convinced me that Patrick's personal involvement had transcended mere legal maneuvers that we could expect from other attorneys, and it was her motherly instinct that compelled us to remain with Patrick.

We accepted the court-imposed responsibilities and obligations as our own, seeking ways to keep Adrian motivated and to maintain a positive attitude. In conversations, we emphasized the importance of his obligations and responsibilities. Along this line, we modified our own rules and regulations, in a attempt to make his home confinement less confining.

Adrian's life had become one huge grindstone, and we tried desperately to explain to him that it would be his choice whether this grindstone would polish him or pulverize him.

Each morning, I drove Adrian and his three other brothers to school, and Dobrila picked them up in the afternoon. We encouraged Adrian to invite his friends over on weekends, provided everyone abided by two rules; no drugs or alcohol, and Adrian's bedroom door had to remain open at all times. Only two such gatherings occurred before his pals decided that we had imposed too many restrictions on their fun. Phone calls continued for a while longer, but eventually subsided altogether.

To compensate, we decided to allow Adrian to have his girlfriend over even during the week to keep his mind preoccupied (no pun intended). She was a stunningly beautiful girl with long blonde hair, a lovely face and a slender, attractive physique to match. She visited nearly every day and stayed until late into the evening. We remained strict on the issue of drugs and alcohol, but relaxed on the issue of the open bedroom door policy, which would, over time, be closed a little more each day, and by the time they were both 18, the door would be closed all the way.

Our constant involvement with Adrian during the initial periods of his house arrest seemed to achieve the desired results. A routine finally settled in. Adrian's ability to cope with his strict confinement and rigid restrictions, despite several subsequent court appearances as well as some confrontations at school, presented no further challenges or surprises for him.

It is said that there are two kinds of parents: those who suspect nothing and those who suspect everything. We had become the kind of parents that did both. We suspected everything and had therefore taken every precaution that should have allowed us the luxury, comfort, and reliance of being able to suspect nothing.

But we were obviously only kidding ourselves.

CHAPTER 18

THE TRUTH BE TOLD

Judges, state attorneys, prosecutors, and police officers are employed by the people, supported by taxpayers, and their sole purpose is to uphold the law and protect the rights of its citizens.

They must do so completely and objectively.

They cannot take sides.

They work for the people, and their salaries are paid by the people's tax dollars.

Any involvement with either plaintiff or defendant, assailant or victim, can only be professional, and must not be guided by favoritism, pity, anger, malice, revenge or preconceived notions of any kind.

Only then can a person be justly tried by them.

So, why then was Assistant State's Attorney Peter Troy, the head authority at the Bridgeview courthouse, sitting in the courthouse next to the accuser's family, engaged in a conversation, smiling and laughing? This was not a good omen.

It took place during the first court appearance with Judge Robert M. Smierciak, on Thursday, January 30, 2003. We had expected and had been prepared for the news media onslaught and their throngs on the courthouse steps. Dobrila, Adrian, our son Eric, and I walked briskly past the reporters, refusing once again to make any comments. We made it to room 110, where Father Klees greeted us. Our case was held until the end of the morning call once again, and we gathered outside the courtroom to talk.

Patrick had previously informed us that the only items of significance that day would be the entry of our "not guilty" plea and the setting of a date for the next step.

He wanted to drag out the court proceedings a bit, in order to allow the media to settle down and not make our case their continued prime objective. He hoped that another newsworthy story might come along and take the heat away from us.

While we stood outside the doors of room 110, Father Klees, who was facing the doors, asked me to step aside slightly, as he had noticed that Judge Smierciak, sitting at his bench, seemed to repeatedly gaze into the hallway through the windows in the courtroom doors. He said, "Judge Smierciak seems like a good and God-fearing Polish judge and I want to make sure that he can see my collar. It could only help." I thought I detected a sly grin as he continued trying to make eye contact with the judge.

Our case was called shortly thereafter and the four youths with their respective attorneys stood in front of the judge. Each of them entered a loud and resolute plea of "Not guilty."

Judge Smierciak turned to the prosecution, asked them to address their motion, a request for DNA samples from the defendants. They had filed it only moments earlier and all of the defense attorneys expressed displeasure over the short notice, but acquiesced.

The motion was allowed and a date of March 10 set for the next session. As we left, Patrick said, "You may want to watch the news, or get a late edition paper. I told a few reporters to call my office later, so that I could give them a statement. I just want to have them focus a little bit on what we have to say, rather than just report speculations from the prosecution." It would appear that Peter Troy's presence and behavior had finally struck a nerve with him.

That evening and the following morning the media trumpeted sensation again. Every newscast and newspaper headline featured the word "sex."

TEENS PLEAD INNOCENT IN SEX ASSAULT
SEX TAPE CONSENT DISPUTED
DNA TESTS SOUGHT IN SEX CASE

Now accustomed to this, our skins had grown thicker and we pretty much ignored it. Once we had gotten past the headlines, however, strange and unexpected things began to appear in the contents of their articles. The *Chicago Tribune* reported on January 30, 2003:

TEENS'S LAWYERS SAY GIRL PERMITTED ACTS

New details have emerged about a 20-minute video at the center of a suburban gang rape case — a tape prosecutors say is sordid evidence of an attack on an unconscious victim, while defense lawyers call it a home pornographic movie instigated by a teenage girl.

A Cook County state's attorney's spokesman said the girl is "semi-responsive" at the beginning of the tape, not unconscious throughout, as prosecutors and police officials asserted.

For the first time, both sides acknowledge the girl is conscious at the beginning of the tape, although they disagree about how conscious she was and whether the girl was capable of consenting. Prosecutors say the girl's inability to consent is at the crux of their case.

All of a sudden, the prosecution conceded that the girl was in fact not unconscious, as they had vigorously insisted until now. The video had been in their possession since day one, and considering that they had claimed this recording was indisputable evidence of a crime involving an unconscious victim, then this admission should have immediately raised several rudimentary questions.

What the hell were they looking at all this time until now? Did they even know what it had been, that they were looking at? How long were they going to harbor this secret knowledge?   Could they distinguish their own ass from a hole in the ground?

Until now, the media had continuously reported that the girl had been unconscious, causing a major frenzy of popular belief, that the youths accused of the alleged rape had been automatically guilty, and should immediately be thrown in jail. The prosecution, who had leaked that information to the media, stood by and basked in the obvious results this information produced.

Next, representations of unconsciousness were made to the Grand Jury, and a 140-felony count indictment had been elicited. And it had been the same prosecutors who had obtained that successful indictment with the same evidence. But now that they had realized their error, you would think that they would take the necessary steps to correct the situation. Their main purpose and objective, after all, is to enforce the law and seek justice. You might expect them to contact the media and advise them that they had been wrong. You might think that they would request another hearing before the Grand Jury and advise them that the evidence was faulty.

After all, it is truth that they are after. The truth and nothing but the truth, so help them God, and definitely not aspirations of a career advancement resulting from a conviction in a high profile case.

But what was it that they did instead? They relied on that tried-and-true political approach of applying a little "spin" to the recent development. They changed their opinion as to what really mattered in this case.

Because of my involvement in this case, I was one of the few individuals who had been allowed to see the tape. And any reasonable person who viewed that video would immediately come to the conclusion that the girl had not been unconscious. She was clearly moving her arms and legs, obeying commands, and giving directions herself. She was talking, and could be heard to be laughing and giggling, as well. But this was now translated by the prosecution as a state of being "semi-responsive."

Robert Kuzas, the attorney for Anthony Roberts, had measured the length of time the alleged victim was moving, talking and giggling. Out of the 20 minutes of recording, she had been doing so for 18 minutes! The prosecution's interpretation of the 18 out of 20 minutes, or 90% of the time, was that she was "semi-responsive" in the beginning only.

Finally, since the recording did not start from the moment they had entered the spare room, but instead from the point in time that the lights had been adjusted, and the clothing of the participants had been removed, no evidence of actual consent was recorded. However, a strong argument could be made that moving about in a co-operative manner, giving directions about what other people should do, laughing and giggling, could be interpreted as such consent. But, since the alleged victim did not specifically speak into the camera and say, "I consent to being fucked by all these boys here," the prosecution automatically precluded the possibility that her behavior was consensual, and pinned their entire case on that slim thread.

Now, they had gone from, "innocent and unconscious girl dragged into spare bedroom and brutally gang raped," to asking, "Was the girl conscious enough to give consent?" It defied any legal or intelligent logic. These prosecutors, like all attorneys, are officers of the law, and as such are sworn to uphold the law. And if they violate their duty, then they are breaking the law themselves. Yet they seem to have no fear of retribution. Instead, it appeared to be business as usual. Put a little "spin" on the truth, regroup, and try again.

Several great minds had something to say about such treatment of the truth:

> *One lie does not cost you one truth, but the entire truth.*
> —Christian Friedrich Hebbel, 1813 – 1863

> *The tragedy is not that a lie had been told, but instead that it created the impossibility of believing ever again.*
> —Friedrich Wilhelm Nietzsche, 1844 – 1900

> *When you add to the truth, you subtract from it,*
> —Talmud

> *To be believed, make the truth unbelievable.*
> —Napoleon Bonaparte, 1769 – 1821

Someone in the state's legal bureaucracy must not have liked the articles that had appeared in the newspapers, or the newscasts of January 30. "Spin" alone was apparently not sufficient to clean their soiled image. Suddenly the defense attorneys were giving interviews and were apparently not going to play by the conventional rules of remaining silent. "Spin" had to be compounded with new methods of offense and tactical interventions.

Bear in mind that every person working in the state's attorney's office is working for the people, and are mandated to remain impartial, as they do not represent the plaintiff nor the defendant (I hope that I have made that sufficiently clear by now). Their job is to remain impartial and to uncover the truth, and not to force nor prevent a conviction (and I hope that this is clear by now). Their salaries are not paid by the plaintiff or defendant, but rather by the tax dollars of working-class citizens (you definitely must know this by now).

Did Jerry Lawrence, the politically correct spokesperson for the state's attorney's office, follow those guidelines in his remarks of January 31, 2003?

Regarding the "not guilty" pleas entered by the accused boys, Lawrence said, "That's an absolute distortion of the facts—it's an abomination. We have the crime on tape."

On the matter of consent: "She had no idea what was happening to her during this humiliating sexual assault. For any defense attorney to suggest otherwise, only re-victimizes the girl."

On the fact that defense attorneys, after enduring months of attacks from the prosecution in the media, finally decided to talk to the media themselves: "They are going to the media to try this case. They are grasping at straws."

I would hate to imagine what he might have said if he were not so impartial.

And of course, I am once again reminded by what another politically correct spokesperson had said about these types of matters. It was Nikita Khrushchev, of Soviet Cold War fame, who pronounced that, despite the differences between the USA and the Soviet Union, "Politicians are the same all over. They promise to build bridges even where there are no rivers."

With the exception of a few status calls regarding the DNA evidence, the first few months following our January 30, 2003 court appearance seemed to go by fairly uneventfully. DNA testing suffered long delays due to busy, backlogged laboratories, in turn postponing the trial date. News reports simmered down to sporadic articles after routine court hearings. The purposeful delay suggested by our attorney seemed to be accomplishing its intended objective.

Dobrila and I had learned to cope with the media's harassment and thought that Adrian had, too. We didn't see the signs of his ongoing anxiety. We didn't realize that, rather than being able to ignore the abuse and discard the adversity, he had psychologically accumulated the fallout since its inception. In fact, it had been collecting and building up pressure within him, like plaque coagulating in the bloodstream of his judgment and reasoning.

Even when we found newspaper clippings in his room, which he had collected and painstakingly highlighted, we failed to perceive it as a symptom of his fragile state of mind. We optimistically interpreted it as a genuine interest to stay abreast of the developments surrounding his case. Relying on the precautions we had taken since his suicide attempt, we blithely put it all behind us, and felt that he was capable of coping with the pressures.

It wasn't until much later that we realized he had only put up a courageous facade. He responded positively to our questions about any difficulties he might be having. No doubt existed in our minds that we considered his plight a top priority, but we nevertheless allowed ourselves to be sidetracked by unrelated problems for much of this time. Life seems to simply be one crisis after another. Or maybe it was because of life's otherwise unpredictable course of direction, which we were experiencing anew and firsthand, that we were not able to diagnose or appreciate the subtle signs that he might have been offering.

Life, after all, is what happens to you while you were making other plans.

Financial issues had consumed us too. Fortunately, we had made substantial strides in recouping and regaining much of our fiscal strength.

But most of all, the biggest reason why we had overlooked Adrian's subtle signals was due to our vision had been unexpectedly eclipsed by new shadows.

I had been diagnosed with inoperable cancer, and was given a life expectancy of less than five years. There were no solutions or remedies to this new crisis, only hopes of mitigating a certain destiny by delaying the inevitable.

We consulted with several local experts as well as internationally renowned specialists at the Mayo Clinic in Minnesota. They repeatedly instructed us to make the most out the rest of my life.

Life truly proved to be a constant, even daily, oscillation between obligations, responsibilities, intentions, and accomplishments, all of which resonate at competing frequencies, and whose harmonies are impossible to be fully understood or appreciated.

Life, after all, is not a struggle between Good and Bad, but instead between Bad and Worse.

CHAPTER 19

DETECTIVES

In June, 2003, Robert Peterson and Jeremy Culp, the two boys charge with misdemeanor battery, accepted a plea bargain. They had inscribed obscenities on the girl's body with a felt tip marker, masturbating and ejaculating on her skin, and wound up spitting on her, all recorded on the video.

In trade for a sentence of probation for two years and thirty days in the sheriff's work program, both boys agreed to testify for the prosecution in the pending trial of the other four.

As I mentioned earlier, I was glad for the apparent easy disposition of their case, and harbored no ill feelings for the arrangements that they had managed to negotiate. However, I do have ill feelings and grave concerns as to the decisions and intentions of the detectives and prosecutors, which led to those arrangements and plea bargains. And these plea bargains had made me start to think more about the detectives and the motives that had guided them.

At the time of Adrian's arrest at 5:34 p.m. on December 12, 2002, their entire evidence was based on the representations that had been made by Jenny Weller, and the unsupported accusations by the alleged victim. No other evidence existed prior to the arrest, as the hospital could not provide any evidence of a rape, and the video recording had not yet been located or viewed. In addition, Jenny had repeatedly informed us that her testimony had reflected that Conny had voluntarily participated in the sexual intercourse: the parts involving Tarek, Adrian and Anthony. It also reflected that Conny had expressed her desire to have the activities recorded.

With that information in mind, the only certain knowledge that the detectives could have based any accusations on was that the alleged victim was two months shy of the age of 17, the legal age for giving consent to sex. And while I agree that a situation involving underage sex should merit an investigation, I disagree that sex among teenagers was a crime that warranted the actions that had been exhibited by the detectives. This, after all, was not a situation that involved a mature (and much older) adult and a young and immature teenager. In fact, on a recent survey conducted by NBC and reported by Katie Couric on January 26, 2005, nearly 50% of teenagers at the age of 16 had had sexual intercourse. A lot of teenagers needed to be arrested if age was the sole criteria by which a felony was determined. Furthermore, there might have been any number of mitigating circumstances that might have justifiably addressed and even alleviated this issue. Possibly a fake identification, possibly talk about visiting bars and clubs, or possibly even facial piercing that are legal at age 18 only, could have misled the boys as to her actual age.

So far, this situation seemed more of a moral issue rather than a legal issue. But what had the detectives done when they were at my house? Did they mention any moral concerns to my wife? Quite the opposite. They told her that our son had been involved in some kind of sex with a tramp. Obviously, no concerns involving any type of moral judgments had crossed the minds of these detectives.

And, with the information that they did have prior to the arrest, possibly some kind of investigation involving a background check of all participants might have been useful. In fact, had they done such a check, they would have found out that she had previously participated in these types of activities involving videotaped sex with multiple partners. This in itself would not justify anything that took place that Saturday morning, nor non-consensual interaction, but it certainly put these activities in a different perspective. It might even lend support to the defendants' insistence that she had willingly participated. At a minimum, it would have increased the probability that she might have participated in this type of activity again.

Apparently, the most important factor in the detectives' mind had been the element of time, as they wanted the benefit of surprise.

The detectives neither looked into her background of sexual conduct, nor did they give any importance to the fact that all of these boys had spotless backgrounds, not a scintilla of scrapes with the law. Yet, they were treated like hardened criminals.

I find it incredible that the only actual evidence, the video tape, had not even turned up until after the four boys were arrested and charged with crimes.

Okay, now let's evaluate the thought process of the detectives after they watched a showing of the tape. Jenny had been the only person to describe events at the party. If they had paid any attentions to her affidavit, they should have accepted the probability that the sexual intercourse had been at Conny's invitation, and with her consent. And they had no evidence or proof that the age of the alleged victim had, or had not, been misrepresented to the boys. The only reasonable conclusion from viewing the tape would be that the sexual intercourse involving Tarek, Adrian, Anthony, and Jimmy, was consensual. Conny had been quite vocal and co-operative, and was performing in accordance with Jimmy's directions. She had been laughing and giggling while she confessed to her enjoyment. She was seen to even have reinserted Adrian's penis into her vagina, and was even heard to have asked Adrian about his girlfriend, and the impact that this tape might have on their relationship.

They had also seen the part where Conny had been unconscious or asleep, and where she was completely unaware of the conduct of Robert, Jeremy and Tarek.

Comparing these two activities, I would find it more reasonable to assume that she might have participated in that portion where she had been conscious and where she had participated, rather than the portion where she had been unconscious. And I further doubt that she would have consented to that latter portion even if she had been awake.

Let me ask again. What could have been the detectives' decision-making process as they evaluated the unfolding evidence? Might they finally have realized they had overreacted? Might they now have recognized that their conclusions had been reached prematurely and irrationally?

What they had done, instead, was to keep the boys isolated from any outside contact while attempting to force written confessions from each of them. These confessions would, after all, be worth a million doubtful speculations, obscure assumptions, vague assertions, and unfounded accusations. A written confession would be a neat and clear substitute for their lack of a proper investigation.

It is this concept of "making a good decision" by which we vest our trust in our politicians, judges, and law-enforcement officials. And philosophers and great thinkers (even some politicians) throughout the ages have toiled with the meaning and interpretation of this concept. Of the thousands of definitions and interpretations derived, I find that the famed political analyst, Theodore C. Sorensen, had offered the most prolific and realistic observation in 1963, when he wrote, "It is a law of life that every gain incurs a cost—and the most efficient decision that someone can make, therefore, is the one which produces the greatest margin of gain over cost." Or simply put, a decision is most often based on the gain it offers.

These officers had four boys in custody. Based on information available to them at that point, only one suspect, Tarek, should have been the only one of these four youths considered for a possible assault charge because of his activities in part two of the video. Nothing supported any charges against the other three. Anthony had never been identified on the video. Jimmy had never touched Conny, and even if his verbal instructions might have been crude and vulgar, they represented no crime. The fact that he was recording a sex act which involving someone whose age he had no way of knowing would at best have been inconclusive, based on what the investigators knew. Adrian's participation in part one of the video appeared to be nothing but consensual, supported by Jenny's statements.

The detectives did have clear evidence of the assault by Robert and Jeremy, as their activities were depicted in the last part of the video. For any number of reasons, including their knowledge about the entire incident, the officers should have picked them up immediately. But they did no such thing.

The news media had a field day with this case. It's amazing how they decide which crimes to sensationalize and which ones to virtually ignore.

For example, in 2003, a 14-year-old Chicago girl was abducted on her way home from school by two individuals ages 34 and 28. They took the child to several apartments in a rough section of the city, where she was repeatedly raped by numerous men over a period of ten hours. The papers carried only two small articles detailing the girl's tragic plight The first brief story appeared soon after the incident was first reported, and the second article was published after the trial was completed.

Another similar outrage took place the next year. A girl, also 14, was beaten and tortured by three men over the age of 25 during a period of several days. They left her for dead, but she survived and was able to escape. This happened in Schiller Park, a blue-collar community of Chicago. The media exposure was again limited to only two small articles.

Maybe though, if the detectives had apprehended Jeremy and Robert, listened to their accounts of the party, paid attention to Jenny's statement, and used some common sense, the whole case would have been handled differently, and the media would have virtually swept it away in the middle pages of a newspaper. Like the tragic little girls in the rough parts of Chicago.

But maybe arresting them would not have produced the "highest margin of gain," as declared by Theodore C. Sorensen.

But this incident didn't happen in Schiller Park or a tough, urban, minority section of the city. Maybe then their sexual misconduct wouldn't have drawn the huge publicity.

But maybe the wheels in the detectives' minds were turning. And whereas my son was certainly not a celebrity by any stretch of the imagination, he did, however, live in Burr Ridge, one of the most affluent suburbs of Chicago. It is a community filled with upper-bracket incomes and impressive homes, and a far distance from the crime-laden blue collar suburbs or urban areas of Chicago. Clearly, a story of rape in this community would be sensational. Names and faces of officials could appear prominently in papers and on television screens. Might even mean a few promotions, or political scores and accolades.

Instead of pursuing the real villains based on the irrefutable evidence, they pursued only those individuals who would provide the most recognition for their efforts.

By the time that Jeremy and Robert had been arrested, the detectives already had the written confessions which they had coerced from the four other frightened teenagers during their original arrest. They really didn't even need these two boys any longer. Yet they promised immunity to the real offenders, if they could collaborate their unfolding story —even if their testimony might be in conflict with the real evidence or the eyewitness account of Jenny Weller.

It appears that they would not allow the truth get in their way of building bridges to their career aspirations.

CHAPTER 20

A MATTER OF SEMANTICS

Semantics, according to the latest Webster's New World Dictionary, is defined as, "The study and development and changes of the meaning of words." And ultimately, my son's case seemed to have been a matter purely of semantics.

The founding fathers of this nation hammered out a document that still stands as the shining example for stating human rights. The U.S. Supreme Court, over a couple of centuries, has refined and shaped those rights to protect innocent suspects from abuse by overzealous law enforcement. It's a great system, but not perfect, and it is manipulated by individual miscreants. Now and then, someone falls through the cracks.

Everyone is innocent until proven guilty, unless irresponsible officials shoot off their mouths and the media amplify it, resulting in a de facto conviction in the press.

On the other side of the coin, we have all heard about a police department fumbling an investigation, which resulted in the declaration of innocence for the alleged perpetrator. Innocence by default. "If it doesn't fit, you must acquit." That's what the law mandates, and that's what the courts must obey and follow. Whether right or wrong, whether you agree or not, it's still the law. Errors by law enforcement officers can let felons slip away, and brand innocent suspects as if they had committed the worst of crimes.

When Adrian was initially arrested, my wife waited in the reception area of the station in Maywood, Illinois from a little past midnight to about 3:00 a.m. for a detective who had picked up our son twelve hours earlier. She waited, hoping to find out about the arrest and the investigation. We would later learn that the detective who gave her all sorts of assurances and promises was solely interested in securing the signed confessions from the frightened teenagers, and as a result was completely ignoring my wife's presence and telephone calls. His subsequent testimony in court revealed that during that entire time, he continued to interrogate the suspects and continued to work on the paperwork relating to this case. He was waiting for the suspects to finally break down and "make" a statement, keeping the four boys under intense scrutiny. For nearly ten hours he watched as their resolve, stamina, and determination were slowly being chipped away. They were isolated in separate rooms, while other officers were making crude and loud comments about their fate. He observed as these boys were intimidated with subconscious threats of violence and possible bodily harm, while they had no witnesses to these proceedings, and no one knew of their whereabouts.

These were experienced, knowledgeable detectives, experts in this type of confrontation. They were dealing with teenagers who had never been in trouble and who had no idea what to expect, no idea of their rights (TV knowledge notwithstanding), and who had nothing to hide (legal interpretation notwithstanding), and wouldn't know how to hide it anyway.

My wife returned at about four o'clock in the morning. She had spent the entire time in the cold, uncomfortable waiting room while both she and the officer on duty at the desk tried to contact Detective Davis. At one point Davis told the officer that he should not let my wife past the reception area. He never answered my wife's countless calls. At 3:00 a.m. he finally did come down, only to convince her to go home. Even then, while he prepared the charges against our son, he was re-assuring and convincing my wife that everything was all right and that she, as a mother, had nothing at all to worry about.

Davis assured her that he, too, was a parent and understood what she was going through. He even shook her hand, smiled, told her that she had nothing to worry about, and said he would drive Adrian home soon, which finally convinced Dobrila to put her trust in him and come home. All the while, our son endured relentless pressure to confess to rape and other sex crimes.

My question is, why would an officer who is supposed to uphold and protect the law be so deceptive? Why couldn't he be honest with my wife as to his suspicions, his intent, and his ongoing investigation and actions? Why did he feel that he had to lie to her? He could have simply said, "I'm sorry and I feel for you, but this is a serious matter, and based on the information we have so far, I have no other choice but to process him and charge him with a crime."

Instead, he told her not to worry. He told her not once, but at least a half dozen times—NOT TO WORRY! Why didn't he want her to know what his real intentions were? Maybe he had been hardened by the ruthless criminals he dealt with on a regular basis. Maybe his experience was such that all suspects and witnesses lied to him, and he needed an advantage by lulling them into a false sense of security. Or maybe he was just full of shit and wanted to make a career move and did not want anyone to interfere with his conclusion. A conclusion he was able to reach without the need of "due process." Perhaps he still hadn't convinced the young suspects to sign confessions, and needed a little more time. Possibly he realized that Adrian's parents probably had the means to secure a competent lawyer at any time of day or night, and this would have been a serious disadvantage in browbeating the suspects.

Or maybe all of this can be disregarded as being pure speculation on my part.

Remember, though, the law requires that all evidence be obtained by legal means. This requirement is designed to prevent biased, overzealous, and even corrupt police officers and detectives from obtaining evidence through short cuts or other illegal means (coercion and intimidation seem to come to my mind).

The next day, Friday the 13th, turned out to be true to its infamy. We were informed by Detective Davis that Adrian had been charged with 140 counts of criminal sexual assault, and that a hearing was scheduled the following day at the Bridgeview Courthouse. Detective

Davis, who had previously assured my wife that our son was a victim of frivolous and unsubstantiated accusations before his arrest, was now suddenly convinced and was charging him as a criminal who had committed one of the most abhorrent crimes.

I truly had no idea that a detective would or could be so misleading. I can accept the fact that he could arrest our son and interrogate him about any crime that he felt Adrian had committed. I can accept the fact that he might have believed that our son was guilty. All of that would be within the law.

However, I do have a problem with the manner in which this investigation had been conducted, the method by which the evidence was obtained, and how the confessions were achieved. "Those who enforce the laws must not break them," is an English proverb from the 17th Century, which offers a small glimpse of the social discontent with the manner in which the law was enforced during colonial times, and may explain in part why our Founding Fathers had such deep rooted concerns regarding civil liberties, and felt it necessary to specify rights in the Constitution.

We know that Adrian's rights were violated when his repeated requests for an attorney were ignored. In fact, all four of the teenagers requested the presence of an attorney. But they were held nearly ten hours in a small cell, with experienced   detectives making all kinds of threats and comments. An assistant state's attorney came in, saying he had their best interest in mind, but nevertheless expressed deep concern for their well-being unless they co-operated. After that, these kids finally broke down and made statements which no defense attorney would have allowed them to do.

We've all seen movies involving interrogations of suspects by "no nonsense" detectives, but perhaps don't realize that they might turn out to be all too true. The interrogator uses all of his skills to trick the criminal into revealing some aspect of the crime. Bright lights, the cigar smoke, the pounding of the table; all of the "good cop-bad cop" routines are usually depicted. This "bad cop" routine was used against our son, with the screaming, swearing, and threatening, while another detective, played the "good cop," apologizing and cajoling, attempting to convince him that he should avoid any further confrontations and conflict and just admit his guilt. Edward Barrett, the assistant state's attorney, told Adrian that even though he was here to protect his rights, he could not guarantee his safety as he did not normally work at this station, and that Detective Davis was in charge.

To the detectives, it was a foregone conclusion, and only a matter of time before the youths would give in.

To Adrian, this was puzzling and frightening. He wasn't sure if his mother knew where he was, because he didn't know where he was. He had repeatedly asked for an attorney, but after what seemed like an eternity to him, no attorney had been made available. And yet the detectives kept threatening and insisting that he had to sign the prepared confession. It wasn't a contest that he could have won. It was more of a conflict involving a young puppy and his master, whereby the puppy was being trained to respond to the desired command. And after fifteen separate attempts by the detectives and the assistant state's attorney, he did.

The puppy didn't have a chance.

Needless to say, all sorts of admissions had been made by the teenagers. Partially due to the fact that by then they were tired, that their will was thoroughly compromised, and that they feared anger on the part of the detectives, and imagined fearful consequences. After ten hours, a statement was written down by the assistant state's attorney, who claimed to be there to ensure that proper procedures were followed. And the teenagers were told to sign these statements, as this was a routine matter. Three of the kids signed. Anthony Roberts was the only one who refused.

The full consequences of the detectives' covert operations became painfully evident during Anthony's trial, who like the other kids, was also charged with 140 counts of criminal sexual assault, even though he was not visible in the taped recording.

In the hearing conducted on September 4, 2003 on the admissibility of evidence for Anthony, namely his unsigned confession, the prosecution put the detectives on the stand, who in great length elaborated on the manner in which the youths were taken in, the way that they were treated during the drive to the station and once they had arrived.

Robert Kuzas, Anthony's attorney, made a point of the fact that no attorney was provided for his client, despite his client's repeated request to have one made available. Furthermore, the mere fact that his client had refused to sign the written statement that was prepared for him, in no uncertain terms indicated that his client did not approve of the contents.

"I have four little words to say, judge," Robert Kuzas offered in his opening statement after the prosecutors had attested to the detectives' proper procedures. "Give me a break," were those words. "These are veteran cops working on a school kid who had no experience with the police. They very well know that when a suspect asks for a lawyer, you stop the interrogation. By doing anything else, they're depriving him of equal protection under the law."

The prosecution responded with their own explanation of what had happened and how the interrogation was performed. The information that they offered was stunning and in stark contrast to the information presented by Anthony, as well as all of the other boys.

The prosecution had a very simple explanation. And this was where the issue of semantics became an issue. First, the detectives claimed that Anthony, and the other boys, were not arrested, and that they went to the police station on their own accord and without any pressure or influence on their part. They insisted that since they had not been arrested, then the issue of admissible evidence did not matter, as all evidence was provided on a voluntary basis. A person who was not arrested obviously did not have the same protection as one who was. Secondly, the prosecutors insisted that none of the youths had actually requested an attorney. They claimed that Anthony in fact had made the following comments:

"I think that I want an attorney."

"I think that I should have an attorney."

"I believe that I should have an attorney."

And to them, none of the above was interpreted as being an actual request for an attorney. It wasn't definitive enough. It was vague and confusing as to what he was trying to say. I suppose that he should have made himself more clear and that he should have made the following request:

"Listen, you motherfucker – I want an attorney, and I want him now. And I'm not going to say another goddamn, fucking word until I have an attorney. So piss off and don't ask me another motherfucking question. It's my constitutional right, motherfucker."

But then, I am not sure that the detectives would have understood that either. After all, they had claimed that he wasn't even arrested.

It was not a matter of what Anthony had said. It was a matter of what the detectives thought that he had not said.

It was all a matter of semantics . . .

Motherfucker!

One important fact which Kuzas unfortunately did not detect involving Anthony's statement at the time, was that the original statement prepared by Edward Barrett, the assistant state's attorney who had been summoned to the station at the time of the arrest, had been corrected after it had been presented to Anthony for his signature. After Anthony had read this original version, he had noticed that his demand for an attorney had not been mentioned therein. Incredibly, the assistant state's attorney promptly complied with his request, and indicated such demand for an attorney on the document in his own handwriting. Yet in court he swore under oath that he never heard Anthony make any request for an attorney.

This discrepancy had gone unnoticed by Kuzas, and no mention thereof had been made in court. Clearly, this had been very unfortunate, as this case could have been won by default, as it would have been positive proof that the assistant state's attorney's oral representation of the truth, given under oath, was in clear conflict with his own written version of the actual truth.

There could be no greater proof of the true intentions of the detectives and the assistant state's attorney, and it was incredibly unfortunate that this had not been noticed by Kuzas.

On September 15, 2003, Judge Smierciak announced his decision. He ruled that the statement could be admitted. In his explanation, the judge said, "The state bears the burden of ensuring the rights of a defendant in any criminal case. One of those rights is the right to counsel . . . If the testimony of the defendant is true, then statements made by him should be suppressed . . . I have viewed the testimony by the sheriff's department detectives, Matthew Rafferty and James Davis, and members of the state's attorney office, and find them to be credible. As a result, I cannot believe the testimony given by the defendant to be credible, and the motion to suppress the evidence herewith is denied."

So far, everything seemed to be going the state's way. It had taken less than three minutes for the judge to reaffirm something which we had really known all along. Yet we had hoped that it would not always have to be that way. But seriously, whom was the judge going to believe anyway. The detectives, after all, had warned us about that back in December.

CHAPTER 21

REVELATIONS

With the exception of Anthony's hearing regarding the suppression of evidence, nothing of notoriety or importance happened for the balance of the year 2003.

Adrian's choice of schools to attend was limited because of the constraints his home confinement presented, so he enrolled at the Community College of DuPage. The campus was located in Glen Ellyn, a mere twenty-minute ride from our home.

Dobrila took responsibility for transporting him to and from school in an effort to keep all potential trouble, real or imaginary, out of his way. However, even the best intentions are subject to foreign influences, and after several months of being his chauffeur, she realized that arrangement could not be a permanent solution. As a result, in February 2004, we decided to give my Land Rover to him, as it provided the most parent-conscious mode of travel. A four-wheel-drive SUV, with exceptional handling, unimaginably slow acceleration, and limited top speed, it was just what every teenager would dream of.

In the meantime, I purchased a new Range Rover for my own use.

My medical condition, diagnosed in 2003, was being maintained with injections of Lupron every four months, as well as daily oral doses of Casodex, both of which were meant to eradicate all testosterone in my body. Testosterone had long been known to be the food upon which my type of cancer fed. It was also known, however, that eradicating the nourishment would not eliminate the cancer, but only slow down the rate of its growth. During the initial months of this hormonal treatment, my PSA level had significantly reduced and leveled off to a consistent reading. Prostate Specific Antigen is a byproduct generated by cancer cells, and the higher the PSA level, the more active the growth of the cancer cells would be.

My condition had already been diagnosed as incurable, as the cancer had metastasized beyond the prostate gland and evidenced itself in two lymph nodes. Whereas a cure seemed improbable, two local experts had recommended two forms of treatment which would slow down the cancer cells' growth rate. Both treatments involved the complete elimination of the prostate; one by surgery, the other by radiation.

And while neither procedure would eliminate the cancer, they would both limit my ability to have normal sex again. It turns out that a nerve, specifically responsible for erections, was located dangerously close to the rear of the prostate, and that any treatment prescribed would almost certainly damage that nerve and render it inoperative.

In short, after every option had been described to me, after all side effects had been evaluated, and after the finality of my condition had sunken in, the real question remaining was one of quality of life vs. quantity of life.

Whereas the answer to this question was easy for my wife, I was not so quickly convinced.

Or maybe I wasn't as willing to give in to defeat yet.

In a desperate attempt to find a better answer, I decided to get one more opinion. Not just any opinion, but an opinion from the single most renowned source for the latest medical innovations and cutting-edge treatments. So, on February 4, 2004, Dobrila and I departed from our home toward the Mayo Clinic in Rochester, Minnesota. Securing an appointment had been a minor miracle.

The trip should have taken no more than fourteen hours in my new Range Rover. However, the weather forecast called for some snow accumulation, and we allowed ourselves ample time to get there. We left at 4:00 a.m. in order to avoid Chicago's morning rush hour. At first, snowflakes barely became visible, but after several hours of being on the road, the storm steadily gathered strength and snow conditions actually elevated to blizzard level. The storm moved southward while we traveled north. Soon, we were heavily bombarded with a steady head-on assault of dense snow and sleet. Visibility reduced to less than twenty feet. But the roads were empty, and my new car handled like the proverbial knife slicing through hot butter. Not daring to fall behind schedule, and risk losing our reservation for one of the last available hotel rooms, but potentially also our appointment, we proceeded to travel at a rate well in excess of 80 miles per hour.

For the most part, the roadway was a two-lane highway in each direction, with a steel guardrail separating the opposing lanes. There were frequent overpasses, and every now and then, the roadway was separated by a low-lying median strip. It was actually more of a wide ditch, the low point of which appeared to be more than ten feet below street level.

Despite the heavy snowfall, not much of it accumulated on the pavement, partly due to the temperature, which would melt the snow upon impact, and partly due to the wind blowing it away before it could pile up. However, at dusk the temperature dropped, and the roadway was soon covered with a blanket of snow. Still, with my car's maneuverability, which seemed to give me the ability to disregard the worsening weather, I became relatively accustomed to the situation. As a result, I didn't hesitate to pass up slower cars which seemed less equipped to handle the weather conditions.

Dobrila, affected by the duration of the drive, the warm temperature inside, the taste and aroma of the soothing hot tea she had been drinking, and the mellow music listened to on the CD player, had eventually dozed off in the seat next to me.

With the dropping temperature, the sleet that had previously bombarded us with low visibility and miserable driving conditions had now changed into snow that was gently falling upon us.

Descending darkness created a mesmerizing and picturesque scenery; an eerie, mythical and dramatically whimsical contrast, created by the endless sea of white snowflakes falling against a background of infinite black sky. This frenzied explosion of white apparitions seemed to cascade toward us in an entropic expression, vividly illustrating nature's infinite magnitude, only to be overshadowed by its delicate, overpowering beauty, in a true testament to the insignificance of man's feeble and petty existence.

It would have been a magnificent spectacle even if one were standing still. But it was magnified a hundred-fold by the velocity of the car I was driving, and its full beauty and magnificence appeared almost impossible to be fully comprehended or appreciated. I was consumed by the pure serenity and peacefulness, which siphoned all clutter from my mind and cleared every congested synapse and conflicting thought. My troubles seemed to have melted away, the same way that the snowflakes would disappear as soon as they made contact with my windshield.

Despite driving at irrational speed under the conditions, I was somehow hypnotized by the quiet serenity that this icy firework had been displaying. To this day, I remember the simple yet magnificent spectacle that I could not escape, as I was filled with amazement and pure awe.

I remember blinking my bright lights in notification to the driver of a dark sedan in front of me that I intended to pass him. This was one of countless such passes during the trip. I overtook him, and after traveling less than 100 feet, I attempted to steer back into the center of the two-lane highway, when I apparently hit a sheet of ice covered by snow.

For reasons still not quite clear to me, instead of simply moving back into the center of the roadway, I inexplicably slid out of control.

As I was spinning like a top, time seemed to suddenly decelerate into slow motion. I attempted to correct my steering, and I expected the fancy automatic braking system of the car to kick in. I remember being concerned about getting hit by the vehicle I had just passed, as I seemed to have been spinning across both lanes.

I saw the car go by without slowing down, and more miraculously, without slamming into me. In fact, I could see his taillights disappear into the snowstorm every time the continuous spinning of my car would position me to face forward.

The next thing I can remember was the feeling of being airborne, as

I had skidded off of the roadway and was propelled onto the median ditch that separated the opposing highway lanes.

The revolving motions must have awakened Dobrila, as I remember the looks of disbelief and horror on her face. I think she might have been screaming as well.

My mind was racing, and I covered my face with my left arm, while reaching defensively toward Dobrila with my right, in anticipation of the imminent crash.

Despite the flurry of reflexive and defensive activities, dreadful anticipations, and overwhelming fear of the unavoidable, and while I was attempting to brace myself for impact, as well as cushion Dobrila, I was still hypnotized by the immeasurable beauty the falling snow had been displaying.

We somehow landed at the bottom of the ditch, headed in the direction we had been traveling.

The probability of us landing exactly where we had was extremely low, as we had spun out of control crossing an overpass, and I had missed a grouping of trees by less than ten feet. In addition, no guard rail had been installed at precisely that forty-foot stretch of highway.

I subconsciously heard Dobrila's exclamations of relief once we had stopped moving. We had both been wearing seat belts and had remained strapped in. I was hunched over the steering wheel, attempting to catch my breath.

Inexplicably, I was still watching the snowflakes innocently fall upon the windshield. Despite their number and magnitude, they still innocently melted away as soon upon contact, and erased every trace of responsibility or culpability.

We looked at each other in disbelief as to what had just happened. While we had spun out of control over an overpass, we did not plunge down to the roadway below. Even though most of the highway did not have a wide divider strip, we landed in a meridian strip. While that location consisted of a ditch no more than ten feet below street level, and any vehicle skidding off the roadway would according to gravity and Newton's physical laws be compelled to roll over and tumble, we inexplicably landed right-side-up at the bottom of the ditch. Furthermore, there was no explanation for the absence of a guard rail at that precise spot, as it had been at all other locations following an overpass. And even though several trees grew within a few feet of the incident, we had managed to miss them as well.

The probability of all of these occurrences happening at the same time was probably close to zero. Maybe even less. I know, as I have almost majored in mathematics during my educational career.

I have no explanation as to why things happened that way. I can only rely on my before-mentioned fatalistic approach to activities which affect a person. But somehow, my belief and determination had been affected by Father Klee's subtle influences.

The only fatalistic determination that I could come up with, based on mathematical probability, and seduced by Christian belief and morality, consisted of a very simple conclusion.

It was not our time to die that day.

Apparently our purpose, obligations, and responsibilities had not yet been achieved.

After regrouping our senses, we effortlessly and somewhat unexpectedly managed to get back onto the highway, and the balance of our trip passed uneventfully, snowflakes notwithstanding.

We returned to Chicago four days later with as much knowledge as we had left with. There would be no miraculous cure for my ailment. There would be no better answers.

Nevertheless, in my heart, I had received a clear and convincing message.

We continued to juggle a multitude of issues during the spring of 2004, including our financial aspirations, my medical endurances, and legal entanglements and ramifications. Financially, we seemed to gather momentum, driven by four construction projects in various stages of completion. Success in any one of them would provide us with much-needed resources. Spring had always been the busiest season for the sale of such luxury single-family homes and we had every reason to believe that this spring would be very rewarding for us.

My medical evaluations, even though not providing the answers I had been looking for, had at least given me an understanding of the direction that needed to be taken. We knew that we could no longer postpone the more aggressive treatments recommended by my doctors. Somehow my preoccupation with financial interests seemed to help, requiring concentration on the execution of business objectives rather than dwelling on the potentially inevitable result of my cancer. It reminded me of the many instances while I had been in college, and had procrastinated in completing a term paper. The more time that passed, the more remorseful and guilty I felt for not having commenced with the task . More emotional effort was spent on contrite feelings than on the physical effort needed to simply complete the assignment. And I remembered the ardent relief that came with actually starting work on the paper. It was that kind of feeling all over again now. We stopped the anxiety associated with procrastination or worrying about the terminal consequences. Instead, we spent effort in evaluating which type of treatment might produce the best results. I busily researched all types of sources that professed to offer insight and answers.

Legal matters involving Adrian slowed to an unusual lull, as no motions regarding his situation had been scheduled for the immediate future due to delays in DNA testing. Conversely, our involvement in civil litigations seemed at an all-time high. We pursued payment for work that had been completed for several of my former partnerships, as well as legal relief involving the malpractice committed by one of my former attorneys, and the final transaction involving my purchase of the mortgage from CIB Bank, to name just a few.

Unfortunately, the slow period in Adrian's case would prove to be the proverbial lull that always leads up to the well-known storm.

On April 8, police officers arrested Adrian as he drove home from school, and charged him with operating a vehicle while under the influence of alcohol. I can't describe the distress it caused for us. It immediately presented a whole new set of challenges and problems.

His home confinement restrictions, imposed by Judge David Sterba, allowed him to go to school and back, and nowhere else. He was arrested in Countryside, a suburb in the opposite direction from his school. Another condition imposed by the judge, and his age, prohibited Adrian from consuming any alcohol. His violation of these terms could very well mean loss of the posted bond and immediate incarceration.

This time around, Adrian refused to give any statements or be subjected to any tests, and instead requested the presence of his attorney. The police officers obliged, and after having needlessly been confined at the police station for several hours, he had finally been allowed to make a phone call. He instantly contacted his mother. Dobrila, in turn, immediately called Patrick Campanelli.

Patrick notified the police department that his client would not make any statements, and would not submit to any tests regarding the verification of alcohol in his system. He then drove to the police station, where he met with Dobrila and me. He was allowed to see Adrian, and after completing the necessary paperwork, was able to have Adrian's release processed. Shaking his head in disbelief, Patrick could give us no immediate answers to our questions about possible consequences that this arrest would have on Adrian's home confinement. Obviously agitated, he stated that he was too upset to wait for Adrian, and informed us that he would call us the next day.

"It wasn't my fault," were the first words out of Adrian's mouth when he saw us. "I only gave a friend a ride home from school and the police stopped me." He spoke rapidly, trying to rationalize his behavior before we would lay into him. "They stopped me for no reason. Maybe they knew that it was me. I did not drink anything. Just ask my friend who was with me." In his haste, Adrian was almost stumbling over his own words.

Rather than let my anger get the best of me, I decided to drive his vehicle back home, while he rode with Dobrila in my car. They arrived first, and by the time I made it home, Adrian had already sought refuge in his room.

"Let him be," Dobrila said as she intercepted me on my way to his room. "He told me that he was dropping off a friend from school when he came upon the police who were stopping everyone leaving a particular house on that block. Apparently there had been a complaint about kids partying and drinking at that house, and the police were stopping everyone who appeared to be rushing out of there. He says that he was mistaken as one of those kids, and because he refused the breathalyzer test, they automatically booked him for a DUI, and of course, once they checked who he was, they realized that this was worthy of further investigation."

I listened to her in disbelief, certain that this unlikely scenario had been offered as a feeble alibi. It sounded and smelled like an absurd fabrication concocted by an immature liar. I was furious that Adrian could have disregarded the orders imposed by the home-confinement deal; that he would have the nerve to subject us to further and redundant scrutiny and recrimination. In all likelihood, it would only serve embellish the prosecution's position and accusations.

This defiance of the law and the judge's demands would definitely compromise the fragile position of the case involving the alleged rape, and seriously undermine the integrity of our defense. It could fuel the prosecution's accusations of leniency afforded to Adrian under the bond ruling. The fact that he had been stopped and accused of driving while under the influence of alcohol was not the real issue. More important were the probable repercussions it would have on his home confinement, and I reluctantly accepted the fact that the prosecution would march back into court and demand strict disciplinary measures for this infraction.

As soon as my temper subsided, I did some research into the alleged events that had been offered by Adrian as proof of his innocence. He had, if fact, given a ride to a fellow student who needed transportation to Countryside. This friend also corroborated that Adrian had been stopped for no apparent reason, and that any allegations regarding alcohol were completely unfounded and unsupported. I also found out that the police had responded to a complaint about a noisy party, and that several other youths had been similarly charged. It would appear that I might have jumped to conclusions, and that I might have been conditioned to anticipate the worst possible scenario.

It must have been the snake-and-worm analogy.

Nevertheless, I was certain that we would be facing new sanctions, as I had painfully learned that the truth is only a side issue to the objectives and motives of career politicians (as in elected state's attorneys), and that their selective versions of the truth are not necessarily correct. Or they could simply embellish the incident and claim everything hadn't been contained in the police reports. And true to my own experience with police reports, they may, in fact, leave plenty of room for interpretation of what might have actually happened. It's a simple analogy of a traveler who, while he had seen a lot more than he could remember, suddenly remembers a lot more than he could have seen.

CHAPTER 22

MOTION TO MODIFY

In the end, while deciding on quality vs. quantity, my wife won. She had chosen quantity, as my responsibilities to my family were, after all, more important than any personal gratifications (as in having a sex life) that she thought I might have been entitled to. Her decision was prompted by the fact that by May, the hormone treatments seemed to have ceased to be effective, as my PSA level had spiked by several points.

As a result, in mid-June, I made the necessary arrangements for the commencement of radiation therapy. It was not a cure, but rather an attempt to delay the inevitable. Prostate cancer was normally a slow-growing cancer, but every examination I had taken suggested that my situation represented a particularly aggressive form of cancer. The fact that it had spread beyond the prostate indicated it to be an incurable condition.

During my initial consultation with Dr. Awan, the specialist administering my radiation treatment, I had inquired about potential life expectancy associated with the treatment I was receiving. I had heard the answer before, but being an incurable optimist, I hoped that his response might have changed after the onset of treatment. If you don't ask, you won't know.

I posed my question in the following manner: "Doctor Awan, I have a collection of approximately 2,000 bottles of vintage wines in my cellar. If I wanted to drink two bottles of wine every evening, when, in your opinion, should I start drinking, so that none of that wine will go to waste?"

He looked at me in disbelief, and after he composed himself, looked at me in further disbelief. "Start drinking tonight," he replied, in an answer that I had expected, but was not necessarily looking for. I reasoned that at least I had a medical recommendation for drinking wine.

Dobrila and I concluded that our children had already been subjected to excessive amounts of pressure, based on Adrian's plight as well as our financial struggles. So far, we had kept my medical condition from them, and decided to continue that policy, at least for the time being.

Preparation for the radiation treatment required a multitude of tests, diagnoses, and scans, which, because of the specific specialties involved, were performed at various hospitals. And even the groundwork for these tests was regimented and quite strenuous. Consequently, both Dobrila and I concentrated on careful compliance with their specifications and requirements. Our various troubles continued to assert their respective potencies in a tilt-a-whirl fashion, for as soon as one emergency would flare up, the remaining problems would somehow fade into lesser shades of urgency.

And this had been the case once again after Adrian's arrest for the DUI charges. Since then, and while my hormone treatments had proven futile, we had faced two status hearings in front of Judge Smierciak relative to the DNA research. During neither of those hearings had my son's DUI arrest been mentioned. That meant we hadn't been forced to consider new defensive strategies.

However, once we settled into the daily routines associated with radiation therapy, the issue regarding the DUI did finally surface. It emerged during another routine hearing on the status of the DNA matter on June 29, 2004, when Patrick received notification from the prosecution of their plans to make new demands. They had decided to file a motion to either rescind the home confinement in favor of incarceration, or as an alternative, push for a greater bond with more strict home-confinement terms.

It was a foregone conclusion that Judge Smierciak would have to react to this infraction in some meaningful fashion, as any noticeable tolerance would send wrong signals to other individuals similarly affected. The judge listened carefully to the allegations presented by prosecutor Michael Deno, while Adrian stood next to Patrick.

As had been expected, Deno first requested that Adrian be immediately imprisoned until his trial, as he had shown himself to be a danger to society once again. In the alternative, if his request were not accepted, Deno requested that the bond be raised to $1,000,000 and that Adrian be confined to his full time, twenty-four hours a day, with no allowances for school.

Judge Smierciak next turned his attention to hear Patrick's arguments. He explained that Adrian had simply given a friend a ride home from school, being careful not to mention that this drive had taken him past his home, in itself an infraction of the home-confinement limitations. The prosecution had not picked up on that bit of information, and Patrick was not about to provide any assistance to them.

Next, Patrick explained that the DUI had only been an accusation, as he had prohibited Adrian from taking any tests of any kind. The judge showed no signs of agitation or concern over the advice that Patrick claimed to have given to Adrian relative his refusal of undertaking any tests. Instead, after inquiring both sides as to any further comments, he made his ruling.

"The motion to amend the bond and home confinement is denied, because the nature of this matter at this time is only an accusation. It might have been different if we had found out that he had been at a bar or something like that."

In retrospect, and at the risk of repeating myself once again, I believe that Judge Smierciak's ruling was sending a message. I wondered if what he didn't say was perhaps the most important part of his ruling. The problem with such speculation, however, is obviously the question of whether his lenience foreshadowed a severe ruling on the main issue later on, or whether it was an acknowledgment of Adrian's innocence, which Smierciak had already recognized, and as a result was offering some reprieve for his unjust persecution.

While Deno was visibly surprised by the ruling, we were actually shocked, and quickly ushered Adrian out of the courtroom in fear that the judge might be tempted to change his mind.

CHAPTER 23

VANISHED

Even though each defendant had his own attorney for most of the duration of the proceedings to date, all of them had to appear for motions involving any one of them. In June, their cases were finally severed so each boy could be tried individually. Whereas this is a fairly routine, normal procedure, it is primarily done in order to accommodate plea bargains by any of the defendants, without affecting the proceedings of the others.

The first attempt for a plea bargain, in fact, followed immediately after the cases had been severed. Tarek's attorney had met with prosecutors behind closed doors, seeking an equitable arrangement for his client. They met with him on the condition that none of the other defendant's attorneys participate. However, all initial attempts at negotiating acceptable terms failed, as the prosecution showed no interest in settling on any reduced terms.

Persisting over a period of almost three months in his quest for a deal, Tarek's attorney was finally offered a plea bargain involving a prison term in excess of ten years for his client. In return, the prosecution would drop all but two charges of the 140-count indictment.

To say that we were shocked would have been another understatement of staggering proportions.

After calculating all possible reductions for cooperation and good behavior, and even educational credits for participating in vocational training, Tarek would still be required to serve a minimum of ten years.

Because of the nature of the felony, Tarek would have spent time in a maximum-security prison, generally reserved for murderers, rapists, and terrorists.

A place which would be the closest thing to hell on earth.

As shocking as this offer had been, the even more stunning revelation was that Tarek actually accepted the offer sometime in mid-August of 2004.

If we felt badly for Tarek after having heard the details, we felt even worse for the consequence that his acceptance might have on the remaining defendants. It would clearly set the scale by which their potential arrangements would be measured.

The terms of his arrangements were formalized in a motion which the prosecutors and Tarek's attorney intended to file jointly on August 27, 2004. At the same time, Tarek would have surrendered himself and immediately be taken to prison.

While waiting for the hearing, Tarek disregarded the terms of his home confinement with total abandon. During that period, he spent more time away than at his home, and he spent more time drunk than sober. He was clearly attempting to squeeze ten years of living into a few precious days.

To my surprise, I found him at our house on the evening of August 26, 2004. He had come to say goodbye to my son and to wish Adrian better luck in the final disposition of his case.

My initial reaction to Tarek's presence was one of speechlessness. I was emotionally crippled the moment I saw him, and psychologically drained within a few minutes of watching him joke and laugh with Adrian. His behavior and demeanor was not in the least commensurate with the amount of imminent pain and suffering he was about to experience, based on the forbidding destiny awaiting him.

With tears in my eyes, I recognized him for the young adolescent that he still was. I saw the transparent portrait of a naive youth attempting to project a mature image, not unlike a young enlisted man during a time of war just prior to departure on a voyage with an uncertain destination.

I had no intention of letting my solemn feelings affect his jovial mood, and waited to collect my emotions before actually engaging him in my dialogue. After several minutes of exchanged pleasantries, I finally broke down, and inquired as to what the hell he had been thinking about when he had accepted such a disdainful plea arrangement.

To my surprise, he seemed unaffected by the tone and harshness of my question, which to me was a clear sign that he had already been confronted in a similar manner. He, in turn, responded in a quixotic and almost sanctimonious manner in defense of his decision.

"My attorney advised me that this would be the best deal that I could have gotten," he stated. "He said we do not have a case—no proof, and that we had already admitted to this at the police station," he continued. "Besides, I'll still only be 30 years old when I get out. And I might as well get it over with."

I could not believe what I was hearing.

I had known that he was of Muslim faith, and that there was a certain amount of pride in facing one's obligations in his religion. But this was not a matter of accepting one's responsibilities, it was a matter of having been ambushed.

I could not believe that his attorney could or would have made such a recommendation. There had been no attempt to investigate the matter at all. We knew that he hadn't interviewed any witnesses. If he had, he certainly would have been in touch with Adrian.

"Besides," Tarek continued as he interrupted my mentally toxic impressions of his attorney. "He told me my defense would cost a lot of money, and that we had already gone through the bond money, which we had agreed to apply towards his fees."

I was left speechless, and knowing that I could not offer any financial assistance, I was reduced to simply wishing him good luck. I left him with Adrian as I sincerely grieved for his ill-advised fate. Remorsefully, I consoled myself that this had not been our fight, and I swore that I would not allow such circumstances to dictate my own son's future.

The following day, Tarek appeared in court in order to follow through with the arrangement that had been made. Because of a particularly heavy schedule, his case was postponed for the afternoon.

However, for reasons that are still not clear, he suddenly disappeared without a trace before his case was called. Vanished. If anyone knew where he went, they weren't saying.

We were shocked and disappointed. But we hadn't seen anything yet.

Less than ten days later, on the rainy night of September 5, 2004, we went into a tailspin.

Adrian disappeared!

Heartsick and frightened, we hoped desperately that he would return in a day or two. Knowing full well what this could mean in terms of probable imprisonment for Adrian, and that the public would take it as a certain sign of his guilt, we did not report his disappearance.

But he did not return. And only a few, brief telephone calls let us know he was alive. He gave us no information regarding his whereabouts.

It didn't take very long before the home confinement officers uncovered his absence through their daily visits.

CHAPTER 24

INQUISITION

We kept waiting for the repercussions. Several days slipped by after we admitted to the home-confinement officers that Adrian wasn't around. We didn't want our fear and despondency to show and set off a chain reaction. They kept coming by to check on him, and dutifully recorded the visits without commotion. It took at least four more follow-up visits before they expressed concern. During every one of those visits they would merely record his continued absence before heading off to their next appointment.

It appeared to me that the notion of movement was clearly being confused with the definition of action, and considering the allegations, along with the degree of persecution previously exhibited by the state's attorney's office, this apparent apathy surprised and confused us. I have learned that the nature of many events over the course of time, whether significant or not, is such that even though they may take much longer to develop than expected, once they begin they usually occur much faster and go much further and deeper than anyone might possibly anticipate.

So too, on a mid-September morning, a series of incredible events was set in motion. I am a fairly well-educated person, with a degree in chemistry from the University of Illinois. I have conducted several successful businesses, and I read books, magazines, and newspapers regularly. I try to keep up with current events and generally understand

and appreciate how and why things function the way they do, be they political, business, legal, or social. Over the years, I have had ample experience with the law, mostly civil litigation. However, the events which were about to unfold have taught me a far greater lesson than the sum total of my entire education, knowledge, and experiences combined.

That September morning, my wife and I were sitting on our deck in the backyard, drinking our morning coffee as usual. It was still very warm even though the leaves on the trees and bushes already hinted of golden hues that would soon transform our forested backyard into an expressionistic masterpiece of colors. With the exception of the chirping of birds, and the occasional "V" formations of ducks flying overhead, which usually would prompt our dog to bark his displeasure over their the brazen invasion of his airspace, quiet reigned over the land. My wife and I sat deeply engrossed in thought about the events of the past few days, all focused on Adrian. We both knew what was on each other's mind, which limited our need to express these troubling perceptions

It's a strange phenomenon that memory is often completely independent of one's will, and that no matter what, memories will interruptwhateveryouaredoingorthinking,withoutconsciouscontrol. They may trickle into your mind without warning, overwhelming you with an avalanche of joy and happiness or remorse, guilt, anger, and sadness. These days we had an abundance of it all, reeling off yesterday's painful answers to today's uncertain questions.

At this time, we still kept the iron gate to our property closed and locked. Originally, the purpose was to prevent the siege of our home by hordes of reporters and camera crews scavenging for news about our son's accusations, which we had first experienced nearly two years earlier when the state prosecutors had first involved the media. Our side remained mostly silent throughout this time, and based on the advice of our attorney, released no information or details of any kind. Our attorney had cautioned us again to stay out of the media in order avoid entrapment by saying something inaccurate, which could be held against us at the time of the actual trial. After all, a closed mouth gathers no feet.

While we remained circumspect, the prosecution adopted just the opposite strategy and showered the media with information. They apparently believed that the more often you hear a particular story, the closer to the truth it had to be. Maybe they were just trying to convince people that if it's in the papers or on television, it must be the truth, even if didn't happen. Hitler's propaganda minister, Joseph Goebbels, propounded the theory that lies told often enough were eventually accepted as truth, and it worked in Nazi Germany. People all too often confuse what they hear in the media with the facts. And I am talking about all types, from random groups to highly educated individuals such as doctors, architects, and judges. It certainly appeared as if the prosecution's goal was to have this case tried in the media right then and there, and in the process, evoke an angry outcry of public concern along with a demand for convictions in court.

The message was loud and clear. Since our son had run away, he must be guilty. Why else would he run? Information containing horrendous accounts of what supposedly transpired at that party two years earlier had been released to the media again. This was the second major opportunity to present itself, and the prosecution was not about to let it go by without taking full advantage. So, the information they released contained only their versions of the facts.

Reporters, in efforts to solicit comments from us, boldly threatened to continue their one-sided assault, because, as they explained, they did not have any information other than what they had received from the state's attorney's office. Never mind that the media had reported every possible scenario, their obsession with the case inspired relentless pursuit of even more compelling tales to entertain the public. They looked for slants that would present yet another new and previously unconsidered angle of the alleged victim's drama. Hysterical editorials expressed astonishingly misguided opinions. Explicit details appeared, based on uninformed, unsubstantiated, and purely biased theories.

So, reporters camped outside our home again and waited for "breaking news" to occur. The ubiquitous "Do Not Trespass" signs we had posted since their last assault only served as a background commentary to the stories they were spinning, and apparently were meant for less-privileged people than these purveyors of yellow journalism.

But we remained silent once again, reluctant to get involved in any type of conflict or contest with someone who bought ink by the gallons and paper by the tons, or whose nightly accounts of world affairs were watched in millions of households on a regular basis.

Both my wife and I were startled when we heard a heavy knock at the front door of our house. A quick glance at each other confirmed that neither of us expected anyone, and heightened our disappointment that the gate did not prevent these callers from gaining access to the house. At the front door were two gentlemen who identified themselves as agents from the FBI.

Startled, but anticipating that they might have news about our son, we invited them onto our backyard deck so that we could talk more comfortably. Instead of furnishing information, however, they were here to obtain information from us regarding Adrian's disappearance. Federal laws had been broken, they believed, which might have serious consequences for anyone involved, including the missing person and his parents.

To say that we were surprised would be a major understatement, as I found it unfathomable that the FBI would have the time, interest, budget, and apparently idle resources to get involved in such a matter. There were murderers out there who needed to be brought to justice. Drug dealers and smugglers who were poisoning society and causing unthinkable, heinous crimes, or terrorists who threatened the further large-scale bloodshed of innocent Americans. Almost daily broadcasts were aired in the weeks and months following the 9/11 national disaster, showing various spokesmen of the FBI painstakingly complaining about how underfunded and undermanned their efforts to fight terrorism were. They emphasized to Congress the importance of increasing their budget in order to hire more agents in order to watch over cargo planes, shipping vessels, trains and trucks, all of which might be target in future terrorist plots.

And then there was my teenage son, whose pursuit seemed worthy of the same effort as rooting out those criminals.

This feeling of surprise quickly turned to anxiety, dismay and even panic. In my mind, this mirrored what must have been the feelings of citizens who were subjected to the Spanish Inquisition,, or the American residents of Salem who surely expressed similar terror when accusers appeared at their doors. Notwithstanding the errors of their ways, or the misguided righteousness exhibited by persecutors back then, the end result always was the victim's demise and the suffering of their families (and friends, if any remained), all due to unsubstantiated accusations for crimes that had supposedly been committed against society.

Maybe you think I was overreacting, but until you have faced such an onslaught, it might be difficult to understand this emotional maelstrom. Please glance backward in time with me for a moment, and consider the persecution back then, the unfounded accusations, the cruel methods employed to enforce the arrest, the shoddy evidence, and the manner in which guilty verdicts were elicited. Powerful officials, cheered on by the hysterical public, pursued suspects without ever considering the possibility that they might actually be innocent. All that seemed to matter was that he or she was caught and punished, often by hanging or burning at the stake.

I'm certain that parents in those days, too, suffered torment when their offspring were subjected to unjustifiable condemnation. As was the case then, so has my son now been accused of crimes under dubious circumstances. Arrests were made with complete disregard of his civil and constitutional rights, and an indictment was elicited from the Grand Jury based on evidence presented only by the accusers who leveraged the evidence to their advantage. Incorrect and contrived information was leaked to the media in order to create an outrage and a demand for punishment. Officials and the public alike appeared to overlook one of our most important values, a presumption of Adrian's innocence until proven guilty beyond a reasonable doubt.

So far, I thought, this certainly sounded, smelled and looked like a "witch hunt" of a bygone era. Or maybe it was a little more civilized, perhaps more like the devastating persecution of imagined communist sympathizers under the McCarthy hallucinations that had ruined countless lives not so long ago. But our consolation throughout this period was the belief that the more you stretch the truth, the harder it will snap back at you.

An old saying, whose origin I have long forgotten, kept coming to mind: "The law is like a spider's web. It scares the innocent, entangles the weak, is broken by the guilty, and is always spun by the powerful."

I was by no means asking for any special treatment for my son. He had been a participant in suspicious activities. The extent of his involvement remained to be seen. All I was asking for was that he be treated with the civil rights long-established in this country's system of justice, and not be branded as a convicted felon in advance of trial. None of the actual evidence had been evaluated yet. And while his flight looked bad, it certainly was not evidence of guilt. I still believe that the judicial system in America is light-years ahead of any other country's. But some pieces still fall through the judicial cracks, and this particular crack involving the persecution of suspected juvenile sex offenders is unusually wide, and is dangerously positioned in ways to entrap countless innocent youngsters.

If history teaches us anything, it definitely teaches us the mistakes we are going to make again.

The two FBI agents, generic stereotypes who wouldn't be given a second glance on a public street, declined a cup of coffee, but accepted Dobrila's offer of fresh lemonade. Agent J. Stover, the younger man probably in his early thirties, Caucasian, remained standing while his senior partner, Agent P. Araya, possibly in his mid-thirties, perhaps of ancestry from South or Central America, sat down with us and explained the reason for their visit. He spoke English without any trace of an accent.

It is clear and apparent in retrospect that agent Stover was surveying the situation and seemed poised to react at the slightest sign of trouble. He obviously represented the "bad cop" while Araya was the "good cop." But back then, I wasn't paying that kind of attention, as I was confused, impressed, and most of all, intimidated by their presence. After all, it wasn't the local police, the sheriff, or even the detectives. IT WAS THE FUCKING FBI!

Despite their nondescript appearance and congenial manner,

they projected power and elicited fear. Fear stemming from the known accusations that had been brought against our son. Fear of the unknown information they might possess. And most of all, fear of the far-reaching consequences their involvement could imply. Simply put, they were the spider and we were trapped in their web.

Voltaire said it best when describing this type of encounter. "It is dangerous to be right on matters on which established authorities are wrong." We were certain of our son's innocence and clearly felt that it was dangerous for us to be right with regard to this matter at this time. So we remained non-confrontational and attempted to hide our righteousness and fear with politeness and friendliness. We felt that these two agents were our enemies, but like Abraham Lincoln had said, we thought that "we could defeat our enemies by making them our friends."

The two officers were also polite, even friendly. But I doubt that their behavior was based on anything other than total conviction of their own righteousness. They showed compassion and sympathy, even concern for our son, as they talked about their experience with young fugitives. Without passing judgment regarding the alleged crime, they elaborated on the punishment associated with fleeing from the law, and the implications of crossing state lines, which could carry an additional penalty of up to ten years in prison. They cautioned us against aiding our son in any way, as that would be considered "obstruction of justice," punishable by law as well. Citing their experience, they said that young fugitives, even if they were innocent of the crime that made them flee, often turn to crime after their money ran out, and as a result would expose themselves to more potential criminal charges. This was knowledge we didn't really want to learn, as our capacity for bad news had already exceeded its limits.

We should contact them immediately, Araya said, if we heard anything from our son, as his voluntary surrender would be well received, and would have a positive impact on his potential sentencing for evading the law. They even promised that they would drop all federal charges, meaning that there would be no additional prison time from the federal government for fleeing, if he were to surrender himself voluntarily within the next 30 days. This promise, however vague and obscure, was finally the first piece of good news we had received.

Even they expressed a certain amount of surprise that the FBI had been called in on this case, and agreed with us that their services were needed more urgently elsewhere. However, they assured us in no uncertain ways, that it would only be a matter of time until our son was captured. Not if, but when. It was inevitable since they had the complete and limitless resources of the most powerful agency on earth at their disposal. The comment was a clear reminder to us that they were the spider.

The course of our conversation took many directions, including discussions of the other youth, Tarek, who had also skipped bail, the potential sixty-year jail sentence facing each of the accused boys, the method by which they had originally been arrested, and the manner in which they were interrogated.

Finally, the real reason for their visit became apparent, as every now and then, they would ask something specific about our son's disappearance. They would generally seem satisfied with each answer and move on. A few moments later, however, they would return to that previous question, and would ask it a different way, ask it from a different perspective, or ask us to elaborate further on our previous response.

Another old proverb states, "The guilty think that all talk is about them." Even though we were not guilty of any crime, the agents had redirected the spotlight of interest directly on us, seeming to imply that we were somehow guilty of something. These FBI men had made it clear that we had the right to consult an attorney before we gave them any answers. However, if we appeared reluctant to openly discuss this matter with them now, it might send a message that we were hiding something. This in turn would only intensify their suspicions.

While being thoroughly intimidated by their mere presence, and concerned about their insinuations, we nevertheless considered ourselves smart enough not to fall into a trap by speculating or saying too much. After all, we really didn't know anything relative to Adrian's whereabouts or the circumstances of his disappearance. Adrian had not yet contacted us, and we were completely in the dark about his situation.

With a certain amount of admiration, I recognized their subtle interrogation techniques. Despite this, and our intention to abide by the lessons learned through our son's experience, we nevertheless had this compelling and incorrigible urge to discuss this matter with these officers. Even more importantly, we felt it necessary to convince them of our son's innocence. Somehow we were inclined to throw caution to the wind and forget our resolution to remain silent. The media's persistent assault had finally taken its toll on us and had broken our will. Immobilized by fear, paralyzed by intimidation, and worn out by the blitzkrieg of misinformation, we appealed for understanding and compassion. At last, we succumbed.

So we breached our silence, and went on to explain exactly what had happened, how it had happened, and why it had happened. All along we were seeking their understanding, and attempting to elicit from these two agents an expression of belief in Adrian's innocence. We were ready to give them written and sworn testimony of all important events which had, or had not, taken place. We were ready to spell out all of our assumptions, confess to all knowledge we had, and even promise the accuracy of everything we hadn't even thought of yet.

Even though we didn't know exactly where we were going by volunteering all this information, we nevertheless used any available roads to get there. In retrospect, I am amazed how easily these officers convinced us to cave in. After all, we had been forewarned, and were rational adults. We should not have been intimidated, coerced, or tricked into any sort of confession. But this wasn't a confession. It was the truth that finally needed to be said—or so we thought back then.

The more suspicious the agents appeared, the harder we tried to convince them of our son's innocence and our ignorance relative to his whereabouts. Based on our limited experience with these officers, I am no longer surprised at the ease with which seasoned and experienced detectives could force a confession from young, unsuspecting boys, and trap them into incriminating themselves.

As soon as they left, we immediately contacted our attorney. In fact, we also called several other attorneys handling various legal matters not involving our son. Notwithstanding the criticism and lecture we received for talking to the FBI, their cumulative comments could be summarized as follows:

"Why is the FBI involved?"

"We cannot talk on the phone, it's the FBI." Four out of seven attorneys made this comment.

And my favorite comment, which I swear it is true: "Don't say anything. Don't get them mad. They have guns."

CHAPTER 25

REPERCUSSIONS

At the next scheduled status hearing in September, Judge Smierciak issued an arrest warrant for Adrian and Tarek. He also ordered the forfeiture of the $10,000 bonds posted for each of them.

As had been the case with every previous court appearance, Dobrila and I sat again in the front row during the judge's announcement, and I thought that he made a deliberate effort to look at us both as he delivered his rulings. If he was judging us, a chorus of opinions soon joined him. Nearly everyone we came in contact with expressed, one way or another, their views that Adrian could not have managed his escape without our help. And even though we had not been officially charged with any crime, we had been put on notice that the sum total of all of our actions, opinions, and thoughts, past, present, and future, would be extensively examined and appropriately dealt with.

The media, of course, came out of a brief hibernation and sought to satisfy their hunger for new headlines. They criticized Judge Smierciak's handling of Adrian's alleged DUI with reporting so slanted the words could easily slide off of the paper. They clamored about the FBI's involvement and suggested that the case had escalated into an international manhunt. This led to slurs about our ethnic background, too.

While the media raised as much commotion as possible, the police, the FBI, and even the Federal Air Marshals threatened us with reprisals if we involved ourselves in any aspect of Adrian's disappearance. Meanwhile, we fought our own battles relative to our son's life and safety.

The law prohibited us from assisting Adrian in any way, and the agents from the FBI had repeatedly advised us to contact them should we learn of his whereabouts. However, this request was not mandated by law, and as long as we did not assist him, we would not be violating any statutes.

I confess that we had been made aware of Adrian's general whereabouts through extremely unfortunate means shortly after the FBI's visit, and his safety, rather than any attempts to avoid breaking any laws, had soon become our sole priority and unconditional objective.

The shock waves just wouldn't stop.

We weren't aware of it.

Our attorneys weren't aware of it.

So it came as quite a shock when our 15-year-old son brought a copy of a report he had printed off the Internet at school. It appeared to be the latest list of the FBI's "TEN MOST WANTED CRIMINALS " for Illinois.

It stunned us to see the name of our son, Adrian Missbrenner, included and described as "Armed and Dangerous." A reward was offered for his capture. Tarek Ibrahimovic's name also appeared on the list.

This immediately established a new stratosphere of disbelief. Armed and dangerous? The only arms my son ever had were the arms he was born with, and the only danger he presented was to himself. Such rhetorical insinuations will scare people and, should they come across him, may incite them to react in dangerous and life-threatening behavior.

Equally disturbing was the fact that a reward had been offered. It immediately exposed our son to even more peril. Any number of individuals, including self-styled vigilantes, could find it tempting to pursue him for profit. Greed by someone he might know and perhaps have confided in, someone who might recognize him in the papers or on the Internet, a casual acquaintance, or even a professional bounty hunter in need of some quick cash, could have serious repercussions.

Now, I am not questioning the legality or morality of the pursuit, but rather the possible methods involved. The warning of "armed and dangerous" implied that he carried a weapon, and from a distance, many objects could appear to be a weapon. Some wannabe cowboy might "shoot first and ask questions later." At least the reward poster didn't include the condition, "Dead or Alive."

Being a parent of a son involved in such a disaster-prone pursuit probably accounted for most of my outrage, regardless of how impartial I tried to be. But I could see the danger. I still believe that any rational individual would agree that rather extraordinary and even fanatical methods had been used to capture a young fugitive, especially with the promise of reward money.

After all, despite the prosecutors' allegations, and the press branding him as a criminal, to this point Adrian was still innocent. Granted, he was charged with a crime, but no trial had yet been conducted, so no guilty verdict had been rendered. The highest law of America mandated his innocence at this time. Period!

I have learned that, sometimes, what is said is far less important than what is not said. After carefully scrutinizing the FBI's ten most wanted list of Illinois fugitives, I realized that it contained only six names! Three of them were wanted for murder and one was wanted for sex crimes with a child. Then there were my son and his friend Tarek, who had also skipped bail. As disturbing and shocking as it was to see Adrian's name and picture on the list, the really mind-boggling fact was the four vacancies. My initial reaction, in trying to understand why only six names had been listed, was that perhaps insufficient numbers of fugitives might be worthy of that distinction. A fair deduction, I thought, especially since this list covered only Illinois outlaws.

But then I did some research. And here is what the document didn't say:

I found out that for 2002 and 2003 alone, there were 371 convicted individuals being sought for murders they had committed in Illinois, based on the Executive Summary for crimes by the Illinois State

Police, published in 2004. Yet only three were named on this list! The other 368 wanted killers had been omitted. Furthermore, four spots remained inexplicably unfilled.

As mentioned, one criminal convicted of sexual crimes involving a child was listed. Most people would accept the logic of his name being part of this list, even though others might argue that murder is a more serious crime. But what could conceivably have driven anyone to place Adrian and Tarek on it?

Neither one had been convicted of anything. How could they be included when 368 murderers were not? Scores of killers who had committed the worst possible crime were not on that list.

I still have no idea what conclusion can be drawn from this omission. One can only speculate that the victims of these murderers, or maybe even the murderers themselves, for one reason or another might not be worthy of such widespread attention. These reasons may include ethnicity, economic standing, newsworthiness, or the political motives of someone involved in the case.

Here is the topper. My son's name appeared on another prominent list, one which named the most noteworthy sexual predators for all 50 states, reportedly also published by the FBI. A total of 15 individuals were listed, including Adrian and Tarek. Unlike the list of the "FBI's Ten Most Wanted," this one did not specify a number (as in 10) of people being sought. Yet only fifteen individuals were listed.

In Illinois alone, for the same two years of 2002 and 2003, based on the same study, a total of 11,991 criminal sexual assaults were reported, of which a total of 3,592 (less than 30 percent) were solved. This means that 8,399 had not been solved. To put this into perspective for the entire United States, possibly 400,000 sexual assaults may have remained unsolved for that two-year period of time (i.e., possibly as many as fifty times the number of unsolved cases in Illinois). And of those fifteen, my son, who is still presumed innocent, was included, whereas 399,985 sexual predators were not.

With that in mind, let me take you back to the Constitution, which protects the rights of any individual and requires that any person be considered innocent until proven guilty in a court of law. This makes it illegal to treat any individual as a criminal prior to such a trial, and then he would be guilty only if a jury arrived at that verdict.

However, these two lists have done just that. They proclaimed my son's guilt without a trial. Is it possible that someone has decided that for the "Common Good of the People," this young individual should be classified as a criminal?

My son, based on the Constitution of the United States of America, the very document which defines America's spirit, morals, ideals, and wisdom, was innocent. Yet the FBI had already characterized him as a sexual predator, armed and dangerous, and whose capture was worthy of a reward. Even more startling, at least to me, was a statistic I pulled from the list of sexual predators. At the time of the alleged crime, my son was seventeen years and eight months old. Tarek also was not yet eighteen years of age. The alleged victim was two months shy of her seventeenth birthday. In short, not even one year separated their ages. Yet they were described and prosecuted as sexual predators.

The average age of the remaining thirteen individuals on that list of sexual predators was fifty-five! The average age of their victims was eleven!

Something clearly was not being said!

CHAPTER 26

THE REAL BIG BROTHER

Did you ever have the ominous, menacing feeling that you were being watched? Not casually observed, but studied and inspected continuously, where every one of your actions is being scrutinized and evaluated. The kind of notion that makes you look over your shoulder and feel that just too many coincidences keep popping up. What I am talking about is how it just keeps going, every time you take a shower, or go to the bathroom to relieve yourself. Every comment you make is heard, including the intimate moments with your mate, every time you say, "I love you."

You are being watched.

You are being recorded.

You are being judged.

From the moment those FBI agents left, we had this haunting sensation of being observed and overheard. I don't mean like the standard movie cliche of an ACME Carpet Cleaning van parked outside the driveway, with a rotating antenna barely concealed and Gene Hackman in the back with earphones. No. Now it's new-age, space-science technology, in which the government has perfected the ability to conduct extreme long-range surveillance, possibly from satellites circling the earth which can zoom in on every detail. If you burp, they know it, and are able identify what you had for dinner the night before.

We all have skeletons of various sizes in our closets. But according to the inventory I took of my closet not so long ago, it would seem hardly worth their time and effort to exhume the bones in there. However, there always is a risk they will unshroud some of the long forgotten smaller skeletons. And we risk the possibility that certain people, if they have something to gain, might interpret these tiny skulls and vertebrae as Tyrannosaurus Rex remains. Or, worse, they might miraculously turn up non-existent skeletons you never even knew existed.

My wife and I had concealed one such secret. We had never told anyone, not even Patrick, of the few contacts we had with Adrian after he left home. Furthermore, there might have been a thin line of legality involved. Certain persons might be of the opinion that our brief encounter with those individuals who had made Adrian's escape a possibility might be interpreted as providing assistance to him, and that our subsequent treatment and persecution might be justified after all. However, at the risk of sounding insincere, or even disingenuous, I would hardly equate the payment of the ransom in exchange for our son's life as subversive. And I do not see that payment as any type of assistance, unless one would consider murder to be the equivalent to an acceptable method of birth control. I refuse to believe that trying to spare my son's life can be regarded as assistance to criminals. Morally motivated actions would vindicate the respective infractions.

Besides, while we may have known his location for a brief moment in time, any prolonged certainty had been avoided in order to eliminate just such a catch-22 scenario. In other words, we had a moral obligation to save our son's life by any means necessary, and we certainly considered that a much higher requirement than any laws imposed by any government. It was our duty as parents, and did not abrogate any of the American legal liberties to which we are entitled to.

Nevertheless, we felt like tiny creatures under a microscope being observed 24-7 by Big Brother. This constant surveillance, whether imagined or real, turned our anxiety into paranoia, compounded by fear of the unknown and dread of punishment.

And let me make this perfectly clear. It is not a good feeling , this paranoia-filled anxiety. Our "inalienable rights" suddenly seemed to be as alien as an extraterrestrial apparition. "The right of the people to be secure in their persons, houses, papers, and effects, against unreasonable searches and seizures, shall not be violated." is a key element in the Constitution's Bill of Rights. But it seemed as if the FBI had amassed special powers which test every word of this amendment and which stretch the interpretation to its maximum limit — and maybe beyond. And since 9/11 and the enactment of the "Patriot Act," those powers have been increased and have been shrouded in the greatest of secrecies yet. And dare I say it, these powers are "Solely for the Benefit and Greater Good of the People." Our attorneys advised, "They may not be able to use information which they obtained covertly as evidence in court, but rest assured, they do know what to do with such information." This was advice which only added fuel for our growing paranoid anxiety. To be honest, it scared the hell out of us.

Since "paranoia" is partially defined as "little knowledge of what is going on," and "anxiety" as "reaction to danger," I felt that I had every reason to feel the way that I did. Call me neurotic (in addition) if you wish, but remember that Sigmund Freud in 1920 had postulated that "neurotic symptoms are created because anxiety is sounding the alarm to an imminent danger." In our case, our alarm was ringing loud and clear, and no less, at all times.

There suddenly was suspicion as to why our mail started to arrive two days late. There was concern as to why some of the pieces seemed to have already been opened. There was dismay that a special hold was mysteriously placed on our checking accounts and anxiety over the disruptive problems that this created in our business. There was panic that all of our business loans were suddenly called in and despair that we could not possibly come up with all the money needed to repay the millions of dollars necessary to repay these loans within the time that had been allocated. There was apprehension as to the reason for the FBI's interrogation of our insurance agent (one who had confided this information) and worry as to who else might have been similarly intimidated.

We worried that even our daily routines might somehow be interpreted as illegal, criminal, unconstitutional, or even immoral, and that the next knock on the door would be the inquisition which had determined that our agnostic beliefs in our son's innocence had warranted this "witch hunt." They appeared to be dismantling our life, one building block at a time, and intimidating anyone with whom we conducted business or social transactions. How that might bring back our son from his self-imposed exile is a notion lost on me. But then again it was Joseph Stalin who had proclaimed, "A government must have the resilience and ability to react to any adversity that opposes its policies, immediately and decisively, and not unlike dry water."

This campaign against us nearly broke our will to survive. Soon we lost the courage to even speak openly to one another in fear of saying something which could be considered controversial, be misunderstood altogether, or add fuel to the fire. We didn't dare invite guests to our house in fear of saying a wrong thing, appearing happy, or implicating them in this sinister plot to destroy us.

To quote Voltaire again, "I felt like we were persecuted by everything in the world, even by things which are not." Simply put, we began to fear out own shadows, which seemed to follow us everywhere, and would especially come out at night.

CHAPTER 27

SWEET DEAL

On January 13, 2005, police officers took Jimmy Brown into custody immediately following his plea hearing. By this time, he was 20 years old.

As had been the case with Tarek, Jimmy also negotiated a plea arrangement without any notification, participation, or involvement of other codefendants. Unlike Tarek, however, he decided to adhere to the negotiated arrangements.

Unconfirmed rumor had it that Jimmy's attorney had at one time been an associate of one of the state prosecutors assigned to his case. Be that as it may, Jimmy's attorney was somehow able to negotiate a plea bargain, which seemed extremely favorable and unbelievably attractive.

With the exception of one count of felony child pornography, all other charges were dropped. Felony child pornography is a Class 1 offense and carries a sentence of four years minimum and fifteen years maximum. However, his attorney was further able to negotiate this prison stay requirement down to a four-month participation in the Illinois Department of Corrections Impact Incarceration Program. This program was essentially a boot camp option for marginally guilty individuals.

In addition, he had to register as a sex offender for life. This was a requirement mandated by law and as part of any sentence imposed in these types of cases. Tarek's plea had a similar condition.

We were genuinely overjoyed once we heard of his arrangement and expressed our well-wishes to Jimmy and his parents. In the backs of our minds, however, we were puzzled by this unexpected and favorable agreement. We questioned the motivation, especially in light of the far less favorable arrangement which had been offered to Tarek.

Initial opinions regarding the severity of each of the four defendants had pegged Jimmy's situation as one of the more severe, as he had been 18 years old at the time of the alleged crime. His verbal comments and directions, which had been audible on the video recording, had been extremely insulting, degrading, and obscene. He had been viewed as the director who coordinated the activities during that fateful night.

"Felon's Sentence is almost funny," read the headline in a February 3, 2005 editorial in the "Doings" newspaper, a prominent local publication. That editorial was readdressed in a follow-up article on February 24, 2005. It was printed after the supervisor of the assistant state's attorney's fifth district office complained to the paper about their superficial reporting relative to Jimmy's settlement.

Quoting Assistant State's Attorney Supervisor Peter Troy, the article said, "I would not want to go to the Illinois Department of Correction boot camp. . . . It may seem like Mr. Brown received a benevolent deal, but I think otherwise."

It would appear that Mr. Troy had a fearful opinion as to the activities at the boot camp and the treatment of its recruits (ironically, it was called "boot camp" and not "boot jail" or "boot prison").

In contrast, he had no reservations, comments, or second thoughts about possibly sending Tarek to a maximum security prison for ten years.

And Supervisor Troy was not alone in the defense of Jimmy's arrangement. Prosecutors Michael Deno and Cheryl Schroeder joined Supervisor Troy in an attempt to offer further clarifications.

"There were numerous nuances in prosecuting a case with multiple defendants," they reportedly told the newspaper's editor, Pamela Lannom. Based on this explanation, it seemed to have come down to mere "nuances" in deciding how to prosecute and punish one defendant versus another. So much seemed to have depended on these nuances that I found it necessary to look up the definition of the word.

Webster's New World Dictionary, updated in 1994, describes the meaning of "nuance" as "a slight variation."

Webster's New World Thesaurus, 2003 edition, offers such alternative definitions as "subtlety" and "refinement."

It would appear that the state's attorney's office had considered the difference in the deal pleas offered to Jimmy versus the one given to Tarek as "a slight variation. Ten years in a possible maximum security prison was a mere subtlety in comparison to four months in a boot camp. Jimmy's plea was apparently only a "refinement" to the prison sentence facing Tarek.

"I feel your article was a disservice to our victim," was one complaint attributed to Cheryl Schroeder. Inexplicably, the alleged victim had now become "our" victim in the eyes of the supposedly impartial and unbiased prosecutors, whose sole objective is to find the truth, uphold the law, and protect the rights of the citizen they are supposed to serve.

Further topics of discussion involved other admitted goals of the prosecution.

There was the goal to protect the dignity of the victim. Never mind the character assassination of the youths accused of the alleged crime.

There was the goal to make the victim comfortable with the plea arrangement. Never mind what the law might require, and God forbid that it might be uncomfortable to the alleged victim.

And there was the goal of securing a defendant who might be willing to testify against the other defendants. Essentially, one defendant walks if he simply makes the prosecution's job easier. Never mind that the law is supposed to apply equally to all its citizens.

It's a funny thing, but nowhere in the article did anyone from the state's attorney's office even once discuss doing the right thing, following the law, or just plain doing justice.

CHAPTER 28

A SOUR DEAL

On March 15, 2005, the long awaited trial for the sexual assault of Conny Skinner started, with Anthony Roberts as the first defendant to face a jury. By this time, three of the other five boys had taken plea bargains involving probation, community service, and boot camp, while two boys, Adrian and Tarek, remained as fugitives.

Of the initial 140 counts which the prosecutors advertised for over two years, only two counts survived the intense war waged by Anthony's defense. These two counts consisted of aggravated sexual assault, and criminal assault charging Roberts with forced oral copulation.

This translated into the proverbial good-news and bad news scenario. The good news was that he no longer faced the possibility of up to sixty years in prison if convicted. The bad news was that he still faced six to fifteen years for each count, or a minimum of twelve years and a maximum of up to thirty years, if convicted on both counts.

The drastic reduction in charges actually underscored a serious observation made by Daniel J. Boorstin, the 1973 Pulitzer Prize winning author, who in 1961 wrote, "A deft prosecutor these days . . .must master the technique of denying the truth without actually lying." How else, other than by embellishing the truth (and in so doing, denying the actual truth), could anyone come up with 140 counts, when only two possible counts had existed all along? Obviously, this police work and the criminal investigation was a bold attempt to draw sufficient conclusions (the accusations) from insufficient premises (the actual evidence), whereby truth and reality were crucified on the cross of the prosecutor's ostentatious aspirations, spurious applications, and biased interpretations of the law.

The main piece of evidence the prosecution had relied on, namely the twenty-minute video tape recorded by Jimmy Brown, did not show that Anthony had been involved. However, his coerced testimony after his arrest more than two years earlier linked him to this alleged assault. The new and improved evidence which the prosecutors regarded as their trump card, and which they again flaunted freely and willingly, was the fact that Anthony's DNA was recovered from the spare bedroom where the sexual activities had taken place. As a result, the prosecution felt particularly good about their case as they prepared for trial.

During the weeks leading up to March 15, my wife was an avid supporter, both morally and spiritually, to Anthony and his mother, Sandra. She would spend countless hours re-evaluating and re-assessing his defense with them and their attorney, Robert Kuzas, and in fact, had brought up several valid points in support of his innocence. Dobrila, being one of those persons who possessed extraordinarily good common sense, was applying that common sense and her good judgment in attempting to help address Anthony's problem. Ironically, common sense and good judgment is what one normally gets from experience, and experience seems to be what one usually gets from bad judgment.

A great deal of time was spent on discussing the fact that no noise relative to the alleged rape was heard. Had it in fact taken place, it would have woken up the two younger brothers of Adrian who were sleeping in adjoining rooms. Furthermore, Jenny Weller, who had arrived with Conny, had seen no evidence of foul play, nor did she appear to have any reason to interfere or object to any of the activities that evening. She had assured my wife on countless occasions since then that "Conny did what she wanted to do." And of course, no evidence of torn clothing, bruises, scratches, or the like was ever visible on Conny herself. Only black felt tip markings on parts of her body, which had been the expression of frustration by those boys who had not gotten their "turns," were the only evidence aside from the video tape.

But as eager and anxious as Dobrila was in helping Anthony, so too was she aware and motivated by the fact that any assistance she would offer here, and any positive results which might come from her assistance, would go a long way in the vindication of our son. As the Chinese saying goes, "People in the same boat should help each other."

With all the extensive preparations, the countless meetings and the intensive research and recollections, it came as no particular surprise that on March 14, at about 9:00 p.m., I received a phone call from Anthony. I anticipated some last-minute details, strategies, or questions. Possibly a last-minute "pep talk" about the next day's activities.

What I got instead was quite a surprise.

"Mr. Missbrenner," he said in what sounded like a tearful and slurred voice, "I am going to take that deal that they are offering."

I was surprised and at a loss for words, as only a day earlier he had sounded so convinced and reassured in his belief of vindication and proof of innocence.

"I think that it might be the best thing to do," he continued.

"What does your mother think?" were the first words I offered in response.

"She is telling me that this is strictly my decision to make," he replied. "But I think that she believes that this is best too."

"What is your attorney saying?"

"He thinks that this is the best deal I could get . . . he says that this is a pretty good deal for me . . . he would take this deal if it were up to him. But he says he cannot make that decision for me . . . it's something that I must do for myself . . ."

I was somewhat surprised to hear that his attorney had made such a strong recommendation for accepting this deal, as I had always known attorneys to avoid making such decisions. It's this habit of distancing themselves from certain decisions and allowing their consciences to be clear so they can sleep at night. It is for that reason that I subconsciously questioned whether his attorney had lost all faith in this case and as a result was taking a shortcut to the bond money that had been posted, and which had also been pledged toward satisfying his legal fees.

I could tell that Anthony had been crying, and suspected that he had been drinking. And who could blame him? Here he was, the evening before his trial, pondering, questioning, and maybe gambling away the next thirty years of his life. And not only did he not know what the right decision or direction was, but he also seemed to have no one to really consult with or take advice from. He had no one to truly guide him.

The deal offered that one of the charges would be dropped if he would plead guilty to the other charge. In turn, the prosecution would settle for the minimum prison sentence of six years, of which he would have to serve a little over five years.

This was not an easy decision to make.

He could take the guesswork out of the equation and settle for a definitive term, or he could roll the dice and hope for a vindication and no prison time. If he lost, on the other hand, he could serve up to 30 years.

I could tell that he was tired. I could tell that the constraint of home confinement had taken its toll. He lived in a small house on a busy street. No front yard, and very little back yard. He had practically been stuck for two full years in a home which must have appeared smaller each day and which must have constricted any remaining joy, interests, and actual life out of him. He didn't go to school and, according the court ruling, was not allowed to work. As a result, his daily existence followed the same routine. His mother had to go to work in order to support them and would leave the house early in the morning. His father had abandoned them when he was little, and his sister struggled with her own life. As a result, he spent every day, and every hour of the day, totally alone. Friends who had initially visited him had to get on with their own lives, so visits became few and far between. Granted, he had all the comforts of home. But with no interaction with others, all the comforts would soon be no comforts at all. There were only so many reality shows, so many talk shows, so many sitcoms, and so many dramas one could watch in a given day, much less day after day after day. The daily news had been telling of stories in places far away, places which he could not visit, places which he could not see, and soon could not care about. Changing clothes had no longer been an issue, and bathing or brushing teeth had become a hit-or-miss proposition. Meals consisted of prepackaged snacks, and alcohol had become the only fuel which motivated him to get up in the morning and help him pass out at night amidst his remorseful, never-ending thoughts and painful flashbacks. With only a few exceptions to this routine, it was a mirror image of the lonely descent into depression and moral defeat which I had witnessed my own son succumb to prior to his escape some six months earlier. I understood his pain, realized his desperation, and recognized his cry for help.

I had missed those signals with my own son.

However, this time I heard them loud and clear.

"May I speak to your mother?" I asked in an effort to verify his previous statement, to which he promptly obliged.

"I cannot make this decision for him," she responded to my question. "He is old enough, and I cannot risk him being mad at me for possibly making the wrong decision. And I just don't know. I think it's the best choice, but I don't know," she gasped as the urge to cry overcame her.

She put Anthony back on the phone. He asked, "What would you do if this was Adrian's situation?"

I thought for a moment, and realized that he was attempting to make a decision without the benefit of a father's advice. His mother could not bring herself to make a recommendation, and in fact was afraid to make a decision for him, and his attorney, personal objectives aside, knew that he really could not interfere with this decision.

It was an unsolicited and yet precarious situation that I found myself in.

On the one hand, I had strong feelings about my recommendation as it would apply to my son. I would not second-guess my decision, knowing very well that I would have to live with the consequences of my decision. I had been used to making decisions my entire adult life, and had always been guided by my convictions. But it is said that the strength and weakness of our convictions depend more on our courage than our intelligence, and it certainly appears to be easier to display courage when someone else's fate is at stake. Nevertheless, I was prepared to recommend the same course of action that I would have recommended to my son.

On the other hand, I simultaneously questioned if I had the right to interfere with the life and future of someone whose veins did not have the same blood, and whose philosophies and objectives about life, liberty, and the pursuit of everything else, including one's freedom, may in reality be 180 degrees apart.   Ultimately, the left hand won.

In reaching that decision, I threw all concerns about giving improper advice out the window, and true to my nature, immersed myself totally into my convictions and recommendations. I did not let up, nor take any prisoners, at least not until my decision was completely and unconditionally accepted.

"Son, don't be stupid," I commenced. "You are not dealing with right and wrong; with guilty or innocent. You are dealing with a fabricated story that someone wants to profit from."

Now absolute in my view, I said, "I have seen the video tape, and I have seen worse things on cable TV and 'R' rated movies than on this tape. If this is the evidence that they are counting on, then I am convinced they cannot convict you. There is simply no way that twelve jurors will find you guilty based on that evidence." My words came slowly and deliberately.   "But what about the DNA that was recovered?" he asked in a voice still worried.

I needed to sound positive and resolute in my response.

"Screw the DNA! You'll obviously admit to having sex with the slut, because you did. But, it's not on the video, so who can say that she was not participating; that she ever objected? I didn't see you anywhere on the video. Screw the DNA," I continued like a televangelist soliciting a "Hallelujah" from his captivated audience. "There is no way that twelve jurors will see the kind of evidence on the video that is necessary to convict you. The worst-case scenario is that it will be a hung jury and that the trial will have to be redone. And if that happens, then the prosecutors will make you a better deal, so just hold out, and don't cave in just yet."

I truly believed in the advice I was giving, and would have given the same advice to my son. "This is a chess game now. They have made their move and hope to entice you into capitulating immediately. But if you admit to having had sex with her, then you can take away their argument about the DNA. And there is no evidence, one way or the other, that would suggest that the sex you did have was anything but consensual," I repeated. "If you admit to the sex, then you'll take away the impact of the DNA evidence. You'll steal their thunder," I continued. "It is their burden of proof to show that she did object, that she was raped. And the video evidence does not show any of that." My legal interpretation sounded good, even to me.

"At worst, it's going to be a hung jury, and they will make you a better deal. Then decide if you want to take it. Remember, the first deal is always the worst deal," I continued without waiting for a response. "Don't be stupid." I glanced at my watch and realized that I had talked to him for nearly 40 minutes, and that I must have repeated myself several times over. But this would be good for emphasis. "This may require more than one trial, and if money becomes an issue, I will help you pay for your attorney fees," was the next unsolicited advice I offered without thinking about our own financial hardship. But I could not worry about that now. "Any attorney wants to avoid confrontation when it comes to sentencing, and they don't want to be accused of giving anyone false hope, so they always go for the settlement. You cannot take that bullshit. It'll be a hung jury."

He reluctantly seemed to agree. He seemed relieved. I think that this was the support he needed, and had not received until now.

I was convinced that I had made the correct decision in recommending this course of action to him. I was older and more experienced, and thought that I was offering sound advice. I was hoping to shine a ray of hope into his darkness, while at the same time hoping that this light I was shining, at the proverbial end of the tunnel, would not turn into the headlights of the oncoming train of overzealous justice and reckless punishment.

As I hung up the phone, I could not overcome the feeling that I had convinced him to be the guinea pig who would test the water for my son's trial.

I felt this remorseful emptiness fulfill my mind and dull my conscience, a feeling similar to the sensation that one gets after witnessing a terrible and unimaginable catastrophe. Actually, it was the more intensely dull type of pain one gets while witnessing a dreadful disaster, mixed with the remorseful relief that one was barely spared, while everyone else around one had perished. The worst part being that you felt responsible for the cause of the catastrophe in the first place.

Somehow I hated myself for what I think I might have done.

Yet it was the right decision. There was no doubt in my mind that this was the right decision.

"God help him . . . God help me . . ." were my last thoughts on the matter as I poured myself another glass of wine.

CHAPTER 29

TRIAL: ANTHONY ROBERTS

B uffeted by March winds, my wife and I arrived at the courthouse in Bridgeview, Illinois by 9:00 a.m., as required. We had learned to expect delays, so it didn't surprise us to hear that the trial wouldn't actually start until 1:00 that afternoon.

The courtroom interior appeared much as those everyone sees on television in documentaries and network series. This one was contemporary in its design and furnishings. Dark mahogany panels covered the wall behind the bench while everywhere else the walls were painted in a nondescript beige color. The ceiling consisted of symmetrically installed acoustic panels and light fixtures. Foot traffic in rows around the seating areas had worn down the relatively new carpeting. The judge's bench, consisting of expensive wood panels, stood elevated about two feet above the clerk's station to his right and the witness stand to his left, near the jury box. Two massive oak tables occupied the space in front of the judge, the left one for the defense team and their client, and the right one for prosecutors. Close by stood a microphone-equipped lectern for the use of anyone addressing the court. A waist-high wall with swinging gates in the center separated the audience, who sat in four rows of chairs. Lawyers and witnesses walked from the entry up a center aisle, through the gates which gave off an annoying squeak each time they were used. It amazed me to see that various obscene words scratched on the waist-high wall hadn't been painted over.

With the exception of a clock on the left wall, and the seal of the State of Illinois on the wall behind the judge, no other decorations were visible. Conspicuous by its absence was the familiar phrase consisting of four simple, yet comforting words, which I had seen in courtrooms of other jurisdictions, even very recently, and which I remember having been boldly displayed even here in Bridgeview not so long ago. I thought that it was ironic that continued controversy involving the separation of state and religion had resulted in the removal of those four consoling words, "In God We Trust," while anyone taking the witness stand to give testimony was still required to raise his or her hand and swear on the Bible.

Once the trial did start, the first stage was the selection of a jury from the pool of individuals who actually replied to the mailed summons they had received. None of the jurors looked pleased, and I wondered how many of them where there because they could not come up with a reasonable excuse for failing to show up. I wondered how many of them were angry about their lives being interrupted by this call to duty, and how this anger might affect their state of mind as it might apply to their verdict.

I was informed that I would be a witness for the defense. After all, I had heard Conny kiss my son several hours after the alleged incident had supposedly taken place, and thank him for a wonderful evening. This evidence would support the defense's position that, contrary to her accusations now, she, in reality, had not been harmed and that she had been a willing participant during Anthony's involvement. Aside from the juvenile pranks not involving Anthony, nor Adrian for that matter, she had apparently enjoyed the party. I was very willing and anxious to testify. Anthony's participation in the events had followed those of Adrian, and if it could be evidenced that she was a willing participant with Anthony, then by default, I reasoned, it would be clear that she would have had to have been a willing participant during Adrian's involvement.

As a scheduled witness, I was not allowed in the courtroom during the trial, nor could I observe any other related activities, as any of them might influence my recollection. I suppose that I could be influenced to remember things that might not actually have happened, if it might have helped our cause. But I understood the system. This is a common practice in which every potential witness is isolated from the actual court proceedings until called to the stand.

Jury selection was not completed until the second day, when eight women and four men took their seats, including one woman who had admitted to being a rape victim herself several years earlier. A surprisingly high number of the jurors were African-Americans.

That same day, several technical witnesses appeared for the prosecution, verifying DNA evidence and the manner in which it was collected and evaluated. The defense didn't bother to cross-examine any of them and the trial recessed at five o'clock that afternoon.

On the third day, I was allowed in the gallery since no other actual testimony was scheduled at that time. From the last row I watched Anthony's attorney, Robert Kuzas, aggressively make a point by pounding his left hand with his right fist, and observed Cook County State's Attorney Cheryl Schroeder spread her arms and shrug her shoulders in a defensive gesture. It soon became apparent that Jenny Weller, who had been subpoenaed by the prosecution, had shown up yesterday, but was missing today. Kuzas had questions for her, and was angry about her absence. Trusting the prosecution, he hadn't issued his own subpoena. Schroeder suggested that the girl had misunderstood the summons, perhaps thinking that it applied only to the previous day.

Now, if I were a skeptic, I might have suspected that this was a crafty maneuver and an evasive plot by which the progress of the trial could be interrupted, and which would allow more time to properly or more thoroughly prepare that witness. Suspicion and skepticism notwithstanding, I sardonically remembered the saying, "Suspicion often creates the very thing that it suspects." And my suspicions that the prosecution was guilty of tampering with a witness was quickly becoming a dreaded premonition. In fact, the consequences of such actions would go far beyond a simple premonition, and would imply that the prosecution was not interested in working within the parameters of the law, but would instead use any and all means to further their cause. This would then no longer be a search for justice, but instead it would be a contest with only one goal: to be victorious, no matter how such victory would be achieved.

Jenny and I were the only witnesses Kuzas had intended on using, and he was primarily relying on her testimony to prove Anthony's innocence. Without her, he really had no chance of winning this case. The judge also seemed puzzled, and questioned both parties as to an equitable solution.

For reasons still unexplained, or actually, impossible to explain, prosecutor Cheryl Schroeder recommended to the judge that "Mrs. Missbrenner drive to Jenny Weller's home and bring her to court."

I could not believe my ears.

I could not believe our good fortune.

I could not belief how naive Cheryl Schroeder was for making that recommendation.

My wife, as honest and truthful as she was, could not possibly be neutral and refrain from influencing Jenny, or ask her for information about her testimony she had given to the prosecution or the grand jury. She would not be able to help herself from correcting any of Mary's potential "mistakes," or reminding her of what actually had happened, how it happened, and why she should remember the events exactly so. It would have been the equivalent of asking a starving person not to eat the food being offered to him. Or maybe it would have been more like asking a fox to transport a chicken.

I rushed out of the courtroom in order to find my wife, who was on her cell phone somewhere outside. This opportunity was too good to jeopardize, and I wanted to get her started as soon as possible before anyone could come to their senses and realize the enormous advantage that was granted to us with this decision. Dobrila's disbelief was overruled by my insistence that she react immediately, and she proceeded to Jenny's house. Approximately fifty minutes later, with the trial in progress, she returned, with the information that she could only find a small dog at the house. No one else. Not Jenny, not her parents, not even any neighbors.

The star witness, on whom the defense had relied, was nowhere to be found. This was a tremendous problem as we had counted on Jenny's testimony, based on our many conversations with her, to provide the clear evidence needed to absolve Anthony.

Robert Kuzas expressed extreme concern, and was virtually

devastated by not being able to put Jenny on the stand. He clearly had committed a grievous error in judgment by not issuing a subpoena, and he acknowledged his mistake. I had known him only for a relatively short period of time, but his admission of having, as he had bluntly put it, "simply screwed up," was consistent with his character. At no time did he dwell on his misfortunes, nor did he follow the usual practice of attorneys by blaming someone else.

I was shocked at Kuzas's decision to continue with the trial, rather than request a continuance until such time that Jenny could be located and brought into court. I am sure that no judge would deny such a motion under these circumstances, even if it had been Kuzas's responsibility to subpoena Jenny himself.

With court back in session, I watched from the outside by looking though the small windows in the doors into the courtroom. I also paced the halls and mentally rehearsed what I planned to say during my own testimony. Standing on the outside and looking in, I remember the feelings of helpless resignation and I could hear the ominous, solemn silence as one would enter the courtroom, much like the familiar calm before a storm, which seemed to hover like menacing, dark clouds ready to unleash their fury onto the accused. Watching through the tiny windows, unable to hear anything, I couldn't help but be reminded of the old silent movies, minus the jerky movements. But the silence did magnify the drama and the exaggerated expressions of the participants. Not in a comical way of those old films, but instead in a dramatic manner. On the left side, the defense appeared solemn and apprehensive, with their heads bowed down, taking notes of events that concerned them. It did not project a positive attitude and their solemn physical gestures seemed to mirror their concern or apprehension. In contrast, the prosecution appeared joyous, jovial, and confident. They were shaking hands and patting each others' backs, appearing to periodically laugh out loud. To them it was a job; maybe a promotion if they did well. As a result, there seemed to be no pressure or real concern one way or the other. And if they should lose, then it was on to the next case, and they would repeat their reign of righteous persecution and the pursuit of their sole mandate of securing a conviction.

To the defense, in contrast, it was a much more serious matter. A matter of possibly thirty years in prison for Anthony, who could be fifty years old by the time he would be released. There was little doubt, looking at this silent pageant, that the outcome could be a disaster. And the trial had just barely started.

Anthony's mother, Sandra Roberts, had started a new job and was not able to attend. My wife, who had since struck up a sincere friendship with her, reassured her that she would take her place and would be involved in all maternally instinctive matters of the case. At every opportunity, Dobrila would whisper to Kuzas and provide suggestions and observations. Kuzas soon realized that most of her comments were constructive and pertinent. He developed a habit of consulting with her before excusing a witness. So apparent and visible was her involvement that several members of the courtroom media expressed their support to her in their mistaken belief that she was Anthony's mother.

Aside from the experts giving testimony on the DNA evidence, the other critical evidence presented by the prosecution was the video tape that had been recorded on that early morning. Witnesses included the alleged victim, Conny Skinner, and Jeremy Culp, one of the boys who had agreed to a plea bargain. At the party, he had missed his "turn" with Conny, but had been involved in the activities after she passed out.

During the viewing of the video tape, the television monitor was positioned to allow visibility only for the jury and the judge. The audience could not see any portion of the tape. They could, however, hear the audio and Jimmy's obscene directorial comments.

The taped activities were separated into three segments by the prosecution. Part one consisted of Tarek having sexual intercourse with Conny. Part two showed Adrian having sex with her, after Tarek had finished. Part three showed the activities of the remainder of the boys, as well as Tarek, including their use of a marker pen to write vulgar words on her body, the masturbating, and spitting onto her body, while she appeared to be unconscious.

I tried to interpret the facial expressions of jurors as they watched the tape. However, their stoic demeanor revealed no emotion, and all of them appeared not to be influenced or moved in any way. This, despite the fact that one of the local papers later reported reactions of shock and disbelief by the jurors. I had seen no such display.

Jeremy Culp next seated himself quickly and self-assuredly in the witness chair. He was one of the luckier boys. For reasons which are not quite clear, he had never been charged with the same counts as the other four youths. In fact, despite his participation in the acts which, as it turned out, insulted Conny the most—the derogatory inscriptions on her body, the masturbating, and the spitting—he had escaped from any real persecution. In fact, he was offered probation for any and all possible offenses, in exchange for testimony against the other suspects. Even though it is still not quite clear why he was singled out for this preferential treatment, I suspect that it related directly to his willingness to testify for the prosecution. However, this type of leniency is usually reserved for the "less guilty" accomplice in order to convict the more serious offender. The getaway driver is offered a better deal if he assists in convicting the person who pulled the trigger. Yet, circumstances surrounding this case did not have such clear delineation as to degree of guilt, and it could certainly be argued that the recorded activities in the last part of the tape depicted the more serious offenses. It really wasn't clear who had been the driver and who had been the trigger man.

The detectives' and prosecution's decision to immediately offer such leniency to Jeremy Culp would, on the surface, appear to have been extremely arbitrary and not well thought out, but may actually hide much more serious and zealous intentions. Our attorneys had given us two reasons for that, both of which involved the fact that the valuable suspect, the "rich Burr Ridge kid," had by then already been taken into custody. According to them, Conny either did not remember Jeremy's name, so the detectives could not immediately locate him. In either event, they didn't have time to worry about him, as they needed to strike quickly, decisively, and as I had mentioned earlier, without the interference of any attorneys. Attempts to apprehend additional suspects might have delayed their "blitzkrieg" for swift justice and protection of human sanctity.

As the case may be, and with Jenny's absence, Jeremy now turned out to be the prosecution's main witness. He was quite poignant in his description of his concern for Conny's well-being throughout her supposed ordeal, despite the fact that he claimed no knowledge of the sexual activities which were going on in the spare bedroom during parts one and two of the video tape. He swore not to have been present during any of those sexual activities. He stated that, once he did enter the spare bedroom, he had immediately been worried because Conny appeared to have stopped breathing. He described how he had lowered his ear against her mouth, and how he gently raised her head, in an attempt to hear her breathe, so that he could rest assured that she was still alive and that she had not been harmed by the actions of the other boys. He did not elaborate whether this action had been prior to, or after, pulling down his pants, standing over Conny's motionless body, and masturbating until he ejaculated on her, and then, after pulling up his pants, repeatedly spitting on her.

Watching him give his testimony, I remembered thinking how hard it was to believe that a person in his situation would actually be telling the truth. Then I wondered whether I would not possibly lie myself if I were in his place. It was probably no easy matter for Jeremy to be sitting on two chairs, and his discomfort was clearly evident. For, as soon as he would get comfortable with the notion in support of the prosecution that "something bad was going on in the spare room," he would become immediately uncomfortable with the question as to why he didn't attempt to stop whatever that something had been. He appeared worried that by not stopping it, he could be accused as an accessory for crimes along with everyone who was present during the commission of the acts. Similar to the analogy of a driver being equally culpable for the death of a bank guard during a robbery, even though the "wheel man" never went inside.

Despite Jeremy's efforts to be a good soldier for the prosecution, his continued self-concern interfered with his ability to paint as clear a picture as the prosecution had hoped. In fact, in most instances, his story was confusing because he would elaborate more on his innocence rather than the real issues at hand. He would spend most of his testimony trying to convince everyone that he had not been involved. In doing this, he inadvertently revealed information which was more valuable than his guilt or conviction. True to his assertions, Jeremy reaffirmed, during cross-examination by the defense, that he touched nothing, didn't look at anything, and most importantly, did not participate in any of the really disgusting sexual activities after Conny had gone into the spare bedroom. Never mind what happened to her while she was unconscious.

Kuzas's cross examination of Jeremy was straightforward. He seemed and sounded supportive of the youth's claims, and he would appear to only ask questions to help him understand Jeremy's innocence more clearly. "So, after she walked into the spare room, you stayed behind in the other room?" The witness concurred. "And, after she had walked into the spare room, you did not know what she was doing?" Another agreement. "In fact, after she walked into the spare room, you could no longer see her at all?" Jeremy said that was true.

Kuzas nodded at my wife and informed the judge that he had no further questions of this witness. The prosecution did not appear to have been surprised or uncomfortable in any way, and excused their supporting actor.

Now it was time for their star, their final witness, Conny Skinner herself.

In most cases involving rape, the victim is reluctant to tell what happened and relive the trauma. In this case, however, the prosecutors were proud of the perseverance, resolution, and stamina that Conny showed by her eager willingness to testify.

Adrian's attorney, Patrick Campanelli, wishing to observe Conny's demeanor and hear exactly what she would say, attended this portion of the trial himself. He had advised us that we should expect her to look like the most pure and innocent victim ever to enter a courtroom. He had painted a vision of her for our benefit, and predicted that she would wear a long skirt, a turtleneck sweater, and a gold necklace with a cross prominently visible, with little or no make-up, and her hair combed back in a pony tail. Anthony's attorney agreed "It'll be for the benefit of the jury," he explained, "to make her as innocent-looking as possible. In fact, not only will she look innocent, but watch out for the halo that the prosecutors will position above her head."

I remember how this comment made me think of the anonymous saying, that it takes a halo to fall only a few inches in order to turn into a noose.

Conny made her appearance. Throughout this procedure, she had been sequestered in a separate room so that she would be sheltered from the repeated agony of the experiences that any of the testimony might cause her. In fact, she was carefully assisted and slowly ushered to the witness stand by one of the prosecutors, just in case she might still be weak from the ordeal she had endured nearly three years earlier.

Contrary to the predictions and our expectations, she didn't wear a halo. Instead of the innocent looking victim, what everyone saw was a mature looking woman, dressed in black, tight-fitting Spandex pants, high-heeled shoes, a tight top and straight, stringy hair. Her make-up was extraordinarily pronounced and highly visible. No gold cross, no halo, no innocence, just the prominently visible camel-toe affliction caused by her excessively tight pants.

Her testimony was equally shocking.

Answering a question by the prosecutor, she said, "As soon as I walked into the room, I was handed a glass. I only took two sips from the glass and immediately became ill. I rushed to the bathroom and vomited up everything that I had drunk. I then became dizzy and passed out after that. I cannot remember anything that happened that evening after that." Speaking softly with a demure affectation, she continued, "The next thing I remember was waking up the next morning, totally naked aside from my black socks, with writing all over my body. I immediately called my girlfriend, who came and picked me up." Dabbing at her eyes with a tissue, she added, "It was just terrible."

The prosecutors, particularly state's attorney Peter Troy, you may recall, had volunteered the information to the media three years earlier, that Conny had been "dragged into a spare bedroom and had been brutally gang-raped by several men." The media in turn had repeatedly broadcast that sensational "news" causing the avalanche of accusations and speculations that fueled this case.

Yet, Conny did not remember.

She did not remember the dragging.

She did not remember the spare bedroom.

She did not remember the raping.

She did not remember anything.

She testified under oath, 'so help her God,' that she did not remember anything that happened that evening.

But after swearing that she didn't remember anything, she corrected herself, and in fact did remember that she specifically did not give Anthony her consent to place his penis into her mouth.

The prosecution was satisfied and rested their case, but did retain their right for redress after the defenses questioned the witness.

Robert Kuzas's cross-examination was peppered with objections raised by the prosecution, as he attempted to establish Conny's history prior to the alleged incident, as well as after the alleged incident. Most of the objections were sustained by the judge, ruling that none of those inquiries would be relevant to the case. Such information was unimportant and prejudicial. The prosecution didn't want anything to compromise the moral character of the alleged victim. The fact, as we had learned by then, that she had group sex on several occasions prior to the party, as well as after the incident, could not be brought up. The fact that she not so long ago had given a person, whom she had met only moments earlier, a "blow job" for a cigarette, was not admissible. Even the fact that she had filed a civil law suit for monetary compensation as a result of this alleged rape was not allowed to be mentioned.

It was not important to the matter at hand, as it had nothing to do with this case. That's the law, plain and simple.

Kuzas obviously knew the legal limitations provided in such matters. Still he made mention of these facts persistently, objections notwithstanding, hoping the bell heard by the jury could not be un-rung.

However, he did not question her actual statements, as he felt that she had helped him enough.

After he finished his interrogation, the prosecution officially rested their case and a break in the proceedings was called by Judge Smierciak. It was about 1:00 p.m. at the time.

As we sat in the cafeteria on the lower level of the courthouse, Kuzas informed me that he would not call me as a witness. I was genuinely surprised, as I believed the contents and extent of my testimony to be important and convincing. I am still not certain of the motive behind this, but he was clearly more qualified to make that type of a decision.

However, his next move surprised me even more. He had wrestled with the idea of whether or not to summon Anthony as a witness, several times mulling over the pros and cons out loud. He finally decided against it, and instead would immediately proceed with his closing arguments.

Even though I disagreed, I did recognize that this was not my fight. As a result, I did not raise any objections. I simply remembered the saying that, "A wise man sees as much as he ought, not as much as he can."

I sat next to my wife in the first row behind the defense's table. Since testimony had been completed, all witnesses had been allowed back in the courtroom. After being called to order by the bailiff and instructed to remain quiet and be seated, it was Robert Kuzas's turn to commence with his closing arguments.

After taking a last-minute review of his notes, he slowly rose from his chair and, appearing to be in a baffled, pre-occupied state of mind, ambled toward the jury.

"Where, oh where, can Jenny be?" Kuzas muttered, as if thinking out loud for everyone to hear. Apparently he was doing his best impersonation of Peter Falk playing bumbling, absent-minded Detective Columbo, from that 1970's television series. "For some reason, Jenny is not here," he exclaimed, as he stopped a few feet from the jury.

"And do you know why Jenny is not here?" he inquired of the jury. "I'll tell you why Jenny is not here," he answered his own question, as he turned toward the prosecutors' table.

"It's because they really don't want her here," he declared directly to them, while stretching out both arms in a visible proclamation that he meant to include all of the prosecutors sitting at the table.

Michael Deno objected, based on the argument that Kuzas could not possibly have known what the prosecutors really wanted. The judge agreed and sustained the objection, instructing jurors to disregard the remarks about what the prosecutors wanted.

Kuzas lowered his head, as if in remorse for having been scolded, and tapped his forehead with his right index finger, in a attempt to seem contemplative and thoughtful. Then, in what appeared to be an illuminating revelation, he said, "Maybe I don't know what it is they really wanted, but I know what I would really want if I had gone through all the trouble and effort to issue a subpoena. If I had engaged a sheriff to serve the subpoena, and if I made sure that the subpoena was served in time, and if I made sure that I had the necessary evidence in support of all that." Turning again, he walked towards the defense table, picked up a document he had place there a few minutes earlier, and raised it to be visible by the jurors. "And this is the subpoena which was issued by the prosecution and served on Jenny."

He paused as he slowly waved the paper back and forth. "This document mandates that she appear in court and provide her testimony as to the knowledge that she has, as it applies to this case." He spewed the words with self-righteous vindication. "This document also provides information as to the consequences of what will happen, if it is disregarded or not complied with." Kuzas hesitated briefly in order to let his last comments resonate with the jurors. "Now, if I went through all this trouble to issue the subpoena, serve the subpoena, and make sure that all of that was done correctly, then I would, sure as hell, be upset if Jenny were not in court as required." For emphasis, he slammed the paper back onto the table. "So, after Jenny does not appear in court, don't you think that the prosecutors would be upset?" he asked, locking eyes with them again, knowing that Deno would again object.

The prosecutor did, and again the judge sustained the objection. Unfazed, Kuzas plowed ahead. "Well, if you were upset, wouldn't you make every effort to get Jenny into court?" he asked with an inquisitive expression while looking at several of the jurors in the front row.

The same objection was sustained based on the same grounds.

Yet, Kuzas persisted. "If it were me, I would be mad as hell," he argued. "If it were me, I would engage everyone available to get Jenny into court. I would ask the sheriff to go get her. I would ask the police to go get her. I would ask the bailiff to go get her. Hell, I would ask the Army, the Navy, the Air Force, the Marines, and even the National Guard to go get her. And if that didn't work, then I would jump in my own car and go get her," he fumed angrily while still facing the jurors.

"But do you know who it was that the prosecution suggested should get her?" he asked teasingly. And as he turned around and raised his arm to point at my wife, he exclaimed, "They asked the judge to instruct Mrs. Missbrenner to go get her."

A slight rumble was audible from the audience, which reaffirmed Kuzas's resolve. "That's right. Of all the people they could have asked to get Jenny, they wanted Mrs. Missbrenner to get her," he repeated slowly and emphatically. "So how upset do you think the prosecutors actually were, when Jenny didn't show up in court, if they sent Mrs. Missbrenner to get Jenny?" Kuzas seemed to answer the question rather than ask it.

While the prosecutors contemplated whether to object or not, Kuzas continued his attack.

"Now, for those of you who don't know who Jenny is, let me identify and explain her importance," he offered, as he once again scanned the jurors' expressions. "Jenny is the person who provided most of the information the police and prosecution have used in making their case. Jenny was brought in front of the grand jury, and based on her testimony, the grand jury issued an indictment against my client. Jenny is the person who alerted the police to the existence of this video tape, and it was Jenny who put together all the pieces of the puzzle for the police and prosecution." He spoke slowly and clearly.

"In short, Jenny is the single most important piece of the equation for the prosecution, because without her, there would have been no evidence, and no case," he explained. "But that is only half the story. The fact that she is not here today is not the real issue. But the answers that she would have given if she were here today are the real issue. And in her answer she would have said that a sexual encounter did in fact happen that early morning," Kuzas divulged.

"But this is only the first answer of a two-part question. And we are told that we have heard the first answer. But we really did not hear the answer, because Jenny isn't here today to offer it. All we heard is what the prosecution claimed that she said. And somehow, they were able to use that which they claim that she said, to make an entire case out of it. But we have never really heard the actual answer," he insisted. "Furthermore, and more importantly, we never heard the second answer to the question. Maybe we can accept the first answer without actually hearing it. Namely, that sex in fact did happen; that a video tape of this was made; that several boys had sex with one girl; that the girl eventually passed out."

Of course, Kuzas knew that Jeremy Culp could have provided the supportive evidence regarding the video tape's authenticity.

"And you know what?" he asked facetiously. "We're not even arguing that fact; we're not contesting the DNA evidence; we're agreeing that my client had sex with his accuser." His face reflected a self-satisfied complacency. "But anything beyond that, are simple and pure speculations on the part of the prosecution. The allegations that a rape had occurred are only speculations, because the evidence presented so far does not support that allegation." Now he sounded unequivocal.

"And this brings us to the second question and second answer. The critical answer. This is where Jenny's presence here today could provide that critical second answer. And the second answer that Jenny would provide would quickly and decisively prove our case," he asserted. "Jenny, you see, is the friend of Conny, who arrived with her that evening. Jenny is also a friend of one of the other boys accused with my client. And Jenny would tell everyone here that Conny did everything that she wanted to do that night. Her testimony would prove that this was not a rape, but a consensual sexual affair," he explained. "But, conveniently enough, Jenny is nowhere to be found. I didn't subpoena her, they did," he pronounced, while waving a finger at the prosecutors. "But they didn't want her here, because they didn't want Jenny to give her second answer," he repeated, knowing that this would again raise an objection.

Again, the judge cautioned the jury not to consider any information on the insinuation by the defense suggesting that they knew what it was that the prosecution wanted. I thought I saw a slightly reluctant smirk on the judge's face as he tried to clear up any confusion about the objection.

Kuzas had made his point about Jenny, so he turned his attention to Jeremy Culp. "Ladies and gentlemen of the jury, the next witness the prosecutors presented, and who they were able to get to appear here in court today, seems to be their star witness as to the events that allegedly happened on December 7, 2002 . . . You've heard that this witness clearly stated that he saw the alleged victim walk into the spare room by her own choice. After everything he said, how innocent and uninvolved he was, he still saw her walk into the spare room. Despite the fact that he was a filthy pig and insulted the alleged victim by writing obscenities on her naked body, by masturbating and spitting on her, he still swore that she went into the spare room of her own free will . . .," he paused temporarily in anticipation of an objection about his characterization of Jeremy as a filthy pig. But the prosecution remained silent.

Surprised, the defender continued, "You have heard him say that he did not have sexual intercourse with the alleged victim. In fact, he testified that he did nothing wrong." He paused again for effect. "And I think he then said that he would never do it again . . . But none of his testimony, the fact that he allegedly did not participate, the fact that he didn't have sex with her, or even the fact that he was possibly innocent, none of that is important here. However, what is important is the fact that he was there. He was at the party that evening. And, ladies and gentlemen of the jury, he, unlike the alleged victim, did not pass out. Unlike the alleged victim, he was able to remember what happened. Unlike the alleged victim, he could remember her walking into the spare room." Kuzas bellowed his litany with conviction.

"So now you have a situation whereby one person clearly remembers what happened, that she walked into the spare bedroom, versus another person not remembering anything that happened." He shrugged his shoulders while raising his palms upwards in a gesture mimicking a person who might want to explain something he didn't remember. "And at this point, we are not even talking about any sexual activities. We are merely recollecting what happened prior to any of the allegations. So, ladies and gentlemen of the jury, I ask you, who would you believe?"

The question hung in the air while Kuzas paced back and forth in front of the jury. "Do you believe the alleged victim who remembers nothing? Who does not remember walking into the spare bedroom? Because, ladies and gentlemen of the jury, if she walked into that spare bedroom of her own free will, then it is more likely that she was a willing participant to the sex that followed. And then she clearly must have lied about having passed out." The defender waited for the information to sink in, while brazenly staring at various members of the jury. "If she walked into that spare room by herself, then she must have lied about having passed out and having woken up the next morning; then all of that testimony is nothing but a bunch of bull," he added as an exclamation point.

"Who are you going to believe?" he asked again, as he reverted back to the Columbo character's maladroit mannerisms. "How about the witness who clearly stated that he saw her walk into the spare room by herself," he offered as a response. "Forget that he is a filthy pig. Forget that he wants to be innocent. Forget that he may or may not have been involved in the sex. None of that is important here." He methodically and slowly re-stated each disclaimer while facing the jury.

"What is important here is the fact that he saw, and the fact that he clearly remembers seeing her walk—into—that—spare—bedroom—by—herself." Kuzas spaced and enunciate each word for emphasis. "And he is their witness. He is on their side. He is telling their interpretation of what happened." This time he knew an objection was coming, and he was correct. Judge Smierciak sustained it and admonished the jury.

Undaunted, Kuzas waded in again. "Because, if you believe Jeremy Culp, the person who remembers everything as to what happened, then you cannot believe the alleged victim, who can't remember anything. And if in fact you believe Jeremy Culp, their star witness, then the alleged victim is obviously not telling the truth about what actually happened that evening. Because, how can you not remember walking into a bedroom if you are making such a devastating accusation? If you are prepared to send this person accused in this matter to jail for 30 years, how can you not remember such an important detail?" Once again he spewed, but this time with genuine disgust.

"But let's also consider the intangible evidence which was not presented. No evidence of any injuries, any bruises, scrapes, scratches, or perforations; no torn clothing, none of that. In fact, after she had gone to the hospital, no injuries or evidence of a possibility of a rape was found. In fact, no proof of any kind, other than her accusation of an event which she does not remember, and a video tape which does not support the claim of events which she does not remember, have been presented so far. In fact, the tape clearly shows that she was moving her arms and audibly responding to the directions of the youth who was taping the activities."

Now speaking more rapidly, he said, "The prosecution has clearly failed to prove beyond any reasonable doubt that a crime has been committed here." Kuzas repeated the observation which my wife had made much earlier in this persecution. "This young woman may have been insulted, but she was not assaulted."

As the defender sat down, he nodded to my wife.

CHAPTER 30

BATTLE TO THE END

The prosecutors, Cheryl Schroeder and Michael Deno, seemed unfazed by Kuzas's closing arguments. Instead, they proceeded with what sounded like a scripted speech. Schroeder approached the jurors and slowly looked at each one as she commenced reading from her note pad.

"Ladies and gentlemen of the jury, you have been gathered here to do that which is morally right to do. Based on the evidence which you have seen, there can be only one way that you can rule. You have heard the testimony of credible witnesses who, without a doubt, have determined that the DNA evidence collected at the scene of the crime absolutely matches the DNA of the man accused of this terrible crime. It is proof positive that this man was involved in this shameful act with this helpless young girl. It is proof positive that he has had sex with this young girl, who had been unconscious and did not know what was happening, and what was being done to her."

She paused to flip a page. "You have also heard the testimony of a young man who was at the party, and who has positively identified the accused. He told you that Mr. Roberts was at the party and that he had sex with the young victim. You have also heard the testimony of this brave young girl, who time and time again has stated that she became sick as soon as she arrived at the party and that she passed out."

Schroeder looked up from her note pad to establish some eye contact, then down again. "You have heard her testimony that she could not and did not give her consent to the brutal rape that followed, and which had been captured on the video recording you have seen."

Unlike the shambling, Columbo-like movements of the defender, Schroeder stood motionless as she delivered her speech. "And you have seen the video tape itself, which clearly shows that the young victim was in a state of mind whereby she could not have given her consent." At last, she lifted an arm and pointed to the television monitor. "Now, there has been some talk over exactly how many drinks this young victim consumed prior to her ordeal. But you know what, that is not important, nor is it relevant to this case," she lectured. "Maybe she did have more to drink than what she remembers. But we are not here today to pass judgment on her memory as to how many drinks she consumed. After all, who of us can object to a young girl's right of passage into womanhood, and the possible experimentation with alcohol? And, whereas this experimentation may be something you or I would not condone . . . this case is not about that." she reasoned.

"Even if she was drunk, it still does not give anyone the right to violate her the way this monster did. And especially if she was drunk, then she could not have given her consent, and whatever followed afterwards was a crime against her," Schroeder claimed, as she flipped another page. "And it is this violation of her right that is really at trial here. It is her right not to be assaulted. It is her right not to be raped. No matter how much she had to drink," she insisted, as she turned and walked away from the jurors. "This trial is about violation of a person's rights, and it is exactly what Martin Luther King stood for and died for." I thought I heard someone groan softly in the gallery. Schroeder pivoted again to face the jury.

"It is the right of every human being, whether you are white, African-American, Hispanic, Asian; man or woman. You have the right to personal freedom and safety," she exclaimed. "And if anyone takes away that right, then he must be punished. This man has taken that right away from this young victim, and it is your job, ladies and gentlemen of the jury, to send a loud-and-clear message that this will not be tolerated." Schroeder thanked the jurors and returned to her chair at the prosecution table.

Her closing arguments seemed short and matter-of-fact, clearly lacking any emotional convictions, moral motivations, or legal urgencies. In fact, I thought that the probability of eliciting a guilty conviction based on her half-hearted effort was equivalent to the success of explaining colors to a blind person.

But no sooner had I become comfortable with her poor performance when I was suddenly concerned about some legal precedence she might have relied on, and which I did not understand or recognize. The judge still had to read jury instructions to them, and I wondered if something in there might legally require the jury to cast their vote in her favor.

I was suddenly worried that she had been wiser than I had estimated, and that she was sufficiently knowledgeable in what needed to be overlooked or stressed in order to make the jurors concentrate on some obscure legal precedent.

And while it is said that doubt grows with knowledge, I am certain that panic grows with ignorance and doubt. While knowing that the defense would not get another chance to address the jury, I was gravely concerned and deeply despaired over the simplistic conclusion that had been offered, while knowing that a conclusion is usually the place people reach after they get tired of thinking.

That afternoon, at about 5:45, we sat in the lower level courthouse cafeteria discussing the trial and wondering how long it would take the jury to reach a verdict. Our case was the only one still in progress, and the entire building had nearly emptied. Even though the sign at the entrance indicated this to be a cafeteria, the only source of food was from vending machines, which mainly offered snacks, soft drinks, stale sandwiches, and diluted coffee at premium prices. By this time of day most selections had already been picked over and only the least appetizing items remained. A microwave oven was available to heat soups, hot dogs and burgers, and consequently, the already stale air was further flavored with multiple aromas generated from its heavy use throughout the day.

Bad food aside, the room itself, as well as the furnishings, were even worse. Drab paint in a nondescript beige covered the walls except for lower sections scraped by contact with metal chairs and tables. Not a single decorative display could be seen, making the damage all the more pronounced. Waste receptacles overflowed with discarded food and wrappers, and litter remained on most of the tables. In addition, discarded newspapers featuring foreboding news of the trial, and Anthony's picture, lay strewn about. Bright fluorescent lights illuminated the windowless room, and on this particular day, one of the fixtures seemed to have burned out. The constant flickering and humming cast a haunting and gloomy omen as to our anticipations of the outcome of this trial.

I remember the sullen premonition which pre-occupied my mind, the elation I felt after Kuzas's well-punctuated closing statement, and the sudden deflation based on the overly simplistic and straight-to-the-point summation offered by Schroeder. I looked at the morbid surroundings, and genuflected over the fact that the stale package of chips which Anthony had purchased might be the last supper he would enjoy as a free man for possibly the next thirty years. A guilty verdict would mean immediate incarceration. What a fitting scene to punctuate this malignant scenario . . . a remorseful thought I could simply not erase.

From Judge Smierciak's comments to the jury, we expected deliberations to extend into the late hours.

Robert Kuzas, visibly nervous, solicited our opinions as to how his presentation had fared, and how convincing his arguments had appeared. He was second-guessing how he had handled some issues, but resolved that he thought that he had done as well as could have been expected, under the circumstances.

Anthony Roberts, as nervous as he must have been, seemed to actually be relieved that this portion of his ordeal had ended. He was probably numb, and the full impact and gravity of this situation would most likely hit him later on. Sandra, his mother, who had been present the entire day, seemed rightfully uneasy, pragmatic, and conciliatory about the trial and the pending resolution. She continued to reassure everyone that justice would ultimately prevail, and that Anthony would in fact be found innocent.

Even though Dobrila and I were both confident, we nevertheless remained concerned and apprehensive as to a guilty verdict. Not only as it would affect Anthony's fate, but even more so, as to the devastating impact that an unfavorable outcome of this trial would have on Adrian's future. We were all concerned about the jury; specifically their ability to comprehend the important aspects which had been presented, their capability to disregard those aspects which did not matter, and their competence and ability to know the difference.

We scorned the prosecution's blatant attempt to sway the African-American jury members by using a reference to Martin Luther King. We satirized their absurd rationalization about the alleged victim's alcohol consumption. We ridiculed the choice and quality of witnesses that they had presented, namely the "filthy pig," who had committed more shameful acts than anyone else, and who now served as their main witness. We mocked the ludicrous proposition that the alleged victim did not remember anything that had happened, and questioned the wisdom of that type of defense.

But most of all, we became engrossed in a discussion as to the situation created by Jenny's absence, and the potential implications. We were all of the opinion that the prosecution had realized they simply could not afford to have Jenny's testimony presented in open court. Unlike the time she had given her testimony to the police or even the grand jury, this time around all aspects would be presented and evaluated. Back then, the police and prosecution could mold the extent of her testimony in ways that would suit only their purposes. Here in court, the defense would finally have had their chance to cross-examine that testimony and present Jenny's original version of the events.

In fact, Jenny, in no uncertain terms, had previously explained that it was Conny's intention to have sex that evening, regardless of who would participate. "I don't care who I meet, I just want to get laid," Conny had said, according to Jenny's recollection of the conversation with her while en route to our house back in December 2002. Those words still resonated in our memory.

Furthermore, Jenny would have testified that Conny had not passed out until after having been in the spare bedroom for at least fifteen minutes, and that she had been flirting, kissing, and fondling most of the boys there. In fact, it had been Conny who encouraged the video taping after Jimmy had suggested it. Without Jenny to support such information, all such knowledge would be inadmissible hearsay. Clearly, this was information that the prosecution did not want to surface, nor could afford to have investigated.

As Kuzas had pointed out during the trial, Jenny had been the integral piece used by the prosecution to build their case. Not utilizing her knowledge and not having her testify after she had been so instrumental was the equivalent, in my mind, of a team not using their star player during the playoffs. Just imagine the Chicago Bulls not using Michael Jordan, who had been responsible for getting them into the playoffs, during those same playoffs. If the information they had released to the media during the past twenty-seven months had in fact been true, then she would have been more valuable to them now than ever before. Obviously, they must have feared that she would have been a liability rather than an asset if she were examined by the defense.

Furthermore, any person who is served with a subpoena, and does not comply with the request, is subject to serious repercussions. They could be held in contempt of court and be subject to imprisonment. Yet the prosecution did not pursue any action against Jenny for her supposed non-compliance with the subpoena. That by itself should have been indicative of the prosecution's real objectives and motives.

The shocking revelation, uncovered several days later by my wife, was the fact that Jenny appeared to have been at the courthouse all along! According to Jenny's mother's explanation, Jenny had been picked up by a taxi that was sent by the prosecution that morning, and had been isolated in a room during the entire trial.

"A lie is often justified in the end by what it achieves," Lenin reportedly said during his ascent to power, and which seemed to be part of the prosecution's adopted conduct of ethics, as they aspired to achieve their own subjugate goals.

In the end, Dobrila and I reasoned, this information would be extremely valuable, if and when Adrian faced trial. We looked forward to presenting appropriate evidence of the prosecution's handling of a witness, as well as the misinformation in which they had indulged.

After approximately one hour, Kuzas went to check on the status of the deliberation. He returned and informed us that no decision had yet been reached, but that the jury had requested to see the video tape again. This, of course, reassured us that the jurors were on the right track. We hoped they could see that the testimony presented by the prosecution should be regarded as unbelievable fairy tales.

Minutes later, we were advised by one of the bailiffs that the jury had made their decision.

We rushed back to the courtroom, and waited breathlessly for the jurors to take their seats. We might as well have relaxed, though. The prosecution requested a delay to allow extra time for the alleged victim and her family to arrive and participate in these proceedings. The judge granted it.

A little later, we watched once again as Conny was helped to her seat my members of the state's attorney's office. In fact, I choked with disbelief as Conny was being consoled by the very individuals whose sole objective should have been to uphold the law, and who had given their oath to remain fair and unbiased. Instead, they appeared to be promoting the beneficial objectives of one person rather than protecting the rights of every person.

With the court in session, we learned that the jury foreman (that title was still used even though a woman occupied the position in this case) had advised the court of a partial stalemate. They had reached a verdict for only one of the two counts, and were unable to unanimously decide on the second count. A reluctant smile crossed my mind as I fondly remembered my premonition of a hung jury only a few days earlier. This was the best news I could imagine under the circumstances. Reassured, I nodded to my wife in a satisfied expression of relief and contentment, as I gripped her hand tightly, in a further expression of good fortune.

Judge Smierciak, however, was visibly displeased, and instructed the jurors to go back and continue deliberating in a stronger effort to reach a decision on both counts.

Still basking in a sense of gratification, we realized that this could be a long night. The possibility that this jury could never reach a unanimous verdict gathered momentum in my mind. We remained in our courtroom seats even after the jurors had been led back to the deliberation room, and were debating where to go to await the verdict, when the bailiff suddenly re-appeared and informed the judge that a verdict had been reached.

It had taken the jurors less than five minutes to reach their decision after they had failed to come up with such a verdict only moments earlier.

This could not be good news.

My premature feelings of joy were quickly turned into remorseful anticipation of a grave conclusion. My fears regarding the jury would prove correct, after all. Most jurors probably had been unwilling participants, and a prolonged struggle to find an equitable resolution seemed secondary to getting home in time for dinner.

Our attorney's forewarning, that most jurors' mindset is usually tilted toward a guilty verdict rather than an innocent decree, would sadly turn out to be a valid premonition. Such a quick turnaround could only spell the surrender of the idealistic few jurors who might have been holding out.

The jurors were led back into the courtroom and took their seats once again. Judge Smierciak asked the foreman if a decision had been reached, and after having been informed affirmatively, the judge was handed several documents.

I focused on his facial expression as he examined the forms, observed a visible reddening, and interpreted this as a definite state of surprise, and maybe even anger. He made no comments or gestures about the verdict that he was reading. I was still mentally evaluating his reaction, when I heard him ask the jury foreman to announce their ruling on the first count.

The foreman cleared her throat and read aloud. "We, the jury, after deliberating the merits of this case, have found the accused, Anthony Roberts, not guilty on the charge of sexual assault."

A split second of deadly silence followed, then was broken by sighing sounds in the audience, as well as the scribbling noises from the dozen or so reporters on hand, busily recording every word of the announcement.

I was pleasantly surprised, but quickly realized that the verdict so far, even though it had cut Anthony's punishment in half, would still only achieve the same penalty that would have resulted from the plea bargain previously offered. It would appear that the justice system would always seek the lowest possible denominator of legal justification, and in the end, accusations, guilt, and punishment, would still find their own common level of indifference.

The pleasant surprise quickly and unavoidably turned into disgust and anger, and it was with a sense of foregone apprehension that I waited for the inevitable conclusion to this nightmare.

As I grasped Dobrila's hand more tightly, I could hear Judge Smierciak asked the foreman for their decision regarding the second count.

Her voice resonated in the completely silent room. "We, the jury, after deliberating the merits of this case, have found the accused Anthony Roberts, not guilty on the charges of aggravated sexual assault."

The celebration that erupted was clearly one-sided. Our group, consisting of Robert Kuzas, Anthony Roberts, Sandra Roberts, Dobrila and me, jumped to our feet while raising our arms in a gesture of well-deserved victory. I heard my own voice crying out, "I knew it! I knew it!" I felt my emotions see-sawing back to rightful and righteous vindication and renewed faith in the legal system.

The reaction of everyone else in the courtroom seemed to be one of subdued disbelief, and I noticed Conny bowing her head while she was being embraced by a member from the state's attorney's office in an attempt to console her.

Robert Kuzas, visibly relieved and overjoyed, yet with tears in his eyes, turned around and first hugged Dobrila, who stood next to me in the first row behind the defense's table. In soft-spoken gratitude, he uttered, "Thank you, thank you. I couldn't have done this without you," in a clear reference to the countless supportive hours she had spent with him on his case.

The courtroom quickly emptied as reporters rushed into the hallway to transmit stories to their respective offices. As soon as we stepped outside, the same reporters immediately surrounded Anthony and Kuzas in an attempt to solicit responses regarding the verdict. I was standing next to Anthony and was glad to hear him comment the way that he did. "I am relieved that this is over and that the truth had finally prevailed. But I will not rest until Adrian and Tarek are vindicated as well. They, also, are innocent of the charges."

CHAPTER 31

A PATH OF TREACHERY

Life presents many opportunities. Just like stumbling blocks and stepping stones, the way you use these turning points can lead to vastly different results.

By spring 2005, it had been nearly seven months since Adrian's disappearance. And even though we had received several calls from him during that time, he had always been careful not to reveal his location or with whom he had been. All attempts on our part to trace his calls had been futile.

We suspected that he was in Serbia, a former republic of Yugoslavia, whose biggest fame in America stemmed from their "ethnic cleansing" campaign, which had resulted in the bombing of Belgrade, its capital, during Bill Clinton's presidency.

Dobrila was born in Serbia, but had moved to France to live with her mother at the age of ten. She still had relatives living in her native land, but over the past forty years they had been mostly forgotten. In fact, with the exception of one cousin, Zoran, who visited us briefly in 1989, Dobrila had rarely been in communication with anyone there.

After Adrian left, we occasionally called Zoran in hopes that he might either know or learn something about our son's whereabouts. We suspected that the cousin might know more than what he led us to believe, but his continued denials gave us no substantial reason for doubting him.

The truth of the matter, however, was exactly what we suspected. We later learned that Adrian had in fact relied on Zoran to put him up with some of his friends after he distanced himself from his original hosts.

Serbia, with the exception of a few metropolitan cities, is an agricultural country incorporating many remote villages, all difficult to access. The other towns and cities seemed to have ignored these rural sites, as most of them were self-sufficient communities needing little involvement or association with urban society. Firewood was used as the main source for heating homes. Unheated outhouses served as bathrooms and the availability of telephones, television reception, and even electricity was a hit-or-miss proposition.

Adrian had sought refuge in these types of villages, but certain drawbacks to that strategy escalated the risks. A stranger in such small hamlets would cause immediate curiosity and concern, combined with the fact that feeding even one additional mouth would present extra financial strain. So Adrian had been forced to migrate from village to village every few weeks.

All this we ultimately learned in late March 2005, when Adrian finally requested permission to return home, and when he elaborated on the pejorative experiences relative to his flight.

We had several phone conversations with him at that time, and were able to piece together his experiences and the baneful chronicles of his journey.

The whole escape was set in motion when Adrian met two individuals in the cafeteria of his community college back in August 2004. He recognized the language they used as Serbian. Considering himself to be at least partially of Serbian descent, he introduced himself with what few words he knew. Adrian had always been an outgoing person who never missed an opportunity to meet new people. Over a period of several weeks, these two young men made a concentrated effort to befriend him.

Gradually, Adrian confided his bleak story and dim prospects. They expressed pained sympathy and painted themselves in the vivid image of Good Samaritans. Thus, as luck would have it, necessity had met opportunity. They seemed to have all the answers to Adrian's countless questions.

He had clearly been looking for a miracle. They, in turn, offered an opaque illusion. "We understand your situation," they reassured him. Their observations about American justice fit right in with Adrian's dilemma. In English, they bombarded him with negative comments. "This system is not just, it's more crooked than a corkscrew. They have to find a scapegoat. You will definitely be convicted."

The pair offered advice. "You have to take matters into your own hands. Your parents really cannot help you." Gradually, they steered him toward escape to their homeland, Serbia. "Your tormenters will never find you there."

Scared by the ten-year sentence offered to Tarek in a plea bargain, discouraged by the continued negative press, exhausted by the limitations of his home confinement, and comforted by the repeated assurances of a viable and alternative answer these two individuals offered, Adrian opted for what appeared as the only easy and logical solution. Once he agreed to their plan, things happened so fast and so smoothly, that in retrospect, one would have to wonder how many times these individuals might have done this type of thing before.

All they had wanted was to be covered for their expenses. A mere $5,000 would buy his freedom. He obtained the needed money by pawning some of his mother's jewelry at a shop recommended by these individuals. They, in turn, prepared everything else.

On that rainy September night, they picked him up in the wee hours and drove straight through Arizona to the Mexican border town of Nogales. There they gave him a fake driver's license, which they had fabricated with his picture, a Serbian passport which also had his photo but had been issued with an unknown name, a bus ticket to Mexico City, a one-way airline ticket to Belgrade, Serbia, and a pre paid cell phone. They also gave him a Cubs baseball cap, which was intended to be the signal for someone who would be waiting for him at the airport in Belgrade.

At the Mexican border, Adrian blended in with thousands of students from a nearby college that Friday night. They all walked across, planning to party in wide-open Nogales. It amazed Adrian that no Mexican authorities questioned him, and how easy the crossing was. He made his way to the bus terminal within a few blocks and climbed aboard. The tedious yet non-eventful bus ride, on a surprisingly new and comfortable vehicle, was mainly along rural roadways and offered little scenic diversion during the forty-hour trip. Adrian drifted in and out of a semiconscious, dreamlike state which lasted for most of the journey.

He finally arrived in Mexico City late on Sunday evening and found transportation to the airport. His flight on Lufthansa Airlines, though, was scheduled to depart the following day. So he spent the balance of his stay in Mexico at the airport.

Even though his trip from home had taken four days without any real rest, Adrian somehow felt no weariness. Two years of home confinement must have resulted in building up ample supplies of static energy, which now provided the fuel he needed in order to accomplish this task.

He felt liberated from the rules and restrictions which had been weighing him down, and which had nearly caused him to drown in the murky whirlpool of subversive accusations, chronic guilt, caustic fear, and imminent punishment. The growing distance from home gave him new courage. He had traveled too far to look back now.

The hardest part had been leaving his home and parents. Especially without saying good bye. But things had gone well so far and he felt rejuvenated in his belief that he could somehow mend things later on. While killing time in the Mexico City airport, he sat in a small bar, eating a hamburger with fries. What surprised him was that no one questioned it when he ordered a bottle of beer. So he took advantage of this new freedom, and guzzled down a second bottle, too.

A constant sea of people, all types, races, and ages, rushed in every direction throughout the terminal. Everyone had seemed to have a destination and was rushing to get there. Adrian felt a melancholic sentiment as he had watched their frenzied activities. Like them, he too had a purpose and had been in a rush to get to his destination. But unlike them, he had no idea of what it really was that he needed to accomplish. Emotions of remorse began to surface once again, and he debated whether to call home in order to let everyone know that he was all right. But he feared using the cell phone and worried that the call could be traced, as he had been convinced that his parents' phone had to have been under surveillance by now.

One thought quickly led to another, and he finally deduced that if he were to use a public phone and a phone card, the call would have no chance of being traced, especially if it was short. At the last second, he decided to place the call to his father's cell phone. It was his first attempt at contacting any member of his family and lasted less than a minute. Yet, after he heard his father's voice, it gave him renewed strength to carry on.

Once aboard the plane, he finally fell asleep, as the strain and fatigue of the past few days' activities finally took their toll. He didn't wake up until the plane's final approach into Frankfurt. It surprised him that instead of feeling physically refreshed, his long sleep had instead seemed to only renew the mental agony of his decision, which until then, he had been too tired to realize. Still, he was able to convince himself again of the righteousness and salvation of his actions.

Adrian spent an eight-hour layover in Frankfurt, all inside the terminal. The technological and architectural differences between this airport and the one in Mexico City amazed him. He had by no means any experience with airports, but these two seemed separated not only by miles, but by generations as well. He had been too busy marveling at the latest technological innovations that had been incorporated even into the smallest of details, that he had actually been able to somehow push his problems into the back burners of his consciousness.

The final leg of his trip lasted only ninety minutes, but was the most nerve-wracking of all. Once again immobilized by the confines of his seat, he found no diversions to keep him from pondering and reassessing profound decisions he'd made. As he watched the minutes tick by, all of his anxieties, apprehensions, and trepidations grew to massive proportions. Unlike the departure from Mexico City, where the scrutiny of his documents had been minimal, he knew that admittance to a city in Europe would be far more complicated. He carried a bogus passport in another name, on which his photo had replaced the original owner's, and had no idea about the methods border authorities would employ to verify its authenticity. A million questions of uncertainty merged with his existing anxieties, causing near paralysis in his body and mind. The original bearer of the passport could be a wanted fugitive or even a war criminal. Maybe he had already died, and the passport had already been canceled. Adrian felt as if he had jumped from the frying pan which had been simmering his former problems, and jumped into the blazing fire of unknown troubles and woes.

All the promises given to him by his two allies had faded into a distant memory. They were still back in Illinois, as far as Adrian knew, making their confident assurances completely worthless.

He felt the blood rush from his head, creating a sensation of unconsciousness as the plane touched down on the tarmac in Belgrade, Serbia.

In an involuntary trance, he helplessly allowed himself to be swept up by the other passengers in their rush to retrieve luggage and exit the plane. Without realizing it, he grabbed his carry-on bag and followed the flow of mindless locomotion into the terminal's customs gates. Resisting forward progress as much as possible, he allowed other passengers to pass him by.

Despite these evasive maneuvers and attempts to delay the inevitable, he soon found himself near the checkpoint. His vision began to blur, and he felt the stress turning into a migraine headache, a condition he had suffered much of his life. Loitering did no good, and he knew confrontation was only moments away.

To top it off, Adrian had an uncomfortable feeling of being watched. Two particularly tall, uniformed men seemed to have fixed their eyes on him repeatedly. Certainty that he had been discovered gripped him. In a vain attempt to deflect the inevitable, and hide his obvious guilt, he repositioned his Cubs baseball cap so that the bill now faced forward and concealed his guilt-ridden eyes. Despite his best efforts, he couldn't resist glancing at the tall officers, who continued their visual scrutiny of him.

Suddenly, without warning, he felt a firm tug on his right shoulder. Before he could turn around he heard the unknown assailant speak in a perfect British accent, "I thought that this might be you." As Adrian turned to face the stranger, he realized that this person also wore an officer's uniform. The cultured voice added, "The way you had your cap positioned, I could not read the logo. Come this way. You don't have to go through the checking process."

The officer ushered Adrian to a side door, unlocked it, and motioned him through. In shock, still frightened, but mostly speechless, Adrian allowed himself to be taken to a dark sedan waiting near taxis, buses, and limousines. His benefactor spoke one more time. "The driver will take you home. But he doesn't speak any English." The car door slammed and the driver accelerated out into the Serbian traffic.

Outside, the weather was dreary, cold, and damp, but all Adrian could feel was the comforting warmth offered by the sanctuary of the speeding car. He settled back into the rear seat and finally felt free to exhale and purge his mind from the horrendous anguish of only moments earlier. Opportunity, he thought, continued to present him with stepping stones, which he hoped would lead him to salvation. And as he focused on his steps in his attempt not to stumble, he failed to see the yawning potholes and unscrupulous stones protruding in his path just barely ahead of him.

Adrian's trip had started in rain, and now the drops started to fall again. After a twenty-minute ride, the mysterious car pulled over to a curb. No words had been exchanged between the driver and Adrian, who still felt a sense of relief for having dodged a bullet marked with his name. At that moment, someone pulled the car door open. Under an umbrella stood a man wearing a bulky overcoat. He snarled in broken English, "Come this way." Adrian obediently followed the husky individual into an old apartment building and up three poorly illuminated flights of stairs. They entered a spacious foyer of what appeared to be a penthouse apartment. From the ceiling, at least ten-feet high, hung an ornate chandelier providing ample light, which reflected off the marble flooring.

A well-dressed man emerged from an adjoining room and greeted Adrian. "Welcome to your new home. My name is Radovan, but you can call me Don." He reached out in what Adrian expected to be a handshake. Instead, Don embraced him with both arms with an energetic hug, then gave him three quick kisses on the cheeks, in what was normally a traditional Serbian welcoming gesture. But in some societies, a greeting involving a kiss on someone's cheek has, throughout history, held a more sinister meaning. To Adrian, though, it meant a familiar and friendly welcome. No one knew it at the time, but to Don, it was intended as a means to lull the newcomer into a false sense of security and good fortune.

It is said that he who can lick, can always bite.

Adrian's limited experience, at age nineteen, had not prepared him to be skeptical or suspicious of a stranger's extreme courtesy or glad tidings. To Adrian, things had begun to look more positive, and this sanguine meeting gave him renewed encouragement about the new future in a different land.

Don could not have been more than thirty-five years old. He was approximately six feet tall and of medium build. He spoke English fairly well and exuded confidence.

Over the next few weeks, Adrian received royal treatment, including being waited on hand and foot. He relished the comfort of having struck up a sincere friendship. Don continually reassured Adrian that his decision and actions had been the only viable option. To pass the time, Don elaborated in great length on the many obstacles he himself had been forced to overcome. He claimed to have persevered in the face of insurmountable odds, and succeeded. Pointing with pride to the prosperous circumstances he had achieved, he encouraged Adrian to follow his example.

To this date, we do not know how much Don fabricated and how much was true, but to Adrian he spun a convincing tale of heroism, patriotism, and a never-ending pursuit of justice. He claimed to have been a trusted member of the Serbian National Defense, SND, during that country's troubles with the other former republics of Yugoslavia. This conflict, in the end, had resulted in the "unprovoked" bombing of Belgrade by the United States.

The SND, he claimed, was a loyal and honorable group of patriots who had taken to arms in order to defend their county's freedom and liberty. He repeatedly compared the actions of that organization to those of the American patriots who had fought for independence from Great Britain two centuries ago. Don's father, he said, had been a high-ranking general in Yugoslavia under the regime of Josip Broz Tito, and after the ascent of Milosevic to power in the post-Tito era, had been rewarded with a coveted government position. However, the ensuing conflict, which pitted Serbia against the world, had resulted in a widespread collapse of most government institutions through privatization. Fraud, graft, and exploitation by the corrupt few, had caused financial ruin to the honest citizens. Naturally, Don's father and his family had lost everything they had worked for in their entire lives. Additionally, in an effort to appease world opinion, Milosevic had distanced himself from organizations such as the Serbian National Defense, which he had originally created. The goal had been to carry out many of the covert "ethnic cleansing" campaigns, which had ultimately prompted America's involvement. Instead of being disbanded, however, many members of this and other similar pseudo-military organizations had gone underground. They claimed territories in most urban areas, which "benefited" from their benevolent protection.

Adrian was impressed when Don proudly displayed his arsenal of weapons, which included automatic assault rifles, grenade launchers, and anti tank missiles, which he had retained from his days of urban combat. With pride, he described his network of residual patriots who occupied positions within the police, customs, and other influential offices.

It is said that man is the only animal capable of remaining on friendly terms with his prey for any length of time, all the way until he has the need to devour it.

In fact, Don's ponderous assertions and ebullient explanations were not simple boisterous affirmations of his self-esteem, but instead were concise and cognitive methods of psychological warfare, conducted to intimidate Adrian into absolute compliance and servile resignation. In other words, Don elaborated on the power and might wielded in order to head off any urges in Adrian to make demands or question decisions. Simply put, he had the power, the means, and the authority to impress Adrian with "shock and awe" tactics designed to keep him obedient and compliant.

To further underscore his reign, Don took Adrian on a few of his business excursions, in which he made a point of passing countless buildings and factories which had been bombed more than ten years earlier, but had been left unrepaired in a clear and demonstrative memorial and as a continued affirmation of the resentment still harbored against Americans. He conducted official meetings and social gatherings with police officers and other uniformed individuals from indiscernible ranks of government services, most of which included the transfer of monies in either direction. Throughout, he persistently assured Adrian that, as long as he remained under his protection, nothing adverse would happen to him. Don also promised Adrian that his time with him had been intended to be only temporary, as he had been working on documentation which would allow him to travel throughout the newly formed European Union.

In order to accomplish that feat, however, he explained that he could not afford any interference from outside sources, and had insisted that Adrian not communicate with anybody. This of course included his parents or any relatives in Serbia. And while Adrian obeyed every instruction and abided by all rules and regulations, Don made a phone call to his parents, which clearly outlined the cost of doing business with him.

I don't know how many times I have heard Adrian say, "But I thought that . . ." Those words have always been the innocent prefix Adrian used as long as I can remember when attempting to explain his actions or an error in judgment.

And he reverted to this once again when trying to reason with Don about why he had used the Internet to communicate with a friend in America during a late night in the first part of October 2004.

"But I thought that the Internet gives you total anonymity and that no message can be traced," Adrian rationalized. Don, however, didn't take lightly to Adrian's blatant disregard of his instructions and disrespect of his rules. To further enunciate his displeasure and anger, he slapped Adrian several times, causing a bloody nose as well as severely crushed feelings.

"You are never to contact anyone again," Don growled. "And if you ever disobey my orders again, then you'll wish you were back in

America to face those little problems instead." Don's verbal assault was far more vivid and painful than the blood that had trickled down his face.

This unexpected treatment served as a wake up call to Adrian, and prompted him to remove the rose-colored glasses which had bathed his new environment as a place with no threats or worry. Gone were the pleasant hues and pastel colors which had clouded his mind, and he immediately began to reassess his situation. It caused him to analyze the events which had brought him here. He remembered how amazed he had been that they were able to produce a valid-appearing passport that had his picture and someone else's identity. He wondered about the ease with which he had been able to enter into Serbia by circumventing the government's customs scrutiny. The cache of arms, the stacks of cash, the constant bodyguards, the covert transactions with the police . . . all of which had seemed so adventurous and exciting, but now lost its luster and appeal. The more he replayed the occurrences and incidents which had defined the actions of his hasty flight, his clandestine arrival and servile residency, the more he came to realize that this was a situation in which he no longer wanted to be involved.

He resoundingly decided that he could no longer remain here, and that he had to take a proactive part in finding a remedy. An opportunity presented itself the very next evening. Don had gone out and left one bodyguard with Adrian in his apartment. While the bodyguard was distracted by a TV program, Adrian pretended to retire for the night in his bedroom. He quietly made a phone call to Zoran, the only relative he knew in Serbia.

The conversation with Zoran confirmed Adrian's worst fears.

Don, he learned, was a well-connected criminal involved in loan sharking, shakedowns of small businesses, and drugs. He had his roots in the Serbian National Defense organization, but for reasons of intimidation and extortion, rather than liberation and protection. He was one of many such former members who had gone into business for themselves after the conflict. And whereas most of them had met with untimely demise, they were particularly fearless and ruthless during their brief reigns. People like them had not built their reputations on things that they were going to do, but instead relied on the horrific memories of what they had done, and the fearful perception of what they were still capable of doing.

Escape from Don's apartment, Adrian decided, should be ruled out as too risky. However, since Don had shown himself to be a person of habit, Adrian was able to predict his routines and patterns of movement throughout Belgrade fairly well. He had a propensity for showboating his self-perceived charismatic personality, and would customarily "grace" some of his favorite restaurants in an extravagant and predictable manner. Adrian had been included in such excursions, and if taken again, might find an opportunity to escape.

The next morning, Zoran surreptitiously posted himself outside Don's apartment building, hoping to see Adrian accompanying Don on a restaurant excursion. As luck would have it, within barely two hours of his vigil, it happened. Don's entourage, including Adrian, Don's girlfriend, and two bodyguards, left the building and drove away in a gleaming late-model BMW. Zoran followed at a safe distance in his rusty, sixteen-year-old Yugo. The destination turned out to be a popular local restaurant, ordinarily closed at that time of day, but opened just for Don's pleasure.

Don had often boasted, "People like me, and they will do almost anything for me. And they like my money even more." To prove it, he flashed wads of money in front of Adrian, both in the apartment and on their outings. Zoran had told Adrian that he would wait outside any restaurant they visited, and stand on the first street corner to the right as one would exit the front doors.

On this day, Adrian watched the warm greeting and exchanges of hugs and kisses between Don and the restaurant's proprietor when they entered. Several tables had been set up toward the rear, and as soon as they all sat down, two more groups of individuals arrived and joined them. It appeared to be a festive gathering, and traditional black Turkish coffee was instantly served to each guest. In a display of chivalry, Don turned his girlfriend's menu down and suggested to the owner that he surprise them by preparing a meal of his choice. The owner acknowledged the honor bestowed upon him with a promise to serve only the best of everything.

Adrian doubted that Zoran could follow through on their plan so soon, so he felt no nervousness or excitement. Instead, he waited for the food to be served. While everyone commenced eating, he asked the waitress, in a sufficiently loud tone for Don to hear, for directions to the bathroom. She pointed toward the back of the kitchen and Adrian nonchalantly excused himself. In his mind, this was nothing more than a rehearsal for the main event to come on a later day. If he established a pattern of making trips to the bathroom, no one would become suspicious.

Unlike strict codes relative to bathroom requirements for restaurants in the United States, no such standards exist in Serbia, and bathrooms are often an afterthought situated in close proximity to the kitchen. Adrian found that to be the case on this day. Not only was the washroom at the far end of the kitchen, but it also was located adjacent to the delivery entrance, which in turn led to the rear alley. Upon discovering this, Adrian regretted the wasted opportunity to take advantage of such a convenient escape route.

Still, just to practice for future occasions, and to test his courage, he decided to see how far outside he could go. Given the stressful activities he had experienced and survived in the past few weeks, this drill seemed relatively inconsequential to him, and without much stress or agitation. Standing near the bathroom, Adrian first scanned around to verify that none of the entourage could see him. Then, he exited the kitchen through the delivery door, and hurried into the alley. After sprinting about twenty feet, he stopped and prepared to return. At that moment, by chance, he caught a glimpse of a car which matched the description of Zoran's car.

A momentary rush of blood to his head and heart caused percussive vibrations in his chest. Maybe this was the moment of escape. Trying to remain calm, he slowly approached the battered car, feeling like winner of the lottery, but fearing that any moment he would realize that it was a cruel joke. As his excitement mounted, he broke into a run, his confidence growing with each stride. In his haste, and overcome with a burning fear that he would be intercepted at any moment, he forgot to slow down and slammed full-speed into the passenger door. The impact caused him to bounce off with a resounding thud.

Sprawled on the ground, he saw a middle-aged man jump out of the driver's side. To Adrian's dismay, it was no one he recognized. He had made a horrible mistake. Then he heard, "Adrian, is that you?"

Within a second, the person kneeled at his side and attempted to help him up. Even though slightly dazed, Adrian spotted a scar on the man's face. He recognized it instantly. The aging process had not been particularly kind to Zoran, and Adrian had trouble recognizing him.

"It's me, it's me," Adrian said, wanting to shout but afraid he might attract the gang inside the restaurant. With Zoran's help, he scrambled up and both of them leaped into the car. Zoran jammed the accelerator to the floor and sped away. Jubilant, Adrian couldn't stop talking. "I can't believe it! Shit. I can't believe it." He turned to see if anyone had observed his erratic escape.

The unbridled feelings of joy, jubilation and inherent celebration filled the Yugo's interior as both Adrian and Zoran repeatedly expressed their mutual disbelief that the escape had been a roaring success. In their minds, the success of his escape had depended in direct proportion to the distance that they would have to travel and separate themselves from his captors. Sadly, they had not recognized that success would not be a distance or a destination, but rather a constant process which could not be measured in feet or even miles.

CHAPTER 32

DANGEROUS MAZE

After traveling for hours in round about ways through the side streets of Belgrade, Zoran and Adrian felt confidant they had left no trail that could be followed. Their time together in the moving car gave Adrian the opportunity to reminisce about the past fifteen years and elaborate on his legal problems, as well as evaluate and discuss the options about the immediate future.

Zoran had been in America and had stayed with us nearly eighteen years ago. He had been a young man of twenty-five back then, and had volunteered to help me with some of my construction projects on numerous occasions. Since he had lived in my house during those three years, he had refused to accept any salary. He had, in addition, learned a new trade by observing and participating with some of my carpenters who had been of Serbian descent as well. He planned to utilize his learned experiences upon returning to Serbia.

To give him a decent start, and recognize his hard work during the visit, I had hidden an envelope with some $20,000 in cash in his luggage upon his return home. He apparently had never forgotten that gesture, as that amount of money in Serbia represented the equivalent of a life's savings. He clearly had intended to now repay my hospitality and generosity by looking after my son, who had been a four-year-old boy back then, when he had played with him and had humored him on a daily basis.

In the wild rush back at the restaurant, Adrian had ripped his jeans in the collision with Zoran's car, and lacerated his knee enough to make it bleed. Other than the clothes he wore, he had not taken anything with him. Even his coat had been left in the restaurant. Even worse, he had no documents or identification.

The collapse of the autonomous government ruled by Milosevic had resulted in a new democratic state. The corruption and intimidation of the old regime had been replaced by a democratic version of corruption and intimidation. The streets were now ruled by democratic teams of rouge police officers, who adjudicated and bartered all transgressions, real or imaginary, on the spot, and democratically divided the spoils of their labor among themselves. It was widely known that getting stopped or interrogated by such officers without proper documentation would have dire and expensive consequences. And a person could get stopped without any provocation or valid reason.

They realized the extreme danger. Without documentation, Adrian's safety would be seriously compromised. He had to not only worry about the pursuit and retribution that Don would probably undertake, but he also had to worry about inquisitions by corrupt authorities, especially since he had entered the country illegally.

The more they evaluated and discussed his situation, the more they understood just how desperate the problem was. No equitable solution came to mind. Adrian was a fugitive from his native country and could not turn back without subjecting himself to immediate incarceration. His escape would only compound the original charges. Now, he was also on the run from criminals who would do even more terrible things to him. And he could not contact the local authorities, as they could take any number of gruesome and atrocious measures. They could persecute him based on the fact that he had entered the country illegally and, given the fact that he was American, could decide to remember the bombings, the embargo, or other grievances for which they considered the United States responsible. Worst of all, he could be apprehended by officers who still had criminal ties, and be simply turned over to Don.

One thing that Zoran decided with certainty was the urgency of contacting us. He realized that the next twenty-four hours would be a crucial time affecting Adrian's life and his future. Decisions had to be made, and Adrian was really in no position to make them. Zoran knew he needed our guidance.

Adrian had convinced Zoran that if anyone was suspected of aiding him in any way, then they could be charged with a felony for aiding a fugitive. Zoran wasn't concerned about it. He was beyond the reach of American jurisprudence.

However, they both had grave concerns about us, Adrian's parents. He believed that our phone lines had been tapped, making any incoming calls subject to scrutiny. Any reluctance on our part to cooperate with investigations of telephone conversations might be interpreted as grounds for such a felony charge. In an effort to circumvent this, they had decided to use a pay as you go cell phone, which Zoran had purchased on the black market. This had been a phone of unknown origin, which would make tracing attempts virtually impossible.

By the time Zoran finally arrived at his apartment in a suburb of Belgrade, it was nearly ten o'clock at night. He lived there with his wife and his two young daughters, all of whom welcomed Adrian with open arms. Adrian used the black-market cell phone to call me on my cell phone. Because of the time difference, it was about three o'clock in the afternoon in Burr Ridge.

The call was short and to the point, as Adrian still had serious worries about the possibility of getting caught if he stayed on the line for too long. I was elated and grateful beyond description to hear from him. He didn't inform me of his location, or whom he was with, but did brief me about his captors and that he had been able to escape. Finally, he assured me that he was safe and that no one had any knowledge of his whereabouts. Before hanging up, he promised to call again in a few days.

His was the second call I received that day involving his situation. The first one had advised me that we would get a visit, and that we had better have the ransom money ready.

I arrived home at about five o'clock in the evening, and in a desperate attempt to find a solution, I took one of my handguns from my safe and waited for the visitors to arrive.

My wife was making her usual run to pick up our younger sons from school, and my attempts to reach her by phone were unsuccessful. I had no way of telling her to not come home that evening. Not that I could have convinced her anyway, especially since I had no intention of telling her the reason for my request. I had no idea yet what would happen.

I had always considered myself an incurable optimist, who could always see an opportunity in every calamity. This time, however, I wasn't so certain that these calamities weren't void of opportunity.

The visitors showed up within minutes after my wife and sons arrived home. All that I had been able to manage was to instruct my sons to stay in their rooms. Then I grasped my handgun under my sweater. While I was contemplating the method of accomplishing my intentions, and evaluating my ability to do so, Don had investigated all calls made from his home and had been able to discover the address for the one telephone number Adrian had called.

One of his bodyguards had been a police officer, and Don and he paid a visit to Zoran's apartment. There they had made things painfully clear. In fact, not only would Adrian suffer, but Zoran and his family would also be punished.

Don and his henchman waited until they received confirmation that the ransom had been paid. There either must have been some sort of honor code, or maybe concern for his reputation, but in either case, Don had kept his word and had not harmed anyone. Or maybe he knew about the problem regarding Adrian's lack of documents and intended to start another chapter of intimidation and blackmail.

Even though the visit from Don and his bodyguard had made perfectly clear to Zoran the precarious situation that he and his family were in, he nevertheless attempted to help as much as he could. My suspicions regarding Zoran's involvement, on some level, had continued to grow, as I had felt that there had been too many coincidences to disregard. The mere fact that the individuals sent to pick up the ransom were from Belgrade did little to allay my doubts. But, having been fearful of repercussions from the FBI ourselves, and not wishing to be forced to collaborate about Adrian's location, we had opted not to pursue our suspicion. The fact that we might have suspected, or even had known about Adrian's location, would obviously not have been a crime. And to the best of our knowledge, we had no responsibility to volunteer any such information to the FBI. We had been cognizant of the fact that we were prohibited from helping him in any way. The problem, as we saw it, was the question about our obligation to tell the FBI of the truth, if they interrogated us about that matter. Had we been asked by the FBI about our knowledge while we had that knowledge, then we would have to reveal it. If we hadn't, or if we had lied, then we would have obstructed justice and would be subject to being punished accordingly.

The less we knew, the safer everyone would remain.

Zoran, based on Adrian's continued pleas to not inform us of his actual situation, as such knowledge would only serve to implicate us, had continued to disavow any knowledge or involvement. His initial attempts had been to secure documentation for Adrian, so that he could at least move about, and possibly even travel outside of Serbia. Countless leads regarding such documentation had been pursued during the first few days. But all such efforts had soon proven futile, as such a feat had been far beyond Zoran's black-market influence and experience.

The constant fear of further repercussions from Don, endured by Adrian, Zoran, and his family, combined with the ever-present tension concerning the authorities, soon proved too much to bear. Every unusual shadow they saw, and every unexpected sound, transformed into ominous signs which fueled that anxiety, and rendered their lives unbearably stressful.

The only viable solution, they finally realized, was to move Adrian as far away from the problem as possible. This was accomplished by putting him up with Zoran's friends and distant relatives in isolated villages, so remote that even time seemed to have forgotten their existence, as life had remained virtually the same for the past sixty years. These villages were basically self-sufficient agricultural communities, with very little outside influence or contact. They were very limited with regards to any resources, and daily life had been pretty much a struggle for mere survival. Every inhabitant farmed his own crops and raised his own livestock of goats, pigs, and chicken. Like the Amish in America, they were close-knit communities, cooperating and helping each other. There were no luxuries, excesses, or riches of any kind. As a result, crime was virtually nonexistent.

Adrian stayed temporarily in several of these isolated villages with a network of Zoran's friends and their extended families. Somehow, they hoped that time would heal all wounds and allow ills to be forgotten, excused, or overlooked. Meanwhile, Zoran promised he would continue his search for identification documents to help Adrian.

But Don hadn't dropped out of the picture as hoped. Before long, he visited Zoran in order to "patch" things up with Adrian. Unfazed by such gullible assertions, Zoran persistently claimed that Adrian had simply disappeared, and presumably had gone to his father's sister, who had resided in Croatia. Croatia had been the main opponent during Serbia's "ethnic cleansing" campaign, and was the one destination Zoran had been confident where Don might not have any influence. It appeared that Don bought into the gambit, because after a few visits, he discontinued any further contact with Zoran.

The village families with whom Adrian stayed labored from sun up to sun down, attempting to accomplish as much as possible during the days of diminishing daylight in the late autumn. There was no social life, as pressures had mounted in preparation for the onset of winter. And while Adrian attempted to help, he actually proved more of a hindrance. Yet, he had been well received by his hosts and had essentially been treated as one of their own. They had held nothing back from him, and he soon gained a tremendous affinity and respect for the smallest and simplest of joys that such modest and barren life offered. Things like late-night card games next to a glowing fireplace, listening to tall tales surrounding the quality of the homemade moonshine brandy which practically everyone made, a kitchen which had still harbored warmth from the previous night's fire the next morning, or just finding an unexpected piece of meat in his stew. Each evening he went to bed fully dressed and even put on gloves and a hat, in order to stay warm during the frigid fall nights.

As isolated as these villages were, snowfall rendered them virtually inaccessible. Whatever had been gathered and stored during the year was consumed during the winter. It had been a vicious cycle for generations, from which there seemed to be no relief or escape for the individuals born into such fate.

The end of February 2005 finally offered some relief from the harsh elements, and it was once again time for Adrian to move on to his next destination, another village. Zoran made arrangements and provided the transportation. Adrian relished the times when Zoran would see him. So too, on this occasion, Zoran picked up Adrian and during the three-hour trip informed Adrian that he had exhausted every possibility of obtaining any documents which would allow Adrian to travel without fear of being apprehended. Local identification papers might be found, but the imminent threat and danger of Don still being on the prowl made that possibility almost useless. A broader portfolio, including a passport, which would allow Adrian to leave the country, wasn't possible without covert connections such as those possessed by Don. Even then, there would be no assurance that such individuals, upon discovery of Adrian's identity, wouldn't repeat a demand for ransom, or turn him over for the FBI reward. Zoran, in fact, confirmed to Adrian that his name and the reward offer had surfaced on the Internet.

Disillusioned and abysmally discouraged by this information, Adrian's once optimistic resolve and enthusiastic perseverance was finally reduced to inert indifference. The persistent failures to find some kind of relief, together with exile in the middle of nowhere, relegated all previous hope to utter despair.

Sensing Adrian's depression, Zoran made a pivotal decision. Instead of taking him to the next destination, Zoran decided to bring him back to his home. His decision was based on the visible distress and dejection evident in Adrian's face and demeanor. It also seemed to Zoran that the crisis involving Don had possibly passed. Still, the move involved a certain amount of risk, possibly placing himself and his family in jeopardy from Don and the local authorities. If they were caught by Don, he might react in vindictive ways because of the perception that Zoran had deceived him. He would most certainly show his displeasure by inflicting ruthless punishment against Zoran or his family. Similarly, the local authorities might discipline him for harboring a fugitive. Or, because of Don's connections within the local authorities, both such scenarios could easily happen.

Too much too soon, and too little too late. This is how Zoran interpreted Adrian's reaction to his apparently destitute condition. Too much bad news had confronted Adrian within a short period of time, while no solution was available even after all these months. Zoran hoped that if Adrian's movements were limited to areas and destinations close to the Belgrade home, the possibility of being apprehended might be minimized. In any event, in Zoran's mind, each problem could be dealt with as it was encountered.

Less than a week passed after Adrian again took residence in Zoran's apartment, when a call came from one of the villagers who had hosted the fugitive. A former lieutenant of one of Serbia's most renowned freedom-fighter organizations during Milosevic's regime had visited that friend and inquired about the American boy hiding out. Despite the isolation of these villages, news of unusual events apparently still managed to somehow travel and reach people who knew how to benefit from such information.

This individual, as had been widely known, had evaded all persecution after Milosevic's fall, and had retained a national network of influence among the less fortunate. These were the disillusioned masses who had been forced to trade a secure and socialist standard of living under Tito's reign for a competitive and democratic contest for survival on all levels of daily living. If Don's threat and power was the equivalent to a virus infecting the safety of his targets, and if the influence of the local authorities was equivalent to a vaccine protecting many but also harming some patients, then this individual's ability to intimidate and strike fear was nothing short of the deadly Ebola virus plague that swept over Africa in the last three decades.

It would be ludicrous to assume that this individual's purpose was to seek a ransom in exchange for a hostage. Instead, it seemed reasonable to assume that his goals were politically motivated and that his intentions were the pursuit of possible favors and the reward offered by the FBI. It would be a gesture on his part to demonstrate to the FBI, and other U.S. government agencies, his willingness to cooperate with their desires and objectives. Serbia officially had no formal agreement with the U.S. government relative to extradition of any fugitives, and an unofficial, unrecognized, and unauthorized individual like this man could perform covert operations which could benefit U.S. agencies without the knowledge or consent of the Serbian government. Granted, this would be a minuscule gesture at best, but every ascent to loftier goals does start with one small step.

For this reason, Zoran's decision not to take Adrian to another village turned out to be beneficial to Adrian's safety. Zoran's friend, who warned him of this development, had informed this "warlord" that Adrian was scheduled to be moved to another village, but hadn't revealed Zoran's involvement in Adrian's transport. However, this piece of missing information would have been quickly uncovered, rendering Adrian's situation as infinitely perilous and precarious. If the FBI showed no interest in reciprocating to this individual's offer, he would most certainly have turned Adrian over to the likes of an individual like Don, or even the local authorities, either of which would have dealt with Adrian in ways not conducive to his health or welfare.

Time had once again become of paramount importance, and it was the fearful specter of this individual's involvement, which caused Adrian to finally seek the help of his parents.

CHAPTER 33

THE RETURN

On a sunny and unseasonably warm day in March 2005, I received the call that I had prayed for from the moment Adrian vanished nearly eight months earlier. Adrian finally resigned himself to the fact that he had made a grievous error in judgment, and that his desperate actions had resulted in dire and pernicious consequences which had only magnified his problems.

He had attempted to buy something he couldn't afford, with money he didn't have, and in the process, had only mortgaged and tarnished his future forever. All too often, the cycle of life and the mere pursuit of survival, which are solemnly reflected in yesterday's hopes and expectations, become today's remorseful realizations and dissolutions, only to be judged as tomorrow's misguided consequences, unexpected burdens, and costly misfortunes.

Adrian's flight had compromised the restitution he sought, and according to the FBI, could have added as many as fifteen years to any sentence imposed on him regardless of whether he was convicted of the original charges involving the December 2002 party.

But none of that mattered to me at that moment. All I cared about was his expressed desire to come home. However, in the back of my mind, I was still apprehensive about any acrimonious implications that our participation in his return might entail. As a result, I informed Adrian that Patrick Campanelli needed to be involved in the arrangement of his return.

Adrian reluctantly gave me the number of his cell phone so that he could be contacted by Patrick. He also implored, "Please hurry! I don't know how much longer it will be safe for me here."

I immediately called Patrick, who invited me to his office the next day. Dobrila, needless to say, was overjoyed when she had heard of my conversation with Adrian. And since we now had a number at which Adrian could be contacted, she couldn't wait to use it. Still cautious, she went to a friend's home and, with the aid of an international calling card, used that friend's cell phone to contact Adrian. All this was done in order to minimize the chances of her call being detected.

As much as I would deny any thoughts regarding preconceived planning of the covert methods employed by Dobrila in her attempt to contact Adrian, the truth of the matter was that we had prepared ourselves for just such a situation. It had been one of many "what if" scenarios we had played out in our minds. No matter what might be demanded of parents, they all are willing to endure the greatest of hardships in return for the slightest of salvations for their children. Such hardships, in the end, might even include acts considered illegal, and the dire and costly reparations for the consequences associated with those acts. However, with the passage of many months, these possible situations became increasingly hypothetical, and by the time of his call, had been reduced to only a distant memory.

With the new development, all that suddenly changed.

In Patrick's office the next day, we listened while he telephoned Adrian. Their conversation was relatively brief and to the point. Patrick simply wanted to hear from his client that he indeed intended to come back, needing that commitment before agreeing to assist in the execution of Adrian's plan. After they hung up, he assured us he would pursue the proper channels to accomplish Adrian's wishes. He cautioned us about the sensitivity of this matter and the necessity for our strict and reticent compliance, especially as it would apply to the media.

Dobrila, more than anyone, embraced the comforting feeling of relief brought about by the knowledge of her son's location and condition, and would call him on countless occasions. Each time she would follow the same routine, heeding the familiar warning of "better safe than sorry." The purpose of these calls was more than just idle chatter or attempts to find comfort and happiness. As Patrick had previously pointed out, the fact that Adrian was willing to surrender himself, rather than be tracked down by the FBI, should be in his favor and go a long way as far as any punishment was concerned. With this information in mind, Dobrila set out to keep Adrian motivated, to continually assure him that this was the right decision, and to keep his spirits upbeat and positive. Equally important, she wanted to express our support so that he would not change his mind.

First, a week went by during which we were assured by Patrick that all proper measures were in the process of being taken, and that this matter could not be accomplished any faster. He was pursuing the standard procedures and acceptable protocol required of an attorney. He insisted that we must remain patient and that nothing we could do would speed things up.

Soon, the second week, while filled with hopeful anticipation, passed without any visible developments. It has been said by many philosophers that "patience is the greatest virtue" and that simply waiting is one of the hardest things to endure. So we attempted to remain virtuous and waited, while encouraging Adrian to maintain his courage and determination. At the same time we pleaded with Zoran to keep Adrian hidden, isolated, and out of harm's way. We passed on the helpful assurances that we had received from Patrick. Luckily, no immediate threats surfaced, and Zoran promised to do whatever it took in order to keep Adrian unnoticed and safe.

The third and fourth week crept by without any reprieve or apparent progress. And whereas we had been exceptionally successful in other areas of our lives during this time, this delay and uncertainty regarding Adrian's situation was relentlessly on our minds. My real estate transaction involving my former partner and the dissolved bank had been completed, and consequently would make a large sum of money available to us. In addition, my medical condition seemed to have stabilized, and I was no longer taking any prescriptions or undergoing further treatments. But rather than enjoying these extraordinary victories, we were relegated to worry about Adrian's questionable safety and contemplated return.

In an effort to encourage and motivate my sons about success and perseverance in life, I often reminded them of a simile I equated to achieving success. This little comparison tells of the premise that in life, one will come across three types of people. The first type is people who make things happen. The second type is people who watch things happen. And the third type is people who don't know what the hell is happening.

After four weeks of patiently sitting by and waiting to see what the hell would happen, we decided that there was a limit at which patience stops being a virtue, and instead becomes a liability flawed by the obvious lack of courage needed to make things happen. As a result, we turned to what might have been the least likely source for help.

We went to the FBI.

Or more specifically, Dobrila went to the FBI.

The really incredible thing she did was not so much contacting FBI agent Pablo Araya in an effort to solicit their assistance, but to also bargain for some measure of exoneration in exchange for Adrian's return. Dobrila is an extraordinarily friendly and outgoing person, whose morality, honesty, and sincerity, along with her genuinely profound virtues and convictions, more than anything else, define her character and true personality. Her principled approach in dealing with problems or addressing adversity, has always been one of her strongest attributes. This would prove to be the case once again, as agent Araya agreed to not only provide his assistance in bringing Adrian back, but also to have all federal flight charges against Adrian dropped. The only condition he required was the stipulation that Adrian would surrender himself to the FBI rather than any other authorities.

While being extraordinarily honest herself, honesty was not necessarily a trait Dobrila expected from other people. With this in mind, she expressed her wish of having something in writing, so that this promise could not subsequently be questioned or contested. Miraculously, this too was agreed to by Agent Araya, and he stated that his office would forward a letter to that effect to Patrick's office. In addition, Agent Araya informed Dobrila that he had been assigned to a case in the Middle East, and that during his absence, all negotiations and activities should be directed to Agent Stover. We knew that name, since he was the partner who had accompanied Araya during their visit to our home back in 2004.

Of course, as with any government effort, everything was delayed. Despite our ardent and continued attempts to accelerate matters, nothing of substance happened for another three weeks.

The letter was finally received on April 16, 2005, and Dobrila in turn contacted Agent Stover, who had been waiting for our call. However, rather than inform us that the most powerful agency on the face of this earth would make things immediately happen, he told us that it would take several days to orchestrate all of the details needed for this operation. First of all, the FBI could not make any arrests in Serbia, so the assistance of Interpol was required. Second, a new passport had to be made for Adrian. Third, Stover had to wrap up some other issues before he could travel to Serbia in order to accomplish this feat. More activity seemed to be masquerading as action.

After several more days of continued, yet innocuous, assurances by Agent Stover regarding the imminent resolution of Adrian's return, Dobrila and I decided to help matters along. Fearful that time was running out on our luck, as it might have applied to Adrian's safety as well as his intention of coming back home, we decided that Dobrila would travel to Belgrade and exert some measure of control and supervision. Our decision for selecting her over me was based on the fact that she had been born in Serbia, and despite her U.S. citizenship, would encounter little animosity from anyone there. I, on the other hand, had been born in Croatia, which together with my U.S. citizenship, is a lethal combination for Serbian contempt. So I would be subject to scrutiny and even possible harassment or retribution at the hands of even the most pacific and amiable Serb.

More than anything to date, this simple action seemed to spark a sudden interest, or maybe concern, on the part of Agent Stover, as he suddenly started to call me several times over the next few days. Each call contained little if any new news relative to progress, and instead was mostly an inquiry about Adrian's intentions of surrendering to the FBI. Any changes, he said, would only result in unnecessary efforts and expenses for the FBI.

Dobrila arrived in Belgrade without any complications and had a long-awaited and tearful reunion with Adrian. Not being there to witness her emotions at that moment, I cannot attest to the melancholic anticipation she surely must have endured during the last few moments of the trip before she was able to hold and hug her son. However, based on my experience in twenty years of marriage, I can attest with insurmountable certainty to the unbridled joy which must have been reflected in her eyes and the radiant happiness and genuine jubilation that must have been evident by her smile, both of which would have smoothed all of the tender lines that her unrelenting love and sacrificial devotion for her sons had long drawn upon her face. Adrian had slept in our bed until the age of eight years, and this had been the longest duration of separation between her and any of her sons. This reunion was a potion more potent and powerful than any medication or drug that could possibly have cured the immense anguish, pain, and fear that had devastated her during the past eight months.

For a brief few days, the world would stand still for her. She didn't dare to think about any consequences or ramifications that her visit entailed. Life's horizon was visible once again, and its luminous brilliance bathed her heart and soul. It erased the immeasurable pain and suffering that had become a constant companion, which had suffocated all meaning and significance from her life. And truth be told, she really wasn't fearful about the consequences, because in her mind, this represented the beginning of Adrian's vindication and ultimate salvation. The FBI had promised no repercussions, and Anthony's acquittal had paved the way for a finding of Adrian's innocence. In fact, all she cared about at that moment was that he was alive, that he was safe, and that she could hold him and tell him that she would always love him and always stand by him.

I have no doubt that after a few hours, Adrian must have been a little embarrassed by being constantly held, hugged, and kissed by his mother. But I am even more sure that his mother could not have cared in the least about his embarrassment.

Later on that evening, Dobrila and Adrian checked into a small hotel in Belgrade under an assumed name with documents that

Zoran had been able to procure from one of his local friends. Despite the fact that all hotels in Serbia required such documentation, very little scrutiny was applied to them, and together with the fact that Dobrila spoke fluent Serbian, the documents she presented raised no suspicions. She had chosen this inn because it was across the street from the more prominent Hyatt Hotel, which was guarded by armed U.S. Marines. Dobrila reasoned that this proximity might offer safety and minimize any potential attempts by anyone to interfere with her mission.

Just like a dog and cat seek each other's warmth and comfort in times of severe coldness, so did Dobrila seek out the protection that the American government still provided to all its citizen, should the need arise. She was also armed with the letter from the U.S. Department of Justice, which FBI Agent Araya had produced. It essentially identified Adrian as a beneficiary of the FBI's protection, which would mitigate any complications in case mother and son were threatened or uncovered by anyone.

The hotel was a small, comfortable inn and offered all the amenities she needed. The surrounding area had everything to offer, and made the need for transportation unnecessary. In fact, its location was far removed from the wanton hardship and subversive depravity of a once-proud nation. This was abundantly evident by the many ruins remaining from the 1999 U.S. bombing and the visible lack of any repairs or maintenance of virtually all public areas. Clear signs served as a grim reminder of the chaotic uncertainty which the recent political unrest and subsequent changes had caused in its population.

The current administration, beset with rampant graft and corruption on all levels, simply did not have the funds and resources to properly address these matters, as they still struggled to meet even the most rudimentary governmental expenditures. What funds were secured and collected did not and could not satisfy the fiscal hemorrhage inherited by the current government. Expenses like payroll for police, firemen, and all other administrative personnel. Expenses like gas, electricity, and even petroleum for their vehicles. And of course expenses like health and welfare benefits, which the entire population was dependent on during this period of rampant unemployment.

And finally, the lingering, ubiquitous need of extricating and assimilating their casualties and national pride.

In the meantime, I had numerous conversations with Agent Stover, who continued to assure me of his efforts to accomplish this task. One particularly reoccurring comment he made during those conversations was his request that Adrian not contact any authorities without the FBI's consent. This naturally included all Serbian authorities, but surprisingly also included any U.S. authorities. It was a repetition of the request Agent Araya had made when he had first agreed to assist with Adrian's return. I wondered why it included U.S. authorities, but I did not dare to question his demand. Instead I simply notified Dobrila during one of our daily conversations. We no longer used any clandestine methods of communicating, as any noticed and recorded communication would, in our minds, only help to accelerate our objectives.

After nearly two more weeks, any action relative to the FBI's promised involvement was still not visible, and Dobrila started to doubt their sincerity. She began to question the possibility of alternative motives and second-guess the FBI's true intentions. A fear possessed her that she had possibly been used as a beacon to locate their prey. Maybe the letter which had promised absolution of any punishment from the FBI was after all not sufficient, or could possibly even be retracted or somehow voided. It was then that she realized with trepidation that the letter contained some vague language relative to a thirty-day time limitation. The letter was dated March 22, 2005 and had not been received until April 16, 2005. However, this was now May 21, 2005, well beyond the thirty-day grace period.

Had they played a game of deception, deliberately delaying fulfillment of their promises until lapsed-time voided them? Dobrila didn't dare mention this to Adrian, despite the fact that her world was suddenly imploding, and the walls which had fortified her convictions were now crumbling and were bombarding her with massive boulders of every possible and reprehensible emotion. She was paralyzed by the fear of Adrian's imminent apprehension and consequent punishment. She was drowning in the violent tide of utter remorse for leading pursuers to his capture. She was sickened by her gullibility at having trusted the government again, despite the fact that they had so far only spread malignant rumors and lies throughout the judicial proceedings. She was boiling with hateful anger for the repugnant, pernicious actions of these traitors who had feasted on a mother's pain by pretending to offer sympathy and hope.

In the end, she was consumed with incessant waves of wistful sadness, which summarized all of her pain and frustrations, and soon eroded into dark depression. She had come so far, only to watch her intentions evaporate into the vast void that once occupied the empty promises and assurances.

She quickly realized that none of those feelings would provide any solutions or improvements, and that she did not have the time to continue wallowing in her misery and misfortune. Time, which had been so abundant until now, had suddenly become precious once again.

It was early evening as she grabbed a single large suitcase that she had stuffed with the most urgent of items and together with Adrian, left the room. She placed the "Do Not Disturb" sign on the door in order to make it appear as if she still occupied the room. They walked past the front desk as they had done on numerous occasions, and greeted the clerks in their usual manner. Informing them that they were going out for dinner to a nearby restaurant, Dobrila said that she was expecting an important phone call and asked that they take the caller's phone number. This was simply another attempt to mislead any observer or pursuer. Assuming that her cell phone had been bugged by now, and that they were being watched and possibly followed, she prayed that all pieces of her entrapment were not yet fully in place. Had that been the case, they probably would already have been arrested. She knew certain limitations existed in official U.S. government protocol, but feared potentially secret and covert actions.

It was a damp and rainy evening, and as they walked briskly away from the hotel, she noticed, for the first time, a stale and noxious pollution caused by unrestricted emissions from the bustling traffic. But it was more than just fumes she smelled as they rushed in the opposite direction of the Hyatt. She had inhaled the vulgar odor of deceit and dishonesty, which had caused her to run without any preconceived plan or destination.

Belgrade was the capital of Serbia with a population of approximately 1,200,000 inhabitants, less than half that of Chicago. Still, she believed that this city was big enough for her to get lost in anonymity, and stay hidden until a more permanent solution could be found.

That evening, Dobrila called me. Her voice, for the first time, sounded desperate. "What are we going to do?" she implored. With Zoran's help, she had relocated into another hotel under another assumed name, and had used a black-market cell phone to make the call. "I don't think we were followed," she replied to a question I did not ask. "But I know that it is only a matter of time. Besides, we cannot stay here forever." Her crying sounds told me that the pressure had finally gotten the best of her.

I, too, was stunned. My hand shook visibly and the muscles in my neck constricted in a clear indication that I was about to succumb to a massive migraine headache. I had suffered from such debilitating pain for the past thirty years, and extreme stress had been a known and common cause to bring about the incapacitating condition.

Feverishly, I looked for a copy of the letter issued by the U.S. Department of Justice that Agent Araya had arranged. I read it several times over. I didn't get the same interpretation Dobrila had seen, but I did notice the ambiguity of the timing. "Don't panic just yet," I said, trying to offer some comfort. "Call back in an hour. I'll call Stover and Patrick in the meantime." I don't think I gave her much reassurance.

It was about 4:00 p.m. and I first attempted to call Patrick. He was not available and I left a message. Next I called Agent Stover, who was available. I didn't want to appear concerned or cognizant of Dobrila's race away from the hotel, and instead inquired about his progress. He advised me that he had intended to call to let me know that he had finally received Adrian's passport, and that he was ready to make his travel arrangements to bring my son home. This could have been a strange coincidence, I reasoned to myself. Or maybe he already knew about Dobrila's actions, and wanted to simply cover any of their tracks of deception.

While I mulled this over, Stover asked for Dobrila's phone number so he could contact her and let her know of his arrival. He knew that she had been in Serbia for some time. Could this still be a coincidental question? I asked myself if it was a crude attempt at gaining information necessitated by Dobrila's disappearance. Up to that point, I was still in doubt about his attempts at deception, but I was now convinced that his inopportune inquiry about her telephone number was the evidence I needed to confirm his deceitful intentions.

Stover said, "I need to be reassured that Adrian is still willing to come back because he has to surrender to us. We cannot arrest him. He cannot even go to the embassy, because they would probably just turn him over to the local police. And then he would be arrested and prosecuted by them and we wouldn't be able to help him." I could not be certain if he was offering a stern caution or giving me a warning.

I compromised by stating, "I'll have Dobrila call you on your cell phone."

After we finished our conversation, my headache had hit like a sledgehammer, and I had to swallow three codeine tablets in order to cope with the relentless pain. I sat back and closed my eyes to allow the medication to take effect, and to think things through.

By now, our involvement with Adrian was no longer a secret, and if we declined to assist in his surrender, we would certainly be accused of aiding him in his flight. We would become accessories and be subject to fines and probable prison confinement.

So much was clear.

We were too deeply involved, and no explanation or decision could excuse either of the two options that we had. If we didn't cooperate with the FBI, then we were guilty of obstruction, and would put the rest of our family at risk because we would be incarcerated. If, on the other hand, we cooperated with the FBI, then we would obviously be guilty of handing our son over to be punished. We would have accomplished what the FBI admittedly could not do.

This, unfortunately, was clear as well.

Dobrila would call back any minute, and I needed to sound convincing and reassuring. Yet my head was now pounding with pain, while my conscience was pounding with remorse for what I had to tell Dobrila, and the decision we had to make.

As promised, she called back, and I told her to use a new phone and a calling card. This would delay anyone's ability to trace her call to Agent Stover. I also told her that we needed to go along with the plan for now and that we could not appear suspicious or doubtful. "Don't worry," I said, as we still had the time and the ability to change our plans, and that the best thing that she could do was to remain strong and positive. I instructed her to call Agent Stover and to give him her new cell-phone number, and to call me back after that. Trying to sound strong and not wishing to alarm her, I said, "Nothing will happen tonight, and tomorrow is a new day."

In fact, there was nothing that we could do tonight.

Within a few minutes, she called again and confirmed that she had given Agent Stover her new cell-phone number. He had advised her that he would arrive in Belgrade in two days and that he would call her then.

The codeine was finally taking effect, and being a synthetic narcotic, ravaged my emotions to their extremes. I had the idyllic urge to keep talking to her. I felt that I had to reassure her not to worry and remind her of the other positive things that had recently happened in our lives. I had to convince her all over again that I loved her and that she should not worry. I even reminisced about all sorts of wonderful things that had shaped our lives . . . and reminded her again not to worry.

All my urgent reminders for not worrying had probably made her worry more.

After we hung up, I took three more codeine pills, and while slowly descending into the familiar, morbid state of painless abdication, I was resigned to mentally rehearse a new plan of desperation, which involved a new kidnapping ploy, in order to save my son from the FBI.

The new day, in fact, did present a new beginning as far as my wife's situation was concerned. It was barely past 9:00 a.m. when I received the phone call which brought me back from sleepy imagination to stark reality.

It was the return call from Patrick Campanelli addressing my concerns as to how the FBI's letter had been worded, and the multiple interpretations. He had also read it several times, but each time his understanding of its meaning remained unchanged. The significance surrounding the thirty-day limitation, in his opinion, did not limit or restrict the effectiveness and validity of the letter, but instead had set a deadline for the FBI to drop all federal charges associated with Adrian's flight.

This would actually be beneficial for us.

Patrick promised to verify his understanding of the letter's contents with Agent Stover, and indicated that he would call me back after discussing it with him. True to his promise, he called within a few minutes, and confirmed that Agent Stover had agreed with his interpretation.

Attorneys, once they are licensed, are considered to be officers of the law, whose proper and legally correct conduct is expected and mandated, as their license would otherwise be jeopardized. In my mind, the fact that an attorney had been given some information by a federal agent gave me a greater level of confidence to believe that this information would be reliable. At a minimum, there would now be several witnesses to attest to the meaning of this document.

It would appear that Dobrila had simply panicked and had allowed her fears to cloud her judgment. Panic usually results from a premonition of some imminent and dreadful occurrence, compounded by a previous incident of a similarly bad experience. And who could blame her? It had been nearly two months since Agent Araya had agreed to drop all federal charges. The ensuing delay and lack of any actions had provided an ample and fertile feeding ground for distrust and concern to be nurtured. This premonition of doubt had then been compounded by the experience she had with the government's prosecutors, detectives, and state's attorneys.

Fear may cause the strong to act, but panic pushes them to react. And perhaps all the little tell tale signs had been coincidental. Yet, all the circumstances surrounding these events over the past thirty months would have caused concern, fear, and even panic for even the most seasoned and experienced individuals, much less a frightened mother who was fighting for her son.

In the end, the FBI and their agents had proven to be honorable and trustworthy, and a far departure from the experiences that we had with other governmental agencies and authorities. In fact, Agent Stover called Dobrila upon his arrival and scheduled a meeting at the U.S. Embassy in Belgrade.

Anticipating that Adrian would be taken into custody at that time, Dobrila, back at the hotel near the Hyatt, packed all of his belongings into a small suitcase. She and Adrian proceeded to the embassy at the designated time. Agents Stover and Stiller waited for them at the entrance and escorted them inside the embassy, where they took pictures of Adrian in order to complete his new passport. To Dobrila's delight and Adrian's surprise, he was not taken into custody that day. Instead, the agents rescheduled a date and time for Adrian's surrender, as certain needed criteria, including his passport, were not yet fully in place.

After having appeared on the "Ten Most Wanted" list of criminals in Illinois, and the "Most Wanted Sexual Predators" list for the entire United States, and after a reward for his capture had been offered by the FBI, the two agents simply said hello and let him go. They shook his hand, exchanged common courtesies, and asked him to come back the following day.

When Dobrila and Adrian returned, it was a repeat of the prior day's events. They verified that the photos had come out okay and assured Dobrila and Adrian that he could surrender the next morning. Again, he was in their grasp, and yet they responded by relying on his promise that he would return.

For reasons that I can attribute only to fearful anticipations, the two FBI agents had scheduled to meet Dobrila and Adrian outside of their hotel the next day, which not surprisingly was the Hyatt Regency. Meeting outside must have been a calculated move to prevent his surrender from being recorded by the hotel's surveillance cameras. There seemed to be a certain amount of secrecy surrounding Adrian's arrest after all. The agents drove him and his mother to the airport and even permitted Dobrila to sit next to her son while on the plane. No handcuffs or restraints of any kind were used, and they even socialized with him during the flight. On the two occasions that Adrian had to use the bathroom, and failed to return within a reasonable amount of time, the agents would show some concern, which was primarily directed toward his safety and the need to protect him from potential harm rather than measures to prevent an escape.

The trip consisted of a connecting flight at Frankfurt, and their arrival there was met by a local FBI agent who escorted them to the new gate. Agent Stiller even bought coffee and water for everyone, and only a minimal amount of attention or supervision was devoted to Adrian during their brief layover.

The final leg passed without incident until the final approach to Chicago was announced. At that time Agent Stover received a message, and while he retrieved the voice mail, Dobrila noticed that he was shaking his head in what appeared to be disbelief over the contents. She watched him pass his phone to Agent Stiller, who seemed equally surprised. Neither agent made any further comments or gestures, and it wasn't until after they had deplaned that they confided in Dobrila what the message had been.

The plane landed at 3:10 p.m. on Friday, May 27, 2005. The agents asked Dobrila and Adrian to wait for all other passengers to exit, then led the way. As soon as Adrian stepped out the door and onto the ramp providing access to the terminal, he was confronted by four armed officers. While two of them stepped between Dobrila and Adrian, with their hands on their guns, the other two grabbed Adrian and snapped handcuffs and ankle cuffs on him. They ushered him through a side door and onto the tarmac. Dobrila had been ordered to step away, and she remembered the consoling embrace that Agent Stiller used in guiding her away from the commotion.

I was waiting at the exit doors by the customs area for their arrival. After what seemed like an eternity, Dobrila finally appeared. She was crying and still being consoled by Agent Stiller. I approached, hugged her, and attempted to console her as well. Yet, the sight of her tears made me cry, too, which in turn renewed her reasons to cry.

When Agent Stover caught up with us, he attempted to apologize to Dobrila for the surprising and clumsy arrest. He explained that he was not aware of the sheriffs' decision to act in the ways that they had until a few minutes before the landing. His displeasure was evident in his face and he expressed it in no uncertain terms. Both men seemed sincerely distressed, and I suspected it was largely a result of their getting to know Dobrila fairly well. Her warm personality, natural charm, sincerity, and common sense had obviously affected them. It may sound like imaginary conjecture or even boisterous exaggerations, but Dobrila has an innate tendency to make people want to befriend her. And these were federal agents who had been extensively schooled to not be affected by any personal feelings or persuasions. Yet they made a point of comforting Dobrila much past the point of normal courtesy, as they seemed to have recognized her to be a genuine and truthful victim who had not deserved this type of treatment.

Agent Stover equated the sheriff's police to hyenas whose actions were those of scavengers moving in for the unearned kill. He characterized their behavior as totally uncalled for, and finally accused them of showboating, motivated by the media exposure. As refined and polished as the FBI had been in their handling of this matter, it was in extreme contrast to the crude, plebeian acts of the sheriff's department. They were transparent in their attempt to gather all the accolades and glory of Adrian's "capture."

The uniformed, armed officers transported him back to the Maywood station, but stopped several blocks away from the entrance, in order to provide an ample opportunity for the media, who had been notified in advance of Adrian's arrival. This allowed time for a storm of strobe lights, cameras, and microphones to be waiting while the posse stoically and victoriously paraded Adrian into the building.

The television cameras caught Adrian's prolonged walk into captivity and thrived on replays of it for days. Newspapers gave it hysterical headline coverage. I imagined that Al Capone's capture hadn't drawn that kind of massive publicity.

It gave us a fair amount of comfort to see that Patrick had taken the time to meet Adrian at the Maywood police department. However, like the media crews, he had been ushered away by the sheriff's police as he attempted to offer some advice and reassurances to his client.

CHAPTER 34

CHANCE ENCOUNTER

To some degree we all have some control over our lives. Some misfortunes and adversities we are capable of bringing upon ourselves, while other troubles arrive in an uninvited and even unexpected manner, and are completely beyond our control. However, no matter how we secure such burden and distress, we always have some control over what we do about them and how we cope with them (this would be part two of my observation and scrutiny relative to the different types of people we come across in the course of our lives).

The financial difficulties that we were experiencing at that time, I have to remorsefully admit, had somehow been invited, as I had chosen to go into business with an extremely unscrupulous individual of extreme wealth, who has been previously mentioned. While my intentions had been to create new wealth from which we would both benefit (a fair 65/35 split in my favor), his intentions had been to modify that split to a more equitable 100 percent in his favor. So we ended up disagreeing. And to make a long story short, we are now in court in order to remedy that situation. The point here being that I had active control over the adversity and I had assumed active control over its remedy. I knew what was happening (he was a crook) and chose to act in such ways that would address the problem (the lawsuit). And in the interim, I coped by wishing him more wealth and fortune which we could both share once my lawsuit was adjudicated.

My medical condition, on the other hand, had surfaced without having been invited. And while I knew what was happening, and had taken the necessary steps to confront my affliction, the extent of this control had been purely passive, as I had to rely on the medication and treatments that had been recommended. The method by which I coped while engaged in my recovery was to start a new hobby. And I had decided to do something that was completely new and unfamiliar to me, in an amalgamous acquiescence, homage and tribute to the unfamiliarity of my disease. I decided to go into gardening. This had been the most unlikely hobby that I had never considered myself to ever be interested in, as I had always considered myself to be a "hunter" and not a "gatherer." However, in order to be successful in gardening, one has to have that elusive "green thumb" talent. And I had nothing like that. I had the exact opposite, commonly referred to as "brown thumb". In fact I had two of them. But I am not one to give up easily, and have often been criticized as being excessively stubborn. And I did not let my early failures of only growing dead plants and weeds discourage me. After a fair amount of research, guesswork, and luck, I had become quite good at this. Soon I was planting flowers, shrubs, and even small trees at every conceivable spot around our house. And after everything had been planted, it appeared to me that things did not quite look right, and I started to replant my initial vegetation. Only this time I planted the smaller flowers and bushes in front of the taller ones, the shade plants in the shade, and the sunny plants in the sun. Somehow, this had been a definite improvement over my original version.

The following spring I decided to take gardening one step further and immersed myself into micro gardening. This was essentially growing plants in containers which could be used to decorate the decks and patios of our house.

The point here being that, while I had no control over the adversity (my cancer) and little control over its remedy (the treatments), I did have major control over how to cope with it. I immersed myself into an activity that was nurturing, creative, and brimming with life (eventually, that is), which was a welcome deviation from the morbid thoughts that would have otherwise occupied and consumed my mind. It was my way of meditating and searching for the elusive inner peace, which only a redundantly mundane activity seemed to offer.

The prized trifecta of my misery was obviously the unexpected adversity involving my son. And in this case I truly did not know what the hell had happened to us. Nor did I have any control over its remedy. Instead, I concentrated once again primarily on ways in which to cope. And the result is the very book which you are reading. While it was still a passive way of control, it was definitely an aggressive passiveness which allowed me to vent my frustrations, anger, and displeasure.

However, while my experiences described herein might have been a nice assimilation of how to make lemonade while life serves you abundant lemons, it was only an introduction to an unexpected event which occurred one morning in early spring 2005. And somehow I can't shake the feeling that fate had somehow offered me a small revelation of support and encouragement, while at the same time providing me with an unexpected jolt of reality. For reasons that are still not quite clear to me, I had decided on that particular day to leave the house early in the morning in order to purchase some newly arrived seedling plants that had been advertised at the Home Depot chain of home improvement stores. The incident which I am detailing will explain the need for the lengthy introduction offered so far. The tail may be wagging the dog here a bit, but it's a good and robust wag and well worth the effort.

After I had made my selections at the Home Depot, and while my shopping cart was fully loaded with countless plants, I proceeded toward the checkout registers. I was turning right onto a main isle when I bumped into someone who was backing up with his own cart. I started to apologize for my infraction while this individual was turning around to face me. To my surprise, astonishment, and horror, I immediately saw that this was one of the two individuals who had been at my house demanding the ransom for my son's life. It was the guy with the blank stare. The one whose exploding head I had visualized as I imagined my bullets piercing his scull. And while I was frozen in place, I realized that he too had recognized me, and that he too was horrified. For what seemed like an eternity, but which probably was only a few seconds, we stood there looking at each other. Silently. Motionlessly. Afraid that any slight move might provoke some terrible response. It was a momentary "Mexican standoff," whose winner would be the one who reacted less obviously. Within a split second I felt the blood rushing from my head, leaving a cold vacuum that robbed me of any initial reaction. But then, just as quickly, I felt this immense pressure built up in my chest, which forced the blood back to my brain and threatened to rupture all rationality and civility. I am sure that I was shivering, but I was attempting to focus on him rather than observe my own reactions. His facial expression also changed from horrified surprise, to momentary uncertainty, and finally to a contrived and nervous attempt of appearing casual and calm. The surrounding noise and calamity had suddenly vanished into a reclusive and ominous silence. The entire store had been reduced to only him and me.

"Hey . . . how are you doing," were his first words, which he managed to express before I could say anything. He spoke Serbian, and while I can communicate in that language, it is not my language of choice, or one with which I can comfortably converse (obscenities notwithstanding).

"I'm OK," was all I could offer in response in English. He was obviously as much at a loss for words as I was.

"How is your son?" was his next unbelievable query, which simply amazed me, and which left me with an even greater loss for words. A million thoughts were racing through my mind. I was reliving the shocking phone call from his brother demanding the ransom as well as the tense moments at my house while I had contemplated that deadly solution. Immediately I realized that my wife was in Serbia at this very moment, and any confrontation right now might put her in eminent danger. Even the fact that he knew where I lived was presenting new problems for me. I so despised him for the pain he was putting me through again. I had barely been able to put that hopeless experience behind me, when his presence now caused me to revisit that cold and desolate corner of my mind once again. I didn't know what I should do. I didn't know what I could do. I knew that I was trembling, and I clutched the handle of the shopping cart as hard as I could in a vain attempt to stabilize my compromised ability to remain rational.

"He's on his way back . . . the FBI's got him," was all I could offer. He hesitated for a moment. His expression once again changed from an uneasy calmness back to visible concern. My matter-of-fact mention of the FBI's involvement had visibly sparked a great deal of concern.

"I hope that our business is done and over with . . . I hope that everything is cool," were his reluctant words, which he finally managed to offer. I realized that he was speaking in English now, as he probably wanted to make sure that I would understand exactly what he was trying to say. Noticing his renewed discomfort gave me some encouragement and I purposely gave the impression of once again thinking twice before saying nothing. Instead I simply frowned and minutely nodded my head, in an unmistaken gesture that I had understood his words. Yet I remained conspicuously silent. I felt that the rushing tide of fear had been in my favor once again, and that this chance encounter was more frightening to him than to me. I realized that I could hear the surrounding noise once again.

"Yeah . . . we're done," I finally offered. "We're cool," were my last words as I turned and slowly and deliberately walked away with my fully loaded cart of pansies, petunias, and campanulas. I felt his eyes scorch my back, but continued to walk away. Of course, in retrospect, and after I had a chance to second-guess my reaction to this confrontation, I wished that I had been more demonstrative and vocal. However, then again, after thoroughly evaluating the significance of this meeting and after replaying the brief events in my mind over and over again, I had come to a more startling realization. I recalled that his cart was fully loaded with electrical supplies. I remembered his unshaven face and dirty work clothes. But most of all I could not erase the blank and tired expression, the lifeless look and dead mentality which he had exhibited after his initial shock. These were the obvious expressions of a person who has had only hardship and suffering in his life. I remembered my son's warnings that all the people involved in his abduction were heavy drug users, and this individual's weary face was certainly an unmistaken proof thereof. All the money that he must have gotten for the jewelry that we had tendered had obviously not changed his life. He still had to do manual work. He was still on drugs. He was still a mess. I hated this motherfucking son-of-a bitch. However, somehow I could not help but hate him a little less.

I recognized that I had subconsciously done the Christian thing of turning the other cheek at a time of potential conflict. My pacifism might have been heavily motivated by fear, but no one ever said that a good Christian wasn't allowed to be afraid. Father Klees might have been proud of me. In the end, I knew that I certainly was. In my mind I exercised control.

I talked to my wife that evening. She was still in Serbia at the time. I did not mention this chance encounter to her, as I didn't want to give her more reasons for concern. Somehow I knew that fate was sending me a message and I pondered its meaning long into the night. I opened a second bottle of my favorite wine as midnight was approaching. It was a 1986 vintage of Chateau Montelena Cabernet Sauvignon. I finally went to bed in the early hours of the morning, wondering if I had watered all of the plants which I had bought that morning.

CHAPTER 35

ROAD TO REDEMPTION

O n Saturday, May 28, 2005, Adrian stood in front of Judge Denise Filan, who was presiding in the Bond Court in Bridgeview that day. The hearing was brief, and the judge ruled that since state statutes preclude a defendant charged with violating a previous bail bond from having a new one set, that Adrian be taken to the Cook County Jail in Chicago, and that he should remain there until his trial.

The media once again came out in droves and hovered by the courthouse doors in anticipation of the ruling. We had made no comments to them when entering the court prior to the hearing, but felt that something had to be said at this point. However, rather than be subjected to an erratic and uncontrolled mob and be bombarded by a barrage of questions, Patrick informed them that he would hold a news conference later on that afternoon at his office. And just like that, the herd of reporters dispersed, satisfied with the notion that the defense would finally make a statement, which by itself seemed to have been noteworthy news, which was reported immediately.

Dobrila, while upbeat and content with the knowledge that her son was back in America, nevertheless remained concerned about Adrian's ability to cope with being incarcerated. And of course she was worried about his ability to get along with the other inmates. Or more accurately, she was concerned over the possibility that another inmate might harm him. Patrick kept reassuring her that violent attacks of prisoners seldom happened in real life, and it certainly wouldn't happen in his case because of the high notoriety associated with his trial.

Despite his positive opinion, it is a mother's prerogative to worry. Never mind optimistic assurances to the contrary.

We arrived twenty minutes prior to the scheduled conference and entered through the rear door to avoid the reporters who had already staked out positions in front of Patrick's office. Patrick briefly outlined to us the topics he would discuss and cautioned us not to make any statements ourselves. I wasn't quite sure what the point of his request was, as I did not see any differentiation or significance as to who would make a statement. Nevertheless, we complied with his wishes and stood silently behind him as he spoke.

A stand with multiple microphones was set up for Patrick's use. It faced the two-dozen reporters and cameramen who had gathered for the conference. After introducing himself, Patrick acknowledged and thanked everyone for their attendance, and proceeded with his speech. He said, "Adrian Missbrenner simply feared the workings of the judicial system, and I think that it was a situation where a young adult did not realize that the judicial system protects innocent people as much as it convicts the guilty. Adrian knew when he returned that he would have to face his accusers from behind jail walls. He is happy he's home, but not pleased to be in the confines of a jail. Fear caused him to run, and now he understands that it wasn't the right decision. However, he is continuing to maintain his innocence. I have been working with the FBI for some time now because Adrian wanted to come back in order to avoid looking over his shoulder for the rest of his life as a fugitive."

Taking his time, Patrick noted that Anthony's acquittal might have played a role in Adrian's decision to turn himself in. Most people had assumed that it would probably influence Adrian, and Patrick felt the need to acknowledge it. It made sense that Adrian intended to take advantage of the decision that had vindicated another person accused of the same crime. But the media had put a cynical and derogatory spin on the issue by accusing Adrian of freeloading on someone else's risky decision to face his accusers. In addition to being a criminal, in reporters' eyes, our son was now also considered to be an opportunist who did not have the courage to face justice until such time that justice was handed to him.

As objectionable as we considered that line of reasoning, we could not argue that it was totally unfounded. Anthony's acquittal did finally shed some positive light on the barrage of unfounded accusations, ulterior motives, and irrational justifications. It had finally offered a glimmer of hope that justice might yet prevail. And, whereas it might not have been the driving motivation behind Adrian's decision, it certainly had been the encouragement that we, his parents, were looking for.

Public opinion is a fickle phenomenon, which, if it could be properly predetermined and identified, could make the objectives of every person in the public's eye easily obtainable. Take public officials, for example. It could make their jobs easy and effortless. However, if a politician has no such intuitions or perceptions regarding public opinion, his career might be troublesome and even short-lived. For example, consider Chicago Mayor Michael Bilandic, who had been the hand-picked successor of Mayor Richard Daily to keep the mayoral seat warm and comfortable for his son, the present mayor of Chicago. However, Bilandic lost his one and only election campaign to a lowly administrative clerk, namely Jane Byrne, after he failed to properly understand public opinion (make that outcry) relative to his slow snow removal efforts during the blizzard of 1979. Clearly, public opinion had a negative effect on the short-lived political aspirations of Michael Bilandic.

On the other hand, look at the political experiences of Washington, D.C. Mayor Marion Barry, who had to vacate his position as mayor during his third term in 1991 because of an undercover drug expose that made headline news throughout the country. Yet public opinion helped him gain reelection in 1995, indicating that nearly anything could be forgotten, ignored, or even forgiven.

The list of public officials whose careers were upheld and furthered by public opinion probably equals that of politicians whose careers were ruined and condemned. President Bill Clinton survived impeachment efforts that were based on moral misrepresentations, whereas President Richard Nixon became one of the most reviled presidents because of the Watergate scandal.

Bilandic and Nixon never acknowledged any wrongdoing and remained steadfast in their denials. Barry and Clinton admitted, albeit after some forceful encouragements, to their errors in judgment. They both survived their scandals, indicating that asking for forgiveness will normally prevail over any denials and cover ups.

Politics is not the only profession influenced by public opinion. In fact, every aspect of our lives is somehow determined by what public sentiments demand. Focus groups work relentlessly in their attempt to find out which TV show, which advertising slogan, and which new song will appeal to the public. Even bona fide singing stars are determined through call in shows, and new idols are created through the process of public opinion.

And whereas this might have been part of the reason that Patrick acknowledged that Anthony's acquittal might have had something to do with Adrian's return, the real reason was to actually keep his acquittal in the news. He wanted people to remember that another person, who had been charged with the same crime, and who had been accused by the prosecution of the same "vile and horrendous acts," had in fact been found innocent of all such charges.

Until my experience with the prosecution and detectives assigned to Adrian's case, I had always lived by the principle that if you couldn't say something good about somebody, you might as well not say anything at all. However, this was a golden opportunity to remind people that the bad things being said were actually very good things.

At the risk of sounding redundant, let me state the obvious once again. Based on the "irrefutable and overwhelming evidence" which the prosecution had alluded to, and without the help of any witnesses in Anthony's behalf, the jury had found him innocent of all charges.

This was certainly something that we wanted everyone to remember.

Following the bond hearing, Adrian was scheduled to be transported to the Cook County Department of Corrections' Facility in Chicago.

The ruling, even though it had been a preconceived notion, certainty left Adrian in a complete state of dejection and defeat, and he stood in front of the judge with his head bowed down in a clear expression that even the last vestige of hope had finally evaporated. It was one thing to anticipate something to happen, and it is altogether another thing to actually see and hear it happen. The convicted or condemned may have no expectations, but still seem to cling to the slightest hope that a miracle might still take place.

It was one of the hardest things for Dobrila to witness, and she winced in pain as she watched his reaction to the verdict. "I love you, please be strong," were the barely audible words she managed to say as guards led Adrian past her.

In order to make his transition from freedom to incarceration a little less traumatic, Patrick had requested that Adrian undergo a medical evaluation because of his condition of frequent and reoccurring headaches. It wasn't much of a delay of the inevitable, but anything that could ease the transition could only be helpful.

Upon his arrival, he was immediately subjected to a battery of medical and psychological examinations, which included blood tests, X-rays, and a series of interviews. He was given his prison uniforms, and all of his personal belongings were taken from him.

He was finally led to his cell in the early afternoon of Saturday, May 28, 2005.

What had been designated as a medical wing consisted simply of a number of cells where beds were positioned in the middle of the cells instead of against one of the walls. This would allow medical personnel more complete access to the inmate-patients.

The only other difference was the restriction placed on such patients' ability to interact with other prisoners. In this division, only one hour per day was allocated for such "out time," leaving the patient isolated in his cell for the remaining twenty-three hours.

While this type of confinement might normally have been objectionable, Adrian actually welcomed it . . . and we agreed. To us, it minimized the possibility for any acts of hostility that might be directed against Adrian from other inmates.

There was nothing to do, and Adrian simply lay down on his bed and visually scrutinized his new home. There were no windows, and he had no concept of time and soon didn't know whether it was night or day. And as the minutes turned to hours, his solitude became his only entertainment. The persistent silence echoed like an eerie symphony of fond memories and wishful thoughts that played in his mind, and he soon started to reminisce, in serene and peaceful imagery, of the simple life which he had left behind in the remote Serbian villages. But no matter how hard he tried, he could not keep the bloodthirsty demons, which defined his present existence, from invading his mind, and ravaging the promising and picturesque landscape that only recently was destined to be his future.

While he dwelled on his past, he was forced to now recognize this path which led to his new future. All that he could rely on for guidance was the dim light which had illuminated and shaped his past to now shine ominously over his shoulder and perilously lead him through the devout and treacherous darkness. And he doubted that this judgmental light would in fact reveal all that which lurked in its shadows.

His pilgrimage had taken him to the exact place from which he had tried to escape. He had embarked on a road to nowhere and had found its promised destination.

And no matter which way he turned, the future would never again be what it used to be.

During these initial nights and days, Adrian had been virtually isolated, and had no diversions, motives, or incentives which would help him from descending into an ever deeper state of depression, consumed with vivid despair and infinite hopelessness.

He realized that he had no future.

He recognized that he only had a past.

After two nights in Division 8, Adrian was moved to Division 11, the maximum-security lockup. It was also the newest part of the jail and incorporated the latest technologies . . . all concrete, metal and glass, but was exceptionally clean and well organized.

His first real introduction to life behind bars came within minutes after his arrival on the very first day. He was placed into a cell with a compactly built man of Mexican descent who spoke English fairly well and seemed to be quite familiar with the routine of prison life.

Adrian had barely introduced himself to his cellmate, when he was startled by the thunderous sound of his cell door being slammed open. Three guards entered the tiny cubicle, and while one of them escorted Adrian to the day room where the inmates congregated during their "out" time, he could hear the two remaining guards scream menacingly at his cellmate.

Within ten minutes, Adrian was escorted back to his cell by the same guard. He was startled again by the noise of the door as it was slammed shut again, and he subconsciously acknowledged that this would be a sound he would never get used to and which would always surprise and scare him.

The cellmate lay motionless on his bed, facing the wall. Adrian attempted to ask what this visit by the guards had been all about, only to be shocked when the man turned toward him. His face was red and swollen. Through puffy lips, he groaned, "I keep making the same mistake," then turned again to face the wall.

Speechless, shocked and confused, Adrian stretched out on his bed. This wasn't good.

All along, Adrian had been worried about the problematic encounters with other inmates and had never imagined or considered this type of treatment from the guards.

His feelings and reasoning had been numbed into a state of withdrawn denial about what had just happened, and while he attempted to find some type of logic or explanation of how to deal with this revelation, he watched in horror as another horrifying spectacle unfolded before him.

From his bed he had an unobstructed view of the room containing the one and only public telephone available for inmates to communicate with the outside world. He watched as a coverall-clad man used the phone in what appeared to be a volatile conversation. The inmate's expressive gestures, his pacing back and forth, and the exuberant waving of his free hand spoke silently of fury and frustration. In the next moment, Adrian caught sight of two men entering the room through a door about forty feet from the phone. They were glancing over their shoulders, obviously on some sort of a covert mission. One of them, apparently nervous, held his hands down as if concealing something.

Adrian, still disturbed over his cellmate's encounter with the guards, watched in total disbelief. The two intruders broke into a sprint toward the inmate on the phone, who suddenly realized the danger, dropped the handset, and scrambled away in the opposite direction. Realizing that they could not catch him, the assailants stopped and retreated back to the doorway through which they had entered.

To Adrian, this looked like something out of a cheap prison movie. He couldn't believe his eyes and felt paralyzed. His eyes focused on the mesmerizing handset of the wall-mounted phone as it swung back and forth with the rhythm of a metronome.

Other inmates had certainly witnessed what occurred, but none paid much attention or ever spoke of it. No one seemed to care.

Within just a few hours of his arrival, Adrian witnessed manifestations of his worst fears. This had prospects of nothing but nightmarish existence. He felt like a sacrificial animal thrust into an arena filled with carnivorous predators and competing with the guards as to who could inflict the greatest damage.

This was a place he might not be able to survive.

We knew that Adrian had been moved from Division 8, but had no knowledge about where they had placed him. Even Patrick could not give us any directions. By chance, Dobrila spoke with Anthony's mother that Sunday, sharing the fears and concerns about our son. Sandra advised her that she had a relative who worked at the jail, and that she would attempt to get more information from him. Lo and behold, she was able to find out that Adrian had been transferred to Division 11, and informed us accordingly the following day.

Dobrila immediately used the number that Sandra gave her and called to verify the accuracy of the information. She also asked about the possibility of visiting Adrian. This was on Memorial Day, Monday, May 30, 2005, and as luck would have it, visiting day for Adrian was on that specific evening.

CHAPTER 36

DETOURS TO REDEMPTION

Adrian welcomed the opportunity to leave his jail cell to be in court on Tuesday, May 31, 2005, and stood in front of Judge Smierciak once again. It was a status hearing to determine the prosecution's plans to proceed with the case.

In our minds, the charges we needed to be concerned about were the original accusations. These consisted of the aggravated criminal sexual assault and the child pornography. And since the prosecution had not included the charges of child pornography in Anthony Roberts' trial, we were hopeful that they would be rescinded in Adrian's trial as well. We were confident that we had sufficient evidence to prove Adrian's innocence, especially with Anthony as a witness. His testimony should be sufficient to result in an acquittal.

Our hopes centered on the fact no witnesses had testified on Anthony's behalf, yet contrary to the prosecution's "irrefutable evidence," the jury had believed that the alleged victim had actively participated in the sexual encounter. Anthony had even admitted to the sexual intercourse with her and had still been found not guilty. Conny had sworn under oath that she did not remember any of the events transpiring that evening. If she changed her testimony in the pending trial now, she could possibly be charged with perjury. We thought that we were in a very good position, because if a jury absolved Adrian from any crime in the main case, then the flight charges should be of no major consequence.

Sure, he could be found guilty of illegal flight, but he had fled because he was innocent, the punishment would be only symbolic in nature. After all, more than anything else it had been the false information that had been spread by the prosecution that had caused him to flee. It was not unlike someone screaming "fire" in a crowded theater and then accusing people of running out. Besides, we had the agreement of the U.S. Department of Justice, who had pledged to drop all federal charges related to his escape.

And we didn't even worry about the DUI charges, because they just meant nothing compared to everything else. They were less than a speed bump on Adrian's way to vindication.

But, as it would turn out, a little knowledge and common sense is a dangerous thing. And just like the student preparing for his final exams, who thought he knew all there was to know about the principles of quantum mechanics, and who would soon learn that they had nothing to do with the history exam he was taking, so too did we quickly learn that we had studied the wrong interpretation of the law. We thought that logic and deductive reasoning would enter into this equation of justice, only to be educated that the prosecution had subscribed to a completely different curriculum.

In this hearing, the prosecutor opted to proceed with the bail-bond violation first. It was their prerogative to choose which charges to discuss first. They had obviously made their decision according to which case would give them the highest probability of a conviction. Adrian had, after all, run away.

Patrick seemed a little surprised himself, but then commented that nothing in their handling of this case really surprised him anymore. He did, however, point to some inconsistencies in the law as it would apply to their decision of trying the flight case first. Peter Troy, supervisor of the prosecutors, had extensively commented to the media that the flight charge was a Class 1 felony, punishable by up to fifteen years in prison. What he failed to say, and this was another example of the prosecution's adaptation of their insidious and unorthodox methods of conducting their classroom, was that the punishment stemming from a bail-bond violation was based on the underlying accusations which had precipitated the bail-bond violation. According to law, any charges for a bail-bond violation should be one category less than the underlying case. And any associated punishment would be based on the category calculated in that manner. In other words, if someone was convicted of a Class 1 felony, and after posting bail, decided to run, then the charges for the bail-bond violation would be a Class 2 felony.

In Adrian's case, the prosecution was attempting to charge him with a Class X felony that, if convicted, would warrant a Class 1 felony for running. Patrick argued that since Adrian had not yet been convicted, that clearly the class of his bail-bond violation could not yet be determined.

It just did not make any legal sense to try the bail bond issue first, as the punishment could not be properly ascertained without trying the underlying case. However, appearances seemed more important to the state's attorney's office than the actual legal ramifications.

Judge Smierciak took the motion and arguments under advisement and said he would later issue a ruling.

———◆◆◆———

CHAPTER 37

DIVISION 1

The prison authorities decided to move Adrian to Division 1, which was reserved for high-profile cases. Visiting days were on Wednesdays, and we drove out there again on June 1, 2005, the day following his hearing for jumping bail. Based on the experience we had with Division 11 only two days before, we thought that we were well prepared for this visit. Nothing could have been further from our belief and expectations.

Unlike the schedule at Division 11, visiting hours here were conducted throughout the day. Dobrila and I had taken our other two sons to school and then proceeded to the prison. Because our trip was in the morning rush hour, we decided to take the side streets rather than the expressway. We drove along Ogden Avenue to California Avenue and then proceeded south to the prison. Once at the facility, which was adjacent to a courthouse, we spent well in excess of thirty minutes trying to find a parking space. The only parking was along a four-block-long street.

Dobrila's was once again in a state of high anticipation and excitement. In a talkative mood, she elaborated on the need to sound positive and up beat in Adrian's presence. "We have to cheer him up," she said, "and tell him that we're talking to our attorney in order to get him out as soon as possible."

I agreed with her wishes, and even attempted to contribute to her euphoric mood. I declared, "It could always be worse. Just imagine all those young men who joined the army because of the benefits, and who are now in combat in Iraq. They certainly didn't expect to wind up in a battlefield. No matter how hard it might be for Adrian, he is certainly in a much better and safer place than they are." I'm not certain my comments helped much.

We had to circle around several times looking for a parking space, and while Dobrila seemed to agree with my rationale, she was really more concerned with observing the pedestrians walking about the parked cars, in an effort to determine if one of them might be vacating a parking spot. The streets were swarming with people, a good many of whom were uniformed officers apparently arriving at their prisons jobs or going home. Compared to the nearly deserted streets we had encountered only two days earlier, this seemed completely non-threatening and safe. I wondered if, despite the fact that the streets were overflowing with people during the day, anyone dared walk them at night.

We finally lucked out and found a space relatively close to the entrance of Division 1. They were the only gates painted white and were therefore easy to locate and recognize. I thought it an ill fitted attempt at a cruel joke on somebody's part, that these gates were painted white, which in my mind was a crude analogy of the pearly gateway to heaven. But then again, maybe these gates symbolized an exit rather than an entrance.

We stepped out of the car into a sunny, warm morning and the early dew had dissipated by this time. I put two quarters in the parking meter, which allowed us the maximum afforded time. We passed a food vendor selling warm, Mexican-inspired products out of his beat up truck. His menu didn't appeal to our appetites. We also passed numerous cars whose drivers had stopped in non-standing zones and appeared to be waiting to pick up someone. All the while, they played their radios at ear-splitting volume, turning the streets into a noisy contest of the pounding beats of "ghetto rap" versus the equally thumping rhythms of Hispanic rap, all in disharmonic noise that only served to thoroughly pollute the air.

Dobrila had stopped talking as the reality of this situation and the thought of entering a prison seemed to have finally set in. She simply nodded her head without saying a word as I commented on the pleasant weather conditions. Her facial expression had hardened and I realized that she was again fighting back her tears. I simply squeezed and held on to her hand in an attempt to reassure her that I also felt the pain, while realizing that any further conversation would be pointless and redundant.

The white gates designated the initial parameters of the prison. While there were no guards present at that point, it was nevertheless an unmistakably clear and distinct borderline offering ominous passage into a different world. As we approached the white entry, we could not miss the assembly of perhaps twenty men, women, and children gathered there in a milling throng. Their appearance and behavior radiated unspoken threats. If not for the presence of the uniformed officers walking the streets, we would not have dared to approach this crowd.

They were mostly ethnic minorities and I couldn't see even one Caucasian. At the risk of sounding narrow-minded and possibly even bigoted, the spectacle confronting us was nothing short of an impromptu carnival of misfits. There was no organization to this crowd, as most of them seemed to hover in groups of two or three individuals. Based on their lack of grooming and unkempt attire, they appeared to be either temporarily or permanently homeless. The women, who generally wore provocative styles, appeared to be working the streets. The men looked like those I've seen in disreputable Chicago areas offering various illicit products for sale. I don't even want to mention the woebegone children, who were probably there hoping to see a father or other relative. Nearly everyone just didn't seem to know what time of day it was. Several of them shouted out loud about some displeasure and violently gestured at some unseen foe for emphasis, while others seemed to simply carry on a conversation with themselves. However, most seemed to just stare at each other in a vain and hopeful attempt to find a solution to the problems that thoroughly preoccupied them.

We were approached by one or two of them with offers of drugs for sale, or requests to buy them. Others asked for handouts. At least we were not obstructed in reaching the white gates, which began to look more pearly in offering escape from this crowd.

Intimidated by them, Dobrila had instinctively grabbed my arm with both her hands and drawn her body closer to mine. We both felt the stares of everyone, as it was clearly we who were the oddity here. I remember thinking how fortunate my life had been compared to that of the people I was passing. Sure, I had my ups and downs lately, but I nevertheless felt fortunate not to be in the same situation as these poor devils seemed to be. As soon as this thought crossed my mind, though, I was reminded of the biblical tale of the nobleman who thanked the Lord because his life had been so much better than the beggar's and was able to give more of an offering and be more productive to society, which he knew that the Lord appreciated. This was a tale of vanity I had heard when I was still in grade school, and I now realize that the ironic meaning of such vanity was not lost on me. I tried to be remorseful for these philistine opinions I had of myself, but no matter how hard I tried, I could only feel sorry for myself because of the low stature and self-esteem I had for being in this place, and how little I actually deserved such a fate.

Once we passed the gates, it was only about sixty feet to the entrance of the guardhouse. This area, while being inside the prison compound, was littered with refuse. This area consisted of two buildings separated by a driveway and sidewalk. On one end of the driveway was a chain-link fence topped with coils of razor wire, and on the other end were the white gates leading into this area.

The entry to the guardhouse consisted of a vestibule controlled by two sets of glass and aluminum doors. Years of abuse and the lack of any repair or maintenance had left these doors in a battered state, discolored by age and usage. They appeared to be no longer properly aligned, as they opened with a raspy, scratching sound and closed with a metallic thud every time the door hit the frame.

Beyond the vestibule, we entered into a larger room which served as a waiting area for visitors who were both coming and going, making it extremely crowded. People visiting were directed to the left by several uniformed guards, and people leaving were directed from the right towards the vestibule. To compound the confusion, each person entering was being patted down, while each person leaving was required to show their identification. This caused a bottleneck effect, slowing the process even more. The entire procedure, moving people in every direction, seemed utterly disorganized. It reminded me a television nature program I had seen depicting the flurry and activities of an ant colony whereby every worker ant entering or leaving the nest was examined and scrutinized by a soldier ant.

As soon as Dobrila and I entered, we too were each scrutinized for contraband or weapons. The officer patting me down was the only Caucasian there. He was a male, in his early fifties, with grayish hair and a distinctively reddish nose, the unmistakable tell tale sign of excessive alcohol consumption. Dobrila was checked by an African American female officer, who was no more than five feet tall, but must have weighed more that 200 pounds.

Once this procedure was completed, we were directed to stand in line in a roped-off section of the room, only to be patted down again at the end of this line. We had moved only about ten feet by this time, and this second examination must have been a result of confusion rather than efficiency or thoroughness.

A technologically advanced apparatus had been set up at this location, and was capable of detecting even the most minute presence of any illicit substances. This piece of equipment seemed grossly out of place, as it was the only modern appliance there. Of course it wasn't in use, and was only taking up valuable space.

All of the officers seemed more interested in carrying on conversations with each other than conscientiously conducting their jobs. Jovial and laughing with one another, their mood and demeanor instantly shifted to anger and animosity in dealing with the civilians. When a Hispanic visitor did not follow the simple instructions of raising his arms during his pat-down, they bellowed their directions in unison at this slight indiscretion, but immediately return to their previous dialogue once satisfied that the offender had been properly warned.

As with the exterior of this gatehouse, the interior seemed equally retrofitted for its present use. Nothing there seemed to have been intentionally designed or constructed for the purposes for which it was being used. A cumbersome old metal desk was positioned at the entrance and served as a counter for the first guard. His only equipment consisted of an equally dated phone, which was in constant use every time I passed through. A few metal chairs were strewn about and did not appear to serve any specific purpose. The concrete floor was covered with mats secured in place with layers of worn and dirty duct tape, and indicated the intended direction of the visitors' foot traffic. The ceiling was made of drop in type panels, which not only varied in color shades due to age, but also displayed a multitude of stains, tears, and holes, which only evidenced their lack of maintenance. Fluorescent lights with varying degrees of brightness offered ample illumination, but like everything else, had certainly seen better days. The interior cinder block walls had been repeatedly painted with multiple layers of gray. Every surface visibly displayed a ground in coating of grime and dirt, and a permanent impression of indifference and neglect.

It seemed to take forever before we were directed toward the rear exit of the guardhouse. We passed a guard sitting in a chair and, despite being obviously asleep, had managed to maintain his balance and not fall off the chair. Past him, we followed directions to Division 1 and traveled along a series of sidewalks flanked by more chain link fences and rolls of razor wire. The distance to the prison building was approximately 500 feet, and the passageway narrowed to less than five feet in width. The overwhelming feeling that I had as we walked toward the prison building was that everything we had seen so far had once been meant as a temporary structure but, over time, had become permanent.

We reached a two-story foyer in front of the prison building, accessible only from the path we had followed. This old building was rather ornate with large art deco sculptures for decorations. It had large, arched windows and two metal plaques, which proudly proclaimed its inauguration date of 1929. However, as grandiose as its ambitions might once have been, its cold reality today only reflected more contrite indifference and continued neglect. The doors leading into the foyer were made of heavy metal and seemed to struggle every time they were used. The flooring inside was polished concrete veined with countless cracks. The sole purpose of this foyer was to provide an access to the second story level through two winding staircases which met at the upper level. These concrete staircases featured heavy, ornate, wrought-iron hand rails, which once again recalled bygone intentions and forgotten expectations. The walls were plastered with countless notifications, instructions, directions, and warnings. All such notices, printed in English and Spanish, warned about any number of rules and consequences. All were faded, and many seemed outdated, yet remained affixed with strips of discolored tape.

The landing at the top of the stairs faced another heavy, metal black door with a twelve-inch square window in the center. Above it was an antique brass knocker. Affixed next to the door was a metal, four-inch square box enclosing a doorbell button. Of course, this button did not work.

A uniformed, armed guard allowed us entry after we used the brass knocker to announce our presence. He unlocked the heavy door with a bright, excessively large metal key, instructed us to step inside, then immediately closed and locked the door. He asked us to empty our pockets. We both carried nothing but our drivers' licenses, and I had my car keys. He placed these items in a wooden, pigeon holed cupboard, and gave me a tattered piece of cardboard with a hand-written number on it.

After yet another pat-down, we were asked to remove our shoes to prove that we carried no contraband. He instructed us to proceed through a detection gate, which did not work, and to a window for further processing. Adjacent to the detection gate was a conveyor belt, which passed through an X ray machine. The machine was not turned on, yet the conveyor belt was continuously running.

The window to which we were directed featured a chipped, orange Formica counter. A female guard sat behind the counter manning a computer. We were third in line at that point in time, and our turn to speak to that guard came about ten minutes later. While waiting, we observed the guard look up the name of the appropriate inmate in a ream of computer-generated names, punch in some information on the keyboard of the computer, get frustrated over the computer's response, or lack of it, re-input the information, look in the ream of paper again, and input some more information, only to stare at the screen for several minutes, while expressing her disbelief for the continued lack of a response from the computer. After several inactive minutes of staring at the screen, she finally pulled out a pad of paper, which contained some pre printed information. She wrote the name of the inmate on this form and handed it to the waiting visitor. She then picked up a phone and gave some type of instructions and directed the visitor to take a seat.

The room in which the officer was sitting in seemed even more unorganized and unkempt than any part of the prison that we had seen so far. Immediately behind her, and along all of the walls, were old and beat-up lockers with all kinds of items piled on top. It resembled a cluttered storage room more than a functioning prison admissions office. Two plastic trash cans overflowed with refuse, and someone's half-finished lunch was left abandoned at the far end of the desk.

The same scenario involving the processing unfolded for the next person in line.

The same scenario unfolded for us once we were at the window.

"Name?" was the stern question she posed to us.

I replied, "Adrian Missbrenner," and passed my driver's license to the woman. This seemed to satisfy her and she simply nodded in the direction of the seating area after she handed me our admission slip. We turned and proceeded to the designated area. It was part of the main room and contained four rows of bright, orange-colored, plastic benches grouped in one corner of the room. Seven other people waited for their names to be called.

One of them was an older Hispanic woman who sat quietly in the front row with a small girl. The child could not have been more than four or five years old. Dobrila smiled at her as we approached the bench, and received a reciprocal grin featuring two missing upper teeth. Her sweetness cheered Dobrila. She stopped to tell the older woman, who had appeared to be the girl's grandmother, how cute the child was. The woman instinctively tensed a bit and drew the little girl closer to her. She still managed to nervously smile back at Dobrila, and in doing so, revealed that her upper front teeth were also missing. "No Inglés," she shrugged, ending the possibility of conversation. This only made Dobrila and me smile even more, which in turn caused the abuela to actually laugh as she lowered her head next to the little girl's in acknowledgment of their dental similarities.

No one else there seemed to have noticed this little humorous interaction, as all remaining visitors were engrossed in their personal, reticent states of mind, while the guards continued to be preoccupied with their ongoing conversations. And I didn't appreciate the full impact that this brief encounter would have on me until some time after our visit that day. And, while I can visualize the toothless smile and weathered face of the old woman to this day, the images which have really stuck to my memory were her mature, forgiving, and even acquiescing eyes, which simply offered a dramatic contrast to the naive, hopeful, and wishful eyes of the gap-toothed young girl that she was holding so dearly. They both appeared out of place and were probably just following their routine of visiting the inmate whom I had assumed to be the young girl's father. Their presence represented three generations of unwilling participants who had been caught up in the legal system, which illustrated the vicious and merciless cycle which can enslave not only the perpetrator of a crime, but also his or her unsuspecting relatives of either generation.

I tried to convince myself that this should not be my problem, and I realized that sometimes you have to lie to yourself to be able to forget.

Other people waiting in that room included three black girls, all about twenty-five years of age, sitting at the other end of the second row and quietly whispering among themselves. One young black male sat in the middle of the third row observing his feet. The last visitor was an older black man in the last row, who was intently staring at nothing in particular.

Dobrila and I sat behind the older woman and the young girl, and as if on cue, also commenced to stare expressionlessly into empty space. No words were spoken. No words were necessary. We didn't really know what to expect once we would see Adrian, but based on the condition of the prison so far, we both knew that we already dreaded whatever it would be. In fact, while waiting, I continued to evaluate the squalid features that defined this waiting area. I noticed two dark brown doors on which were taped pieces of discolored, aged paper inscribed with handwritten words indicating that these were restrooms. Below each of the signs were two more taped-on notifications that both facilities were out of order.

As I stared without thinking at the ceiling, I noticed what appeared to be an airflow vent, useless because a blue blanket had been stuffed into it. Several vending machines lined the walls and appeared to be relatively new. The cement block walls, needing paint, displayed more hand-written notices, prescribing visitor behavior rules, all in both Spanish and English.

I offer all of this detail to emphasize the drab routine Dobrila and I followed for the next 38 weeks during which we made our regular visits to Adrian.

After about 15 minutes our names were called, and we walked toward the hallway to which we were directed, providing access to two visiting rooms. Room "A" was designated for the general population, and room "B" was reserved for the high-profile cases, which included Adrian. We proceeded toward room "B" and passed a secured area, a small passage through the hallway controlled by two sets of doors. The first door would open and allow access into the passageway, while the second door remained closed. Once the first door closed, the second door would open. This was meant to better control and restrict access to the visiting area. Yet we noticed that the first door was held open by a rusted wire clothes hanger attached to the door handle and the adjacent radiator. The second door's closing mechanism didn't work and it remained permanently open.

Adrian was seated behind a three-quarter-inch thick glass window, waiting for us as we reached the visiting room. Dobrila sat on a rusted, metal stool permanently fixed to the floor, and faced the window. The room held a total of seven such stations, but two were marked permanently out of order. Each station had a round metal screen cut into the glass in order to allow for communications between the visitors and the inmates. This screen was completely covered with smut and reeked of a vulgar stench which could only have been attributed to years of total neglect and continuous disregard of any attempts at hygiene, cleanliness, or functionality. There was an unusually deep shelf extending on both the visitors' and inmates' side, which necessitated both individuals to raise themselves from the seat in order to get close enough to the screen so that a conversation could be conducted. This resulted in extreme discomfort, and combined with the offensive odor of the filthy screen, made any lengthy conversations impossible without frequent breaks. The glass panels showed ample damage, mainly in the form of holes which appeared to have been drilled or burned into the glass. All of these holes had been patched with some kind of epoxy fillers, which over the years had also been discolored by embedded dirt. The stained and dirty glass panels reached all the way to the ceiling. The lower portion evidenced an ever-changing array of fingerprints, dried spit, and moist residues of a prior visitor's conversations.

To equate the conditions as disgusting health hazards would have been a positive spin on the actual conditions. Every visit to the prison resulted in the immediate need of a thorough shower and laundering the clothing we wore.

Adrian dressed in the customary tan prison garb. He wore handcuffs and leg irons, ostensibly to prevent escape, which seemed impossible, so I presumed they were primarily for intimidation rather than function. However, there could have been the possibility of violent behavior, and those restrictive measures might have been a suitable precaution after all.

While he appeared in a relatively good mood, we both suspected that this was more for our benefit than an actual impression of his real feelings. Each of our thirty-minute allocations seemed to end all too quickly, leaving inadequate time to express all of our hopeful feelings and encouraging promises.

We would visit every week, and on numerous occasions include our other sons as well. We were allowed a total of thirty minutes for each visit, per person. If four of us sat with him at the same time, we simultaneously used our individual allotments of time, so we soon learned to split up, and talk to Adrian separately. That way, with four of us there, the visit could actually last two hours. Sometimes, it takes a while to cope with strange government rules. And whereas nothing of real importance was ever discussed, these visits nevertheless served as a measure of support and proof of our continued devotion toward a positive resolution and outcome.

In fact, over the course of our regular visits, we noticed a dramatic change in the demeanor and behavior of the guards toward us. It turned out that we had gotten to know some of them on a first-name basis, and more often than not, our visiting time was extended to sixty and even ninety minutes at a time for either of us. Somehow, these guards must have felt a certain amount of compassion, if not sorrow and anguish, for us, as we were among an extremely small number of individuals who visited there every week.

In addition, Adrian was a normally jovial and good-natured young man, and had been given the nickname "Adrian Misbehavin'," because of the continuous jokes and good-natured pranks with which he entertained the guards and fellow inmates.

Dobrila and I left that day of our first visit with the feeling that our observation of the prison's condition was nothing short of an apparition of the fictional prisons of some third-world dictator or a prison of a bygone communist regime, which we thought could only have been possible in movies and fictional novels. In our wildest dreams we had we not been prepared for the conditions that we encountered, and we expressed our outrage and disgust to everyone that we talked to for weeks.

While all of our friends expressed sincere grief and disgust for these conditions, as they might apply to our son, we felt that most people were basically indifferent and really didn't feel much remorse about the overall poor condition of the prison. Without saying it, they all implied, through silence and apathy, that these inmates probably did not deserve any better conditions, and that it had been their own criminal actions which sent them to prison in the first place. And I remorsefully recognized these same sentiments in my own opinions until such time that this issue actually hit home.

And while I continued to remain outraged at the humiliating and disgusting conditions, I have somehow learned since to appreciate the unrewarding task of the guards. Visitors are at best subjected to these conditions once a week. These guards are there on a full-time basis, on the other hand, and have to endure the same conditions almost every day. To this day, I remain hopeful that these guards have received the proper training, adequate incentives, and appropriate rewards which would properly motivate and educate them to deal with not only the deplorable physical conditions, but also the psychological demands imposed upon them by the visitors and inmates. Based on our experiences, both the visitors and inmates seem to have mostly come from less privileged and less educated backgrounds. Combined with the general anger and hostility that must be inherently directed against these guards, as well as the visible lack of protective features, they were presented with a combination of inequitable conditions which could easily mutate into open confrontations. Sure, the guards have guns, but their use, no matter how justified and proper, would certainly explode into a public confrontation of political finger-pointing and second-guessing, all at the cost of the guards and visitors.

I shudder to compare the similarities of the working conditions of these guards and those of postal workers, who have shown a propensity for violent behavior under much less stressful conditions. And let me restate the obvious once again. These guards come to work with loaded weapons.

CHAPTER 38

PRISON HELL

In 2005, national headline news reported the alleged mistreatment of Iraqi inmates held at Abu Ghraib prison in Iraq. The torture and humiliation of prisoners by military personnel was photographed by soldiers and leaked to the news media. Sensational pictures, including images of nude prisoners forced to pose for the amusement of U.S. soldiers, appeared on international television for weeks. It turned out to be a colossal black eye for the presidential administration of George W. Bush and a major embarrassment for most Americans.

Another blow came with accusations of mistreatment of inmates at Guantanamo Bay prison in Cuba, also operated by U.S. Military forces. Senator Dick Durbin, the distinguished Democrat from Illinois, initiated a national crusade of outrage related to the mistreatment of Muslim detainees at Guantanamo. The eyes of the world were watching as Durbin asserted that the USA was mistreating her prisoners. He expressed the opinion that these prisoners deserved humane treatment even though many of them were accused of involvement in terrorist crimes against the United States. The senator also complained about the unacceptable conditions at that prison and the shameful, barbaric treatment they endured.

Members of the Bush cabinet repudiated these charges, and claimed in rebuttal that conditions at Guantanamo were not just acceptable, but that they were actually very good. A spokesperson reported how the United States had spent vast amounts of dollars on this prison facility, and described in great detail how every prisoner was in fact treated with dignity and respect, and how their accommodations included comfortable furnishings, TV sets, and radios; that the prisoners were offered air conditioning, hot water for bathing, and ample time for recreation and the pursuit of social and religious activities. He recalled a recent dinner menu that had been served to the prisoners, which included fried chicken, mashed potatoes, steamed peas, and chocolate cake. In fact, he compared the accommodations and food quality to those of a full-service Holiday Inn Hotel, in a tongue in cheek reference to a popular commercial about the quality of Holiday Inns.

This defense was challenged by Senator Durbin as greatly exaggerated. He felt that it is America's responsibility to set an example for the rest of the world and showcase the high morality and respect with which all prisoners are treated, regardless of whether they were detained because they had killed or had attempted to kill U.S. soldiers and had been implicated in countless terrorist plots.

The opinion of the world was at stake here, and in Dick Durbin's view, the Bush Administration had failed in its job performance. It was simply insulting, deplorable, and unacceptable that America would possibly treat captives in such fashion, or even be accused of such barbarous conduct.

It should be noted that the inmates at Guantanamo were called "detainees" by the Bush administration, rather than prisoners of war, a designation reserved for soldiers who fight for a country with a recognizable chain of command. This label would have guaranteed them certain rights under the Geneva Conventions. By implementing this interpretive loophole, the administration reasoned that they did not have to adhere to such rules and instead could treat them pretty much as they wished. Such treatment included the practice of not charging the "detainees" with any specific crimes and instead holding them for unspecified periods of time.

This criticism may be very well justified and properly founded. In fact, not only did human rights investigators working for the United Nations call on the United States to shut down the prison because of these unacceptable treatments of its inmates, but even former President Jimmy Carter joined this cause and urged the Bush administration to do so.

More bad news came, making this exposé seem to be only the tip of an undercover iceberg, as reports of covert transports surfaced, which alleged that the U.S. was secretly transporting similar detainees to secret foreign prisons which had not turned up on the radar of human-rights scrutiny.

Of course, politics reared its head in the debate. Senator Durbin came under fire by Republicans claiming that his intervention was not so much noble as it was a promotion of his political aspirations. The point here is that the senator from Illinois had made it his obligation to criticize a prison facility in Cuba. And while being thoroughly engaged in exposing the conditions there, the distinguished Senator must either not have been briefed about, or simply disregarded, the conditions of the prisons in his own back yard.

Obviously, the eyes of the world were not observing the conditions of the prisons in Illinois. And it would seem that the senator's own eyes were equally not focused on his own state. After all, the Bible advises, "Let he who is without sin throw the first stone."

After the court appearance on May 31, 2005, Adrian landed in Division 1H at the Cook County Department of Corrections. It was the oldest building in the prison system and dated back to 1929. In fact, Al Capone had been housed in this building during his incarceration at Cook County. And conditions had not really been updated, improved, or modified in the 75 years since then.

A long time ago and ancient history to young people today, President Herbert Hoover saw the beginning of America's Great Depression in 1929. John F. Kennedy was twelve years old, and Mickey Mouse was barely a year old. The Star Spangled Banner was not yet our official national anthem. Israel was still only a dream, Iran was still Persia, Pakistan was still a part of India, itself still part of the British Empire. A Martian invasion was still believed to be a dreadfully viable threat, and most of the world had not yet heard of Adolf Hitler.

Considering the world events that have shaped human history over the past seventy-five years and the technological advancements and innovations that had been achieved since 1929, it should be difficult to accept that any technology would have survived that long and still be used today. More significantly, it would be hard to believe that a government installation would have remained unchanged since then. Especially when the government in question is that of the most powerful and most advanced nation the world for those seventy-five years.

What was described as pure imagination and science fiction back then has for the most part become reality today. In fact, more innovations and revelations have been accomplished in the last seventy-five years than in the entire history of mankind leading up to 1929.

While we are exploring the deep reaches of our solar system and are growing entire mammals from one single cell, we are also still using antiquated and archaic technologies as they apply to the treatment of certain members of our society, whereby "anesthetization with a hammer" might be an appropriate comparison.

Of course, many popular arguments might challenge the notion that criminals should be considered as actual members of our society, as they had probably conducted themselves in ways that are not very "society like," and committed crimes against our society. So why should society be concerned about such individuals?

At the risk of sounding "holier than thou," let me present the altruism that any society is only as strong as its weakest link. In fact, in 1937 Franklin D. Roosevelt, in his Second Inaugural Address, professed that, "The test of our progress as a civilization is not whether we add more to the abundance of those who have much, but instead it is whether we provide enough to those who have little?"

If we, as a philanthropic society, hold ourselves to be, and pride ourselves with our progressive accomplishments, then we must also accept the blame for our haughty shortcomings. I am not on a mission to correct all of society's ills and problems. But I am suggesting that any human being should be treated as a human being, no matter what society's interpretation and designation of him or her might be. At a minimum, everyone should agree that a human being, any human being, has a higher standing in our society than any other organism. The value of the life of a human being cannot be equated with the value of the life of any other creature. Furthermore, the treatment of a human being should be superior to that of any plant, insect, bird, or animal.

The most vile criminals have to be treated better and more humanely than the most lovable puppy. It's not a matter of whom we might like more, whom we fear more, or whom we could forgive more. It's simply a matter of DNA (if you are a supporter of evolution), or a matter of owning a soul (if you are a believer in divine creation).

With that in mind, allow me to elaborate on the conditions of the division to which Adrian was confined. The building, constructed in 1929, houses well over 1,000 inmates and is divided into various sections. My son's section, division 1H, contained nineteen cells and nineteen inmates. Each cell's dimensions were approximately seven feet by ten feet, the size of a small bathroom. Each cell contained two metal beds, a toilet, and a sink. The walls were constructed of metal panels and bars, and the floors and ceilings of poured-in-place concrete. Heating was provided by hot-water radiators and cooling and ventilation by a crudely retrofitted system with marginal operation at best. The sink had a faucet which indicated the availability of hot and cold water. But hot water was never available and the cold water was icy and actually painful to the touch.

The guards' walkway was located on the outside perimeter of the cells and separated them from the exterior walls of the building. All of the windows were in this outside wall, severely curtailing the amount of natural light that actually penetrated into the cells. In addition, the window panes had been discolored by age, and the accumulated layers of dirt over the decades had further restricted the sunlight.

Only one shower was provided, and the stall's metal walls and ceiling were thoroughly rusted and caked with grime and mold that screamed of dangerous and unacceptable health hazards. Hot water was limited here as well, and most of the inmates had to use cold water, making showering an event which had occurred much too infrequently.

Building codes mandate that every commercial and residential building must have some kind of fire or smoke-detection system. Commercial structures exceeding a certain size are required to have a suppression system as well. These are minimum standards established by the government, yet the entire cell block portion of the prison did not have any smoke detectors, fire alarms, or sprinklers. Every single one of the 1,000-man prison population was completely unprotected in case of a fire. Human beings were locked in small cells and could not possibly escape the deadly smoke of a fire of any size. Yet there were no alarm or suppression systems that might be instrumental in saving their lives.

Upon admittance, Adrian was given a used mattress, one used blanket, one used pillow, and two used bed sheets. All of them prominently displayed an assortment of stains from the previous inmates' use. A moldy and offensive odor accompanied the stains, adding malevolent insult to injury.

I recalled Adrian's bitter criticism during my first visit, whereby he drew a parallel of his conditions and treatment at Division 1H to the conditions and treatments of animals in a zoo. He had been to several zoos, and offered a valid indictment that the animals there were prized and valued more than the human beings here. In zoos, he explained, a high priority has always been placed on matching the environment for the housed animals to their natural habitats in the wild. In the prison, on the other hand, the only priority seemed focus on keeping costs associated with the inmates' environment as low as possible. The safety, comfort, and convenience of the inmates didn't seem to rate any concern or consideration.

Some might argue that animals penned up in zoos never did anything to deserve incarceration, while the great majority of prison inmates committed crimes ranging from heinous to annoying. Human rights advocates, though, believe that compassion should motivate at least equal treatment for animals and human beings.

In zoos, a careful diet is established for the captive animals, which provides all the required nutrients regardless of cost. In the prison, a diet had been implemented which again seemed to be based solely on cost, regardless of the nutritional value. And taste was an altogether unknown concept. In fact, the food served to the inmates was not just tasteless, but was actually repulsive. Not only were the cheapest ingredients used, but they were prepared in such fashion that any taste had been thoroughly compromised. Adrian had been in charge of feeding our two dogs at home, and he insisted that the smell and appearance of their food was far more appealing than the food he was served in prison. He joked about the fact that he had never tasted the dog food, but was certain that it would be better than his food in prison. This situation regarding the dreadfully sordid food must not have been unknown to the individuals in charge, as they had implemented a system whereby inmates could purchase additional food items from a catalogue delivered once a week. The costs associated with the purchase of these food items was heavily laden with service fees, which easily exceeded triple the normal costs of the items themselves.

Another drawback existed with the purchase of this extra food. If it needed to be cooked or heated, the prison offered no facilities to accommodate such tasks. Ever resourceful, the inmates found a solution to that dilemma themselves. They simply saved all cartons from the milk that was served and used them as fuel. They would light a fire in their cell, use the metal grid of their bed as a grill, and cook the food they purchased. They heated water by the same method. Prison authorities officially disapproved of such practices, but in practice allowed them to be "secretly" carried out, as it seemed to provide a simple solution to a problem that they didn't want to acknowledge or worry about.

I am no expert at fire prevention and the damage caused by smoke inhalation, but the practice of open fires in a poorly ventilated and enclosed space, which in addition is not equipped with fire alarms or fire suppression systems, certainly resembles images I have seen in historic documentaries about prisons in underdeveloped countries or of a bygone era. It will undoubtedly take a major catastrophe involving the lives of numerous inmates before administrators of these prisons will be motivated to make any changes regarding these conditions. And I can only hope that this neglect will then be considered a crime rather than just an oversight. Maybe if the administrators were subjected to living under such conditions, then some changes might come about.

Despite the dreadful living accommodations, the disdainful food quality, and the disparaging apathy regarding normal and mandatory code compliance and human safety, the real crime to which the inmates have been subjected to is the indifference regarding their spiritual and psychological well-being. The real story involves the scornful attitude and unscrupulously high disregard that the people in charge of the prison system seem to have for anyone who is destined for incarceration.

Granted, inmates are at best third-class citizen and arguably do not necessarily deserve any compassion and pity. Inmates and convicts are there in order to make some measure of reparations for acts they committed against society and the laws which preserve and protect our humanity, democracy, and quality of life. Prisons, after all, do not just punish the offenders, but protect the rest of the population from these offenders by putting them away.

In order to protect the many, a few individuals must be held accountable and suffer the consequences that our society deems fit and proper. This was the case with Joseph Stalin, who punished dissidents for the good of the people. This was even the case with Harry S. Truman, the 33rd president of the U.S., who justified the use of two atomic bombs on civilians as an effort to end World War II quickly, and save many military lives in the process. These are obviously dramatic analogies, which on the surface might be hard to accept or agree with.

Yet not all such similarities should be discounted, especially if one considers that some prison inmates might actually be innocent of the crimes they were accused of committing.

Notwithstanding the foregoing, the various and disparaging opinions involving the proper and appropriate treatment of inmates range from "turning the other cheek" to demanding "a tooth for a tooth." The underlying truth still demands the recognition that these inmates are human beings, regardless of the acts that they might have committed. Because if we do not recognize that simple fact, then we are no better than the very criminal who is being judged and condemned. The standard by which America is known, and wants to be known, is that her people are guiding themselves with moral values and objectives that are higher than those of any other nation. Yet, let me restate, that the strength of these values and objectives is only as strong as its weakest link.

Bertrand Russell, the 1950 recipient of the Nobel Peace Prize for Literature and one of the world's most noted logicians and mathematicians, pointed out, "We have two kinds of morality side by side: one which we preach but do not practice and another which we practice but seldom preach."

The treatment of prisoners in America, in my opinion, is a precise example of this dual line of reasoning and logic. And until I was forced to witness this disparity of America's perceived morality and the morality that is being practiced, I too had the same preconceived opinions about the treatment that prisoners should deserve. There are countless laws which presuppose and mandate the treatment of inmates. The execution and performance of these treatments appears to be subject to conflicting interpretations. In essence, the system that addresses the incarcerations and rehabilitation of convicts is a perfect example which has exhibited every aspect of this multiple concept of morality.

The good. The bad. The ugly. The unknown. The disregarded.

The Cook County Department of Corrections in Chicago altogether houses approximately 11,000 inmates and supervises another 4,000 individuals in various alternative projects. It is one of the largest correctional facilities in America. This facility houses mostly individuals who have not yet been completely adjudicated and are incarcerated only because they could not post the required bond or have not been eligible for a bond. Each prisoner has been accused of a crime. Most have not been found guilty of anything. Some have been found guilty, and await sentencing hearings. A few have been returned from state prisons to be retried after appeals courts overturned the original verdicts.

The inmates who have not yet been tried either have been accused of crimes so heinous that bail is precluded, or of lesser crimes subject to bail. In the latter instance, these people simply could not raise the money to post the bond. All of these inmates are waiting for their day in court. Some were similar to Adrian's case. They had been accused of an unproven crime, had posted the required bail, and because they disregarded conditions of the bond, were incarcerated to wait for their respective trials.

Up to this point, the only thing that Adrian had been found guilty of was failing to obey the bond restrictions. The most serious charge against him was his failure to appear in court on the specified date and time. This automatically equated him to the same degree of guilt as those individuals who were not eligible for a bond, or those individuals whose crime required a bond amount that was purposefully too high for them to possibly be able to satisfy.

It's one of those situations where general apathy and disinterest by the public, relative to the determination of an appropriate and equitable treatment of all criminals, has resulted in a chaotic and indifferent resolution. It is a popular belief that prisoners are in prison for a reason, and while it may not necessarily be for the right reason, the fact that they were implicated in a crime would lead one to believe that some amount of guilt must have existed.

After all, where there is smoke, there must be some kind of fire.

It has always been better to be safe rather than sorry!

One of the most disturbing elements of this chaotic system is the failure of the authorities to understand that inmates of Cook County Department of Corrections are not all the same. Even though these people have not been convicted of the current charges, and must be regarded as innocent until proven guilty, common sense dictates that differences exist in their backgrounds. Some are simply more volatile and dangerous than others. It doesn't make sense to mix hardened career criminals with young men who have spotless backgrounds. It is callous arrogance to lump together inmates who are charged with savage, heinous serial murders in a cellblock with someone who has made a stupid error in attempting to flee.

The caliber of inmates with whom my son was placed should shed some light on this disparaging and inappropriate process. Here are a few of the inmates housed with Adrian and the crimes charged against them:

Johnny Ruffin: First degree murder; gang-related.

Edward Leek: Conspiracy to commit murder. A former policeman charged with paying someone to kill his partner.

Carlos Magna: Reckless homicide, killing two people in a car accident.

Rafael Belbonte: Two counts of the first-degree murder of his wife and her lover.

Markith Lambly: Attempted murder and robbery.

Isaac DelRio: Aggravated kidnapping of his girlfriend's baby

Cornell Milton: First-degree murder of his daughter.

James Degorski: Seven counts of first-degree murder involving the Brown's Chicken massacre.

James DeKalewe: Two counts of aggravated kidnapping and rape of a child.

Paul Runge: Seven counts of first-degree murder including the rape and murder of a ten-year-old child.

John Luna: Seven counts of first-degree murder involving the Brown's Chicken massacre.

Wayne Willis: Four counts of rape.

Antwon Hill: First-degree murder in a shooting.

Stanley Gardner: First-degree murder of his son.

Robert Spurlik: Multiple child molestations during his tenure as a schoolteacher.

Jim Pender: First-degree murder of his wife with a hammer.

Mike Prodanic: Illegal alien, crimes unknown.

With the exception of Prodanic, the last individual on that list, all others had been caught and charged, the evidence against them supported by DNA evidence, fingerprint evidence, or the collaboration of several credible witnesses. These men faced trials for kidnapping a baby, molesting children, raping a kidnap victim, serial rape, multiple murders, and gang murders.

Confessions, undisputed evidence, and eyewitness evidence to heinous crimes were the reasons these individuals were incarcerated. Adrian was thrown into that mix of horrors for one reason only: he had violated bond conditions and failed to appear in court. Of course, he faced trial for the alleged crimes at the party, but that was not the reason for his imprisonment. He hadn't kept his court appointment. Nothing more. The other boys charged along with Adrian had been arraigned without any prison time. One of them had been completely acquitted, one had served only boot camp, and two had gotten off with probation only.

I could not help but be reminded of the corollary Adrian had cited involving the prison and a zoo. And I am reminded that in a zoo, all animals are separated by their temperament and behavior. The young and inexperienced are separated from the mature and violent. The grazers are separated from the carnivores.

It wasn't until much later into his incarceration that Adrian finally confided information about these men, and said that life with them consisted of nonstop intimidation and threats, and the slightest of perceived indiscretions could provoke a violent confrontation. Most of these inmates would never be set free again, and the consequences of their actions now did not concern them in the least. The method by which the prison officials had decided to deal with such potentially volatile situations was to allow only five to seven inmates outside their cells at any one time. And such time was limited to only four hours per day. During that time, they were allowed to watch television programs, make phone calls, or visit the recreation room and play cards or exercise. The remaining twenty hours they were locked up in their cells without any TV, radio, or even a clock, and forced to simply vegetate and endlessly ponder the futility of their fate. If an inmate created any commotion, then the entire division would be under a "lock down," and the out time would be reduced to only one hour.

In the end, after everything had been said and done, the clear intent was to break the will of every prisoner, and force them to accept the inevitable "herd mentality" of conformity. And while this probably achieved the initial stages of such conformity, it was more analogous to the inherent resistance of a caged animal toward its captor. The prison into which Adrian had been thrown certainly resembled the cage into which these ruthless predators had been captured.

It was a place that one would not want to visit, much less want to live in. And it certainly wasn't a place that any righteous politician would want to experience himself. Even if it was in his own back yard. Unless, of course, it was used to manipulate a political campaign scenario.

To quote Carl Jung, Swiss psychiatrist and philosopher, "As in the beginning of the Christian Era, so we are once again faced with the moral dilemma that our social conscience has failed to keep up with our scientific, technical and industrial developments."

CHAPTER 39

SURVIVAL

Someone with a great deal of insight into human behavior coined the phrase, "Those who can make a difference—do, and those who can't—teach. Since my ability to make a difference is probably very limited, and since I am not qualified to teach, I can only do the next best thing—complain. And while I might not yet be ready to stand in front of the gates of a prison in order to make my discontent known, I am nevertheless willing to point my fingers at the foes who have attempted to remain invisible and conspicuously unaccountable.

One person who attempted to make a difference, and who actually had also taught as a professor at a university in California, stands out in my mind. She was one the FBI's most wanted fugitives, was associated with the Black Panthers, and yet ran as a candidate for the vice presidential position in the 1980 and 1984 election campaigns. Angela Davis, whether you like her or not, and whether you agree with her or not, certainly deserves credit for putting her life where her convictions stood. Instead of political rhetoric, she actually took up arms in order to voice her opinion and to support her beliefs. And where I may not necessarily support her actions and decisions—I acknowledge that I am a mere savant as it might apply to the political movements of her times—I do applaud her experience, insight, and understanding of human suffering. She was willing to stand against the forces in power at the time, which are much like the powers that still exist.

In 1971, Angela Davis professed that, "Jails and prisons are designed to break human beings, to convert the population into specimens in a zoo—obedient to their keepers, but dangerous to each other."

And while my son's interpretation of the conditions inside the prison have a common denomination with Davis's summation, they were formed as the result of mere "synchronistic" coincidence. Their views were derived independently, albeit humiliatingly and degradingly, of each other. Nevertheless, they support and give credence to each other, and while generations apart, still resonate with the same indifference to human dignity and disregard for moral values

No matter how you say it, or what simile you use to make your point, the simple matter of the fact remains that a prison is a very dangerous place. Unlike populations in a regular prison, which generally gravitate toward their respective social groups, the inmates sharing space with Adrian remained unaligned for the most part. While this did not create a hostile environment based on ethnicity, it did establish a situation where safety did not lie in numbers, and a hierarchy was instead generated based on physical strength and the severity and reputation of the charged crimes.

The need to make friends with a dominant individual soon became painfully clear to Adrian, after he was initiated into the ranks of subservient acquiescence. Adrian was still attempting to make sense out of his situation and tried his best to get used to the routines of prison life. He wanted nothing more than to simply blend in with the rest of the inmates, and avoid drawing any attention onto himself from either the guards or the other prisoners. He was the youngest person there, and having heard every story of inappropriate sexual behavior by inmates in general, and especially by inmates with reputations for rape and murder, kept to himself as much as possible.

It was June, and the weather was warm. He looked forward to getting out of his cell, going outside, and enjoying the sunshine with breezes that occasionally swept through the exercise yard. He cherished just sitting in the open air, closing his eyes as he faced the sun, and allowing the warmth to gently tan his face. The brightness penetrated his eyelids, almost painfully so, but to him it was a pleasurable pain, cleansing his conscience and burning away all sorrow and hardship that had taken hold of his deepest emotions.

So, on one particular Thursday afternoon, he sat down on a patch of dirt at the far end of the yard, and leaned back in an effort to get comfortable. He was attempting to drown out the shouting and noise of the basketball game at the other end of the yard. As he looked up he noticed a bird tangled in the sharp razor wire atop the surrounding chain link fence. The bird appeared to be dead, but its wings continued to flap and move in the breeze. Adrian shaded his eyes with his hand in an effort to see what kind of bird it might be, as the analogy of a free and innocent creature getting caught in the sharp vices of the prison's restraints was akin to the sad irony of his own experiences. The fact that the bird seemed to have died in its struggle to regain freedom was, however, an ominous prophecy, which he ruefully acknowledged and realized as well.

Because of Adrian's visual and mental preoccupation with the bird, he hadn't noticed the approach of another inmate, who squatted beside him. The tattooed prisoner grunted, "What's up, bro?" Adrian turned and tried to focus his eyes on the intruder, and heard him say, "Why you sittin' here all by yourself?" Without waiting for an answer, he growled, "You think you're better than us?"

"No, no. Not at all," Adrian replied, trying to avoid the menacing stare and preparing to get up and move away. His worst fears about prison seemed to finally be coming true and were unmistakably crashing down on him. He could feel the blood rush from his face and he desperately looked around to see if anyone was observing this ambush.

"There's no one here to help you, bro." With each word, the wiry man grew more aggressive. He slapped a heavy hand on Adrian's shoulder, preventing him from getting up. The unwelcome touch had a paralyzing effect on Adrian, freezing him in his helpless sitting position. He felt sweat beading on his face, and struggled to keep from hyperventilating.

With a condescending smile, the encroacher said, "Relax. I wanna be your friend. I'm gonna watch your back, bro. And I know that you wanna be my friend, too. And since we're gonna be friends, we'll be sharing our shit, you know. I see you buying all this food, so we're gonna share that food, you know what I'm sayin'."

Reluctant to believe that this threat was only about the meager weekly allowance he received from his mother, yet visibly relieved that it might be so, Adrian finally looked back at the inmate and managed to nod his head in approval.

Rising to a standing position, the aggressor said, "See, it's all good, bro." Adrian was still sitting on the ground, with his palms pressed against the ground in order to support his upright posture. Believing this ordeal to be over, he relaxed and finally exhaled a sigh of relief. Just then, the inmate turned back again, and crouching back down in order to get closer to Adrian again, he snapped, "And by sharing, I mean all of it, motherfucker." And without any sign of any provocation, purpose, or reason, he viciously hit the back of Adrian's palm with his fist.

The intruder's actions were too fast and completely unexpected, completely catching Adrian off guard. Within a split second, he felt an excruciating pain in the hand that had been hit. A pain far greater than any mere punch could have caused. He instinctively looked down just in time to see the inmate open his fist and reveal a plastic stick now embedded in the back of Adrian's hand. In the blink of an eye, the inmate removed the stick, leaving a bloody gash in Adrian's hand.

"Just a little reminder, bitch," he hissed before rising and ambling away, as if leaving a friendly conversation.

Adrian realized the weapon used to stab him was a sharpened toothbrush handle. His new "protector" had used it to demonstrate his superior position in the hierarchy and to underscore the seriousness of his demands. It was an ominous warning, and Adrian heeded it. He did not tell anyone of his injury. Instead he sought a way to find a means of real protection within the sentient confines and limitations of his situation.

The answer lay in befriending another inmate named Wayne Willis. A black man, who at 6' 5" and well over 300 pounds molded into an extraordinary physique, Willis towered above everyone else. He held the rank of undisputed chief of these inmates. Luckily, Adrian was blessed with a great sense of humor and jovial mannerisms, and Willis was a man who appreciated these characteristics. Adrian was able to get a lot of mileage (and protection) from the jokes he used to entertain this serial and brutal rapist.

He also became friendly with Paul Runge, another tall and powerful inmate (one of the hardcore inmates I mentioned earlier). In February 2006, Runge would be convicted and sentenced to the death penalty for the multiple murders and rapes he had committed.

Lastly, he was taught all of the rules of prison life by Mike Prodanic, who had been incarcerated for some time for a crime to which he never admitted nor ever elaborated on. Based on his Serbian nationality, Mike found a common bond with Adrian, who, to this day, speaks fondly of the friendship they shared. In fact, it became an animated truism that it takes far fewer degrees of separation (than the famous six degrees involving Kevin Bacon) to come across a Serb in any walk of life or life experience.

After all, it was Nikola Tesla, a Serb employee of Thomas Edison, who has been credited with helping invent the light bulb. It was Gavrilo Princep, a Serb national, who killed Archduke Ferdinand, precipitating World War I. And it was the Serb ruler, Milosevic, who committed the most heinous atrocities in Europe in the last 60 years. And these are only a few events to which the Serbs have admitted.

For Adrian, it had become a matter of survival, and I would like to think a matter of intelligence, for him to adjust his behavior and intellect to fit in with those inmates. With the exception of Mike, he humored, supported, and even agreed with the opinions of those individuals who were able to protect him from further harm. Adrian realized his lowly position in the chain of command of this prison regime, and simply became a voluntary, if overly conspicuous, member of those high-ranking inmates' entourage.

Intimidation, perception of strength, and power was the standard method of gaining and maintaining respect, and any association with the upper echelon of the inmate hierarchy was extremely helpful to the less powerful. Adrian took every opportunity to be constantly in the company of Wayne Willis or Paul Runge, and through this persistent association, gained a tremendous and insightful understanding of their reasoning, motives, and psychological behavior.

It came about that Adrian had one more conversation with the inmate who had accosted him in the yard on that June afternoon. This time, the "protector" offered his apologies and assured Adrian that he had meant no harm, and that he no longer wanted to share any of his "shit," and that he in fact didn't want any shit from Adrian at all.

The most gripping association Adrian formed while locked up was with the serial killer, Paul Runge. As luck would have it, Adrian's out time had primarily coincided with the out time of Runge. Through this coincidence, Adrian became well acquainted with him.

While waiting for trial, Runge made no secret of his barbarous character and predatory inclinations in order to maintain his position of respect with the other inmates. He confided in Adrian some of his darkest secrets and most vile perversions, revealing the multifaceted composition of his sinister and demented character. It amazed Adrian to hear Runge confess that all of his murders had been premeditated, and that his ultimate goal was the experiences and feelings he would get from watching his victims die. It was a craving and hunger that he knew he would never be able to eliminate, and which could only be satisfied by intently observing the sheer panic and fear in the eyes of his helpless victims when he told them of their imminent deaths. And this hunger grew progressively more intense, and the cravings more perverse, and had finally culminated in the most gruesome crime imaginable.

Runge spelled it out in gory detail. He had forced the mother of an 11-year-old girl to watch as he raped the young child, sodomized her, and then killed her by slitting her throat. The acts, said Runge, didn't provide the real pleasure. Instead, the thrill came from forcing the mother to watch the cruel torture and painful death of her young daughter. His satisfaction was achieved by seeing the mother helplessly observe what he was doing. He feasted on her infinite agony by looking into her eyes in order to witness the greatest human pain and the most unimaginable suffering that could possibly exist or be imagined. After the daughter was dead, he laid her body on the bed next to her mother and raped and sodomized her as well, while she was holding her daughter's lifeless body. Finally, he slit the mother's throat and set their bodies on fire in order to destroy the evidence.

Adrian wondered why Runge chose to tell him of these horrific events. They were a series of summations whose measure of sheer gruesomeness grew worse and more painful with every conversation and encounter that Adrian had with Paul Runge, and exposed Adrian to the level of sheer madness that knew no taboos, bounds, or limitations.

One of Sigmund Freud's favorite expressions, borrowed from an ancient Roman philosopher, was, "Man is wolf to man."

Runge was far beyond that description or any other categorization in man's feeble attempt to describe the ultimate ghastly behavior.

During one particularly animated encounter with Adrian, Paul revealed a braided strap that he had fashioned from strips of torn bed sheets, and which he kept around his waist at all times. Paul assured Adrian that this strap was a much more reliable means of killing a person than the normal weapon of choice, such as a filed down and sharpened toothbrush, to which Adrian had already been introduced to. In fact, Runge offered to kill anyone who was giving trouble to Adrian. No reasons would have been needed and no explanations required. It was simply a favor he was prepared to do for Adrian.

The lessons came hard and fast to Adrian. He had quickly learned that it was much safer to be mad with the entire world, than to be sane alone. Needless to say, he never questioned, corrected, or clarified anything that Runge would do or say, and he never won any card games against him that involved wagers or money.

The value of one's life in prison can easily be measured by this type of example, and it provides some evidence as to the dangers of being in the company of such criminals. The environment that is being created is clearly a two-sided weapon of society. On the one side, it punishes the criminals for the crimes they committed against society. On the other side, it sharpens their lawless skills, helps them learn new methods of dishonest conduct, and further warps them by exposure and influence from other criminals.

But everyone realizes this. God knows that thousands of studies have proven the insidious effect of prisons; that they are fertile incubation grounds for sprouting new and improved criminals upon their release.

Paul Runge had been incarcerated at the age of 17 for the murder of his first victim. Because of his youth and the circumstances surrounding his crime, he was released after approximately eight years. Now someone might make the point that I have just gone through a rather painfully expressive narrative on the madness that must have possessed him and driven him to commit six more murders after his release, rather than describing or suggesting anything that he might have learned during his initial incarceration. And that would certainly be a valid point as long as you are a pathetically ignorant bureaucrat who works for the type of institution that I was criticizing, and whose sole purpose is to avoid blame and ignore any problems that might interfere with your employment objectives or career goals.

Because his life story is exactly the point that I am trying to make. At age 17, he committed a vile crime. In fact he was diagnosed as being mentally disordered, and incapable of understanding the consequences of his actions. That's what the state-appointed professionals determined back then. But then he was put into prison, and received his apprenticeship to bigger things in life.

It is said that man is the only leopard that can change his spots, or if you prefer, the only tiger that can change his stripes (in either event, they are both carnivores). Most people have heard of these metaphors. Most people have also heard of the analogy that man is the only animal who drinks when he is not thirsty, who has sex at any time of season, and (as I had already mentioned) can be friendly toward his prey until the time that he eats it.

So, let's put two and two together and determine the startling answers that politicians in charge of prison reform can come up with.

First, you have a young individual, like Paul Runge, who has committed a serious crime.

Second, you have a professional who determines that he is mentally unstable and that he should not be held totally accountable for his actions.

Third, you put him into the very environment which breeds and nurtures the very thing that he has been found guilty of, or other anti-social behavior.

Fourth, you know that man, by nature, is worse than an animal that adapts, and is really capable of doing almost anything, in order to survive. He might even be devious enough to convince gullible or unqualified mental health experts that he is cured and ready for release.

Fifth, you allow a bureaucratic system to administer all the remedies and draw all the conclusions from their self-declared expertise.

According to my math, the simple conclusion one gets from this compound equation is the creation of a Paul Runge.

Certainly, I'll be the first to admit that I have oversimplified the variables of this equation to some degree, but somehow one of the biggest problems seems to be the continued practice of putting the grazers of society in with the meat-eaters of civilization. Placing a 17-year-old, immature or mentally challenged youth with seasoned criminals is a crime in itself. This also applies to incarcerating suspects not proven guilty, or guilty of a relatively minor infraction in cells with the extremely guilty.

Or to paraphrase, can we, as a society or civilization, really call it progress, if our cannibals are now using knives and forks?

Adrian did the best he could to survive and fend off the negative influences that could destroy his whole life. He could no longer see the sun rise, and he could not watch the sun set. He was locked in a cage for twenty hours each day, with nothing to occupy his time. No television. No radio. Not even a clock that would let him watch the minutes tick away like hours.

Panic and fear, which once had filled his mind and lodged in his chest like molten lead, had soon turned to solitude, seclusion, and even indifference. It slowly conquered his mind and inexplicably offered him a strange relief from the pain that had been his constant companion. It felt like someone had slowly turned down the thundering volume of his screaming conscience and instead had offered a soothing silence that was brought by the indignant surrender of one's will. This transformation was the exact thing that Campanelli had cautioned us about when he discussed his concerns about the effects of an extended incarceration.

The human mind and body is a wondrous thing, and the true

workings have not yet been fully explored or understood. In the case of a comatose individual, whose body starts to shut down vital organs simply to prolong the life of the individual, so does the mind start to shut down certain functions and memories to protect its sanity. Adrian could feel this happening to him.

Twenty daily hours of living in isolation allowed the other four to offer mixed emotions and only conditional relief. During those four hours, he had to watch every other inmate in fear of being injured again. Or maybe even worse. And he had to listen and show compassion, understanding, and even support for the vile crimes that the group of inmates sharing his out time had committed, if he wanted any type of security. After all, the saying goes that if you walk like a duck, talk like a duck, and are always in the company of other ducks, then you must be a duck.

In his case, the reality was that if you walk like a menacing criminal, talk like a menacing criminal, and are always in the company of other menacing criminals, you may not be one, but you'll have a better chance of survival if these menacing criminals find you entertaining, agreeable, and humorous.

But in truth, this act provided only a temporary truce, which could be broken at any moment by the unstable and endlessly volatile nature of his protectors. He had to learn how to survive all over again. And the only way that he could learn was from his mistakes. His worst nightmare had become a brutal reality. He was living the life he had feared the most, and the horrendous experiences of his visit to Stateville Prison nearly four years earlier had now become an everyday experience.

The reason for his incarceration wasn't the same reason that had forced him to run. He had fled due to his fears, especially the worry that he could not get justice for the alleged crime. The media, in their relentless pursuit of sensationalism and self-adjudicated justice, had already convicted him of the charges nobody had yet proven. The prosecution had pursued him like a hungry lion after a young gazelle. Police detectives involved in his case had gained promotions for their extraordinary job performances. And judges, from their sacrosanct, elevated benches, had shown no inclination to toss out fabricated testimony by witnesses who would benefit from such deliberate duplicity. Clearly, they could only rule based on the evidence that had already been molded into the conviction promised by the prosecution. And relying on a jury to make the just decisions, while being forced to serve, was the equivalent to betting on three-legged horse at an endurance race.

Conny had prophetically said, "You'll be my second victim," during that December party which kept replaying in his mind like an annoying commercial that never goes away. Little did he know that her words would turn out to be such literal truth, and that the sex involved that evening would ultimately get him fucked in ways he could never have imagined. He remembered her prophecy every time that he had to light a fire in his cell in order to heat up the miserable food that he had to eat. Every time he had to heat up the ice-cold water in his cell in order to wash himself.

He remembered how she had moaned in pleasure and approval, every time he had to listen to the sick and perverted stories of his jailhouse companions. He remembered her playful threat, that he would get his just reward for having sex with her while he had a girlfriend, every time he was shackled and chained to make an appearance in court for some arbitrary and predetermined ruling.

He remembered her boastful proclamation about her sexual experiences and that this would be one fuck he would remember for the rest of his life, every time he heard the prison cell door slam shut.

He remembered all those fateful incidents during all those twenty hours that he was locked up every day.

And while he was still angry, his fury was really no longer directed at Conny. Those wounds had been healed by time. He knew that she was the source of his problems, and that he should be furious and unforgiving. But he could not change his feelings. The injuries caused by her lies had been callused over by the new skin of perseverance that he grew to simply survive the torture, pain, and suffering inflicted by the piercing claws of blood-thirsty vultures disguised as justice-seeking persecutors.

While he was still sorry and remorseful, it was no longer for himself, but rather for the pain it had caused his family. Though he still hoped to find justice, such hope was reduced to only a remnant of a fleeting thought.

Adrian had been locked up for months, diminishing his early hopes for a speedy trial. More importantly, he had regressed into accepting the routine demanded by his desolate circumstances, and had even become accustomed to the conditions and adversity that it warranted. Everything he did was colored by the simple desire to survive, and he considered any day that passed without a threatening incident a tremendous success. His mind was decomposing and deconstructing and he simply accepted the herd mentality of survival.

While our son endured this unwilling transformation to this level of mentality of survival, it saddened us to hear his depressed comments. "It doesn't matter." "I don't care." These were his answers to any questions we asked of significance, reverence or importance. His descent into this level of depression had been Dobrila's worst fear.

Patrick had warned us that, "There comes a critical moment in time, where his resolve and reasoning will be broken, and all of his future actions and decisions will be influenced by this crucial acceptance of helplessness and inability to control his own destiny." This observation was based on clinical fact and experience with thousands of inmates over extended periods of time, which also noted that the pivotal breaking point generally occurs after the first three to six months.

It was hard to fully appreciate and digest the information from Patrick as he expressed his concern for Adrian's prolonged incarceration. His explanation served to precipitate the anger we already felt with a feeling of intense disgust and contempt reserved for the most dire of situations, like having your innocent child locked up with dangerous murderers and rapists.

Adrian was locked up with the worst kinds of predators, such as a sadistic killer with psychological problems who boasted about his ability and propensity to kill anyone in the prison community at will and without fear of any consequences. Adrian was not locked up because of the alleged rape accusation. He was locked up because he did not show up in court at a specific time and date.

The penalty for not showing up was the forfeiture of the $10,000 bond which we had posted. That money had been pledged and lost.

I am not totally insensitive and ignorant about the consequences relative to a person's flight and the possibility, or probability, of a person running away again. Even as it applies to my own son and my own financial investment. "Fool me once, shame on you," and you know the rest of that proverb.

But it is also a common proverb that the punishment should fit the crime. In fact it's the basis of our legal system.

And somehow I fail to connect my son's punishment with his crime of running away because he was afraid of not receiving a fair trial.

As I am writing these words, and as the remorseful tears of despair and helplessness are pouring down my cheeks because of the unnecessary and inappropriate punishment that he has had to endure, I can only hope that my solemn voice will not be a totally vain attempt, nor be drowned out by the jubilant screams of joy and satisfaction of the prosecutors who have caused his imprisonment. If these prosecutors, detectives, and judges portray themselves to be the messengers of justice, then they are the messengers who, in an attempt to prove their cause, have completely lost the very message they were sworn to pronounce and deliver.

CHAPTER 40

TRIAL ONE: JUMPING BAIL

"**N**o condition so low but may have Hopes . . . none so high but may have Fears," wrote Thomas Fuller in 1732, compiling a summation of the human condition.

Adrian's trial, in the end, would be more about the positive powers of hope than about being right or wrong.

The court date for hearing the charges for jumping bail was finally set for Monday, August 8, 2005.

By this time, Adrian had been held at Cook County Jail for over two months while waiting for his trial to begin. The charges included the original 140 counts of sexual improprieties as well as the new charge of jumping bail and fleeing to a foreign country.

The prosecutors had elected to proceed with the bail jumping based on a very simple premise. The outcome, as you will see, based on the allowable evidence, was obviously heavily slanted in their favor. And getting a guilty verdict, and some jail time now, would somewhat lessen their burden of having to get a guilty verdict in the main case later on.

It would be the fuel to keep their endurance burning, and which might pressure us into accepting a plea arrangement after all. It might be more reasonable for us to avoid any further potential or unknown damages by settling on a negotiated penalty of known severity.

They would get their pound of flesh.

It also would perhaps quench their thirst for blood, especially after the scathing beating they suffered in the Anthony Roberts trial.

However, at the risk of sounding somewhat self-serving and personally motivated, let me ask the following questions:

Was it really fair and proper to allow the prosecution to proceed with the bail-jumping charge first rather than the main case?

Might there not have been some mitigating circumstances relative to the main case that might have made him run? A person doesn't just run away for no reason. They run away from something.

And this questionable decision gets compounded and further shrouded in mystery by the fact that the charges of the underlying case were not even allowed to be brought up at all in the bail-jumping trial.

Essentially, none of the possible reasons and explanations as to why he might have run could be presented as evidence in his defense.

But wait, one might say. If the horrendous accusations of the underlying case could not be brought up, then Adrian would not look like the monster that he had been made out to be. Would that not be helpful to the defense?

And on the surface this might be perceived as having been beneficial for the defense, because no one was supposed to have known the severity of what he had been charged with in that case. Which might be a good point if no one had any knowledge of that underlying case. However, the alleged atrocities had consistently been one of the main topics in the news for the past three years. And unless every juror had just moved here from a foreign country (as in two seconds ago), or had just come out of a coma (also two seconds ago), then they absolutely must have had some knowledge of the underlying case.

In fact, it appeared all over the news on the very morning that the trial of Adrian Missbrenner was scheduled to start. Furthermore, the frenzy and commotion created by the media on this, as well as any trial day, would certainly have given anyone some idea of what might have been going on here.

And yet it was expected that the prospective jurors would not know about the underlying case?

Before arriving at the court, every candidate for the jury had the opportunity to read heavily slanted stories in the papers, or see Adrian's face on television and hear the loaded words, "rape, unconscious girl, sexually assaulted," and more. If they missed it on the morning news, they would be inundated with it that evening. With their interest piqued, they could read or hear: "Innocent, unconscious young girl was dragged into a spare bedroom and brutally gang raped . . ."

Or maybe the news would report the prosecution's revised version: "Innocent young victim was too drunk to give consent for gang rape . . ."

Somehow I think that any juror selected would have known about the underlying case by the time this trial got underway. I also think that the media might have done a good job in persuading every person without an opinion to form one.

Now imagine if every juror had knowledge of the underlying case, then it is probably safe to assume they had probably already formed an opinion about Adrian's moral character and guilt in the underlying case. And armed with such knowledge and opinions, how do you think they might perceive his attempted escape from the justice he deserved to face?

Having said all this, I think that it might be abundantly clear that even if the underlying charges were not allowed to be addressed, every juror nevertheless would have such knowledge. This could do immeasurable damage to the defense because no evidence of his innocence in the underlying case could be presented to perhaps change any juror's opinion of his guilt.

And if jurors thought that a prison term would be the proper punishment in the underlying case, then they would probably conclude that Adrian was trying to avoid justice, so he was guilty in this matter as well.

All of this might sound a little bit confusing, so let me try to clarify it with a hypothetical example. (I am determined to convince you yet.)

Let's assume for a moment the following facts: Bill shot Bob. Everyone had heard of how Bill shot Bob, that it was a terrible injury and that Bob had suffered tremendously as a result. Bob was a very likable person. The crime of shooting Bob, and his suffering, were widely reported. But it turns out that Bill actually shot Bob in self-defense. However, Bill wasn't allowed to tell anyone about it, and none of the reports about the shooting had mentioned it.

If we applied the rules of my son's trial to Bill and Bob, then Bill would be tried for shooting Bob based only on the simple fact that he had shot him. Bill could not mention the fact it had been self-defense.

However, to be fair, after the trial which determined whether Bill had shot Bob, and an appropriate penalty had been imposed, then Bill could have another trial to prove that he had shot Bob in self-defense.

OK, so far so good. Bill still had a chance.

But even if the second trial proved it was self-defense, what if Bill could not change the outcome, or the penalty, of the first trial in which he was found guilty?

Adrian's and Bill's scenarios were obviously very different, but the logic applied to the pursuit of justice was identical.

Bill cannot be tried without bringing in evidence relative to his self-defense.

By the same argument and rationale, Adrian should not have been tried for running first. And the basis upon which he decided to run should not have been disregarded during his trial for running.

But then again I think that any parent might be somewhat biased as it applies to their child's rights and treatment. And since we had no options on the sequence of trials, nor on permissible evidence, we proceeded with the trial under the imposed guidelines (as in restrictions.)

Every one of our friends and acquaintances asked us why we would go to trial on the charges of jumping bail rather than save time and money and just plead guilty to the charges. What defense could possibly be offered in order to make a jury question whether he had run away or not? It was a very simple question and premise. He either ran or he didn't.

Wouldn't pleading guilty to something that was really unavoidable and unquestionable make us look favorable in the eyes of these judges, who always preferred matters to be resolved by agreement between the parties, rather than forcing a decision from them? Especially in a case as convincing as this. Wouldn't it make us look as if we wanted to simply waste the court's time and efforts, which was never a good idea?

However, Patrick, our attorney, insisted that we proceed with a trial. And he based that decision on four factors.

First, it automatically gave us an opportunity to seek an appeal with a higher court, if we felt there had been any improprieties conducted by any of the parties involved. This included improprieties on the part of the judge.

Second, since this was our first actual trial in front of Judge Smierciak, other than just addressing or presenting responses to motions that had been filed, it presented a good opportunity to test his demeanor and evaluate his temperament. This was at a minimum of risk on our part, as the outcome was a foregone conclusion. Yet we could modify and adjust the method of our defense based on the judges actions, reactions, comments, and behavior, in the main trial that really mattered. Of course, we also had the same opportunity to scrutinize the methods employed by the prosecution.

Third, this was a good practice for Adrian and our witnesses. A trial run where we had the opportunity to test the depth of the water with only one foot, rather than jumping in with both feet, so to speak.

Fourth, we could just get plain lucky based on any number of events.

"Don't ever count out luck," Patrick insisted. "I have seen very strange things happen in court where the outcome was based entirely on luck." With a little smile, he added, "And I do have an idea, a-one-million shot that might work. It's a technical thing and jurors most likely will not grasp or accept it. But it's something we have to try," he explained. "And I'll take luck any day if it wins me a case."

This was essentially a warm-up for the real test. Even though the outcome seemed preordained, the sentencing was still critical and undecided, and in fact was entirely up to the judge. A guilty verdict could result in a sentence of up to fifteen years, based on the charges filed by the state alone. There could have been an additional ten years from the federal government, had we not negotiated a resolution with them ahead of time.

In fact, this trial was not an issue relative to guilt. Instead it was an issue of sentencing and the penalty that the judge would deem appropriate.

Because so much of a critical decision was still vested in the judge's decision, I repeatedly questioned the shrewdness of possibly angering the judge by asking for a trial. It was my opinion that showing faith in the judge's wisdom, and throwing ourselves at his mercy, would be perceived by Judge Smierciak as a positive gesture. He might show some compassion for that reason and reduce the sentence as a result.

Yet, Patrick insisted, and I finally conceded to his wishes.

Nevertheless, in an attempt to mitigate this risk as much as possible, I decided that we needed to show our belief in the serious nature of this trial, and possibly convince the judge that we regarded it seriously. So we arranged as many spectators as possible to come and watch the trial. In doing so, I hoped that the judge would realize that we felt it important enough to get "mobilized," so that we did not take his time for granted. At least twenty of our family and friends occupied the gallery seats.

This maneuver was clearly on par with the argument involving luck. But, based on Patrick's assurances, stranger things have happened in court.

Day One

The morning of August 8 presented some new and unique challenges for which we had not been totally prepared. And while they involved the coordinated effort to reach the courthouse on time because of the uncoordinated methods of attempting to accomplish that feat by our four sons, the ensuing commotion did reduce some of the anxiety about the dreaded activities we were about to face. While all of my sons had been lucky to inherit their looks mostly from my wife, they had also been blessed with my propensity for fashion and inclination to always look my best, with which I had been preoccupied during my own youth. As a result, shirts, pants, and jackets had to be re-ironed, neckties had to be reevaluated, and hairstyles had to be perfected. Even our eight-year-old showed signs of his own style and flair.

Adrian would be brought to the courthouse in his prison uniform.

It would be prejudicial for the jury to see him in this in this garb, so we were instructed to bring a change of clothes for him each day. He could change into apparel that would make him appear less guilty.

Anyone living in Chicago knows that, unlike other parts of the country, the region has only three seasons. The extreme cold season, the extreme hot season, and the construction season. This August was no different. What started out as a hot early morning became an unbearably hot mid-morning. And as soon as we exited our air-conditioned car, we were drenched in sweat, which was quickly absorbed by our formal attire. The short, belabored walk to the courthouse exhausted us and I remember thinking that this trial might become one hot issue after all. To our surprise, only four news crews were positioned in front of the courthouse, and their movements were equally lethargic.

The lack of any larger number of media crews made me think that we had finally reached the saturation point, and that this issue had finally reached its limit. Little did I realize that these crews had ample experience with jury trials, and they most likely knew that this day's events would be fairly uneventful, featuring the tedious jury selection process only. They were correct.

We entered the courtroom and took our customary seats on the left side of the gallery. Patrick and Cheryl Schroeder were standing in front of the bench involved in a discussion with Judge Smierciak. I strained my hearing in an effort to pick up their conversation, but was able to discern only incoherent sound bytes. "But it could be a parolable offense . . ." was one such partial comment I heard from Judge Smierciak.

Patrick came back to greet us and I asked the meaning of that conversation, specifically the judge's comments. He explained that Smierciak had asked them if there was any possibility of a settlement in this matter, and those specific comments involving "probationable" applied to the range of the potential sentence, should a guilty verdict be obtained. Shrugging his shoulders, he said it was an unusual comment, but expressed doubt of any hidden message in it.

As Patrick returned to the defense table, I could not help but feel a sense of wistful relief transcending the lawyer's disclaimer. I could not help but believe that my interpretation might prove more sagacious and prophetic as to the judge's true intentions. I could not believe this was a mere coincidence, but didn't allow my hopes to soar unreasonably high.

The balance of the day was fairly uneventful. Groups of potential jurors were led to a sequestered area and interviewed by the prosecution and the defense while we waited in the gallery. Dobrila and I scrutinized the potential jurors, taking note of their appearances and looks, in a clear and definitive attempt to judge a book by its cover. We tried to decide who might be a good juror for our cause, using lessons we had learned from Anthony's trial as a guideline. That jury had reached a not-guilty verdict, and we wanted people just like them, and passed our choices on to Patrick. He patiently listened.

Needless to say, his experience in these matters far exceeded ours, and any of our recommendations were really redundantly unimportant. Yet we felt compelled to help, even if our assistance was not needed. Or not wanted. Our prime candidates were those individuals we thought would find that running away was not considered such a terrible crime compared to the underlying accusations that he would have to face in the near future. We sought someone with an attitude of, "He's just a kid; let's not hammer him just yet; he'll get his 'reward' soon enough." Under the circumstances, that's all we could hope for.

This deductive reasoning obviously eliminated any intellectuals, young females, and anyone who might have young children. Our prime candidate would be a young male, preferably black or Hispanic, who might have had trouble with the law himself, and middle-aged parents of older teenagers who might understand their volatile minds. Everyone else was in that gray area of uncertainty.

While we were observing and scrutinizing the potential jurors, I noticed that a Hispanic woman in her late thirties was repeatedly looking in my direction. It appeared to me that she even smiled at me several times that our eyes met.

It was past five o'clock in the evening when the jury selection was suspended at Patrick's request. It turned out that Adrian had suddenly developed a severe headache and could not continue. And the law requires that any accused be able to participate in all phases of his or her trial.

The judge was visibly displeased, as he had made it clear that he wanted to have the jury selection completed the first day.

Going into the second day without a full jury would compromise his schedule.

That was obviously not a good sign.

Day Two

The jury selection continued during the morning of August 9, and we waited patiently in the courtroom for its conclusion. At once point Dobrila returned from a restroom break, extremely excited, even frantic. She grabbed my arm and started to drag me out of the courtroom while feverishly exhorting me to hurry up.

Outside and out of earshot of everyone else, she started to explain the reason for her excitement. "On my way to the bathroom I happened to come across one of the potential jurors . . .and she recognized me," she gasped. "It was Anna, the girl who worked for you when you had your office in Lyons!"

As soon as she mentioned the name, I recognized that this was the Hispanic woman who had been smiling at me the day before. I had to momentarily collect my thoughts in order to figure out what this might mean to us. I had not seen her for nearly seventeen years. And even while she had worked for me back then, it was strictly professional and without personal involvement of any kind. I had divested myself from that business under good circumstances, and she had stayed with it. I could think of no ill feelings that might hurt us now.

But what could that really mean?

Should we go back and try to talk to her? We knew that wasn't allowed. But, hell, the prosecutors and detectives had done dozens of things that were not allowed.

Could we expect her to actually do something illegal? Like not disclose that she had known us? All we would need was one juror who would vote in our favor, and then possibly convince everyone else to do the same. Even if no one else would decide in our favor, her vote could make it a hung jury.

But what if we attained a not-guilty verdict without her help, and it would be discovered later that she had known us? I wasn't sure if double jeopardy protection would prevent a retrial under these circumstances. I knew that, at a minimum, she might be in serious trouble for concealing her acquaintance with us.

The more I thought about this situation, the more possibilities presented themselves, and the more confused I became.

In the end, and primarily because I could not think of a positive and definitive manner in which to apply this situation, I decided not to pursue it at all. However, for the duration of this trial, I kept pondering what the probability factor of such a coincidental encounter had been in mathematical terms. At least a lucky million-to-one chance. In the end, she was not chosen as a juror.

The jury was finally selected, and the first witnesses were called after the lunch break.

The prosecution's burden was to prove that Adrian had run away and voided his bond provisions. Nothing more and nothing less. And this is what they explained during their opening statements. If he ran, they insisted, then that's the proof that he was guilty. End of story.

Patrick's opening statement was a little more involved. He explained that the conditions of the bond contained a provision that allowed a person to return from a possible flight within thirty days from the date he disappeared. He further explained that if that person does not return within that time frame, his failure must be based on a willful intent of not wanting to return. In other words, if the runaway wanted to come back, but could not due to circumstances beyond his control within those allocated thirty days, then the law says that he was not guilty of running.

In fact he read that requirement out loud from a textbook of the law.

Holy shit !

I could not believe my ears.

I could not believe that Patrick had kept that little morsel of information to himself. He later confided that he did it on purpose, as he didn't want any unintentional leaks relative to the methods of his attack to reach the prosecution.

This was now definitely more than a million-to-one chance of winning.

The prosecution seemed unfazed, and stayed on their course in simply relying on de facto evidence that he had run away. So they called to the witness stand a clerk who had processed the paperwork attesting to the fact that Adrian had disappeared. They presented evidence from the home-confinement department that Adrian had not been where he was supposed to be. And they presented FBI agent Stover, who had gone to Serbia to bring Adrian back to the United States.

It was short, sweet, and to the point. In fact, the prosecution rested their case by 3:00 p.m.

Patrick's first witness was FBI agent Araya, with whom he had negotiated Adrian's return. Araya confirmed that he had been in discussions with Patrick for some time prior to Adrian's actual return. He also confirmed that the FBI had dropped all of their charges against Adrian.

Next, Patrick recalled Agent Stover, who testified that Adrian's return was made possible only because of his surrender. He affirmed that, while they had a general idea as to his whereabouts, they would never have been able to get him from Serbia themselves because of international restrictions.

Finally, Adrian took the stand.

Patrick had obviously coached him with questions that he intended to ask, along with the right answers.

But, it's a funny thing that often happens to a person in that witness chair. And anyone who has been there will know exactly what I mean. In fact, this was one of the four reasons why Patrick had wanted to let this trial take place, namely to give the witnesses an opportunity to experience just such an event. For some reason, most people draw a blank as soon as they hit that witness stand, and the best-laid plans and most-thought-out deliberations are simply forgotten. In addition, unrehearsed information suddenly has a tendency to surface.

And this is exactly what happened to Adrian.

He pretty much had forgotten the things that he was supposed to have said, and instead said things that took everyone by surprise.

Even Patrick was astonished.

The intent was to verbalize his vain attempts of securing the needed documents for returning to America; to elaborate on the steps he had taken in his attempt to accomplish this feat. Patrick wanted Adrian to explain that despite his best efforts, he was unable to get anything done within the thirty-day window of opportunity afforded under the law.

In fact, the reason why Patrick had questioned the FBI was to demonstrate that they had a difficult time themselves, and that it had taken well over thirty days for them to even respond to requests of securing Adrian's return, much less accomplish the actual task.

However, what Adrian said instead was that he had been kidnapped (which Patrick did not know about) and that he feared for his life. He told of hiding out because the Serbian mob was after him, and that alone had consumed more than thirty days.

Naturally, upon cross-examination, the prosecutors asked the type of questions about his kidnapping which made the whole story appear fabricated and just pure fiction. They asked for names which he didn't know. They asked him about dates and times, which he could not remember. And they asked for proof, which he could not provide.

By the time the prosecution had finished with dissecting Adrian's testimony, it certainly appeared like a pack of dramatic lies.

This second day, which started with a surprise about the possibility of a former employee being a potential juror, offered a startling possibility of salvation through a legal loophole, and finally ended with the revelation that, by telling the truth about his ordeal, Adrian managed only to sound like a shameless liar, who would make up any far-fetched story in order to support his innocence.

DAY THREE

With witness testimony completed, the balance of the trial was limited to closing arguments. The prosecution elaborated on the fact that he had not returned until he found it convenient for his own purposes, which was well beyond the thirty-day grace period. They condescendingly portrayed his story about the kidnapping as an absurd and unbelievable fable, and that he was simply a spoiled rich kid who had really been traveling leisurely throughout Serbia.

Dripping with skepticism, they said he had finally gotten bored and decided to return to America, while knowing all along that his parents would get a good lawyer to get him off the hook. "Don't let him make a fool of you, ladies and gentlemen of the jury. Don't think for one moment that all of his actions were not clearly thought out . . . He came back when he was good and ready, and not one moment sooner."

Of course, Patrick presented quite a different interpretation of the same evidence and testimony. Any good attorney, after all, should be able to paint a contrasting picture with the same evidence. While the prosecutors' rendition of the evidence was matter-of-fact, his presentation was emotional, unscripted, and genuinely from his heart. Despite my own ample experiences in courtrooms, I had never witnessed any attorney perform as emotionally as he did.

While the prosecutor had stood behind the podium and mostly read from a prepared statement, Patrick paced around the courtroom, using his hands to emphatically gesture every point and continually varying his enunciation and pitch in order to underscore the urgency of his message. "It's so easy for them to criticize and argue about something they have never experienced," he began. "They never had to fight for their lives. They never had to wonder if today was their last day, if this meal was their last meal. They never had to ask themselves if the next person you meet would be the one to get you."

Patrick's voice trembled, "It's so easy to slander someone's struggle when you are safe and sound in America. But that place was not America, and it was not safe and sound. In fact it was still a battlefield from the time that America had bombed the hell out of that country. And do you think for one moment that it was safe for an American boy to wander about that country afterwards?"

Intent on keeping the jury glued to his every word, Patrick said, "This young boy was fighting for his life. He didn't want to return because he was bored; he wanted to return because he wanted to live. And the FBI themselves admitted that it took a major effort to get him out of there; that it took several months just to get the paperwork done; that they never would have caught him if he hadn't voluntarily surrendered himself. And even then it took them several days to guarantee his safety."

He paused and wiped the sweat from his forehead with a tissue. "He wanted to come back, but he couldn't. It wasn't willful. It was not willful," he concluded slowly in order to let the last words resonate in the jurors' minds.

With the close of the attorney's summations at a few minutes before noon, the judge ordered a break for lunch, but asked the jurors to start deliberations while they waited for their meals to arrive.

Anticipating that a verdict would not be reached for some time, Dobrila and I invited every one of our family and friends to join us at a nearby restaurant for lunch. Most of them accepted our offer, and the restaurant of choice had to reposition several tables in order to accommodate our group. We had reviewed the menu and had barely placed our beverage orders when Patrick called and advised me that the jury had already reached their decision.

We rushed back to the courtroom and arrived at 1:30 p.m. As is customary, we all rose in honor of the jury's arrival, and upon the bailiff's signal, sat back down after the jurors made themselves comfortable.

Next, Judge Smierciak asked the foreperson if they had reached a verdict, which was affirmed immediately. The bailiff handed a copy of the written verdict to the judge, who briefly looked at its contents and handed it back to the bailiff. She in turn handed it back to the foreperson.

"Please read your verdict," Judge Smierciak instructed.

There was a deadly silence in anticipation of the verdict. Both the prosecution and the defense were standing. I held my breath as Dobrila clutched my hand.

"We find the defendant, Adrian Missbrenner, guilty of . . ." was all I could hear as I somehow blanked out everything else that followed. I felt my eyes well up with tears and I instinctively wiped my cheeks. I heard commotion and an unintelligible murmur from the audience, which consisted mostly of reporters along with a sketch artist.

The bailiff sternly asked for silence, as Judge Smierciak announced that he would conduct a sentencing hearing on September 9, 2005.

Patrick at that point petitioned Judge Smierciak to consider delaying the sentencing until after the sexual-assault trial in order to prevent the contamination of that trial's jurors.

The judge declined that request and notified the jurors that their lunch had arrived.

We had embarked on a desperate journey toward an elusive and hopeful destination. And while there were many paths that could have led us there, we chose the longest and most difficult in hopes of finding a different answer. All along we had been burdened with the heaviest of baggage, the knowledge of its foregone conclusion. Because no matter which direction we chose, and no matter how much effort we exerted, we knew the predetermined destination all along.

But human nature is such that hope, no matter how slim and how elusive, will provide the nourishment and strength needed to persevere in one's struggles. It's the antidote to despair, futility, and desperation.

Miraculously enough, and despite the countless disappointments of unfulfilled wishes, hope will always resurface from its eternal spring and continue to be a beacon that will guide us to shore during life's turbulence and storms.

So, while all hopes for an acquittal had been crushed, we maintained our hopes of an equitable and just penalty that the judge would impose. And I continued to hope that the portion of conversation involving the "probational offense" between the judge and the attorneys that I had overheard was the beacon by which we could navigate.

As expected, the media feasted on the jury's decision. Starting with the afternoon edition of the news, the guilty verdict made headlines again. The next day, the *Chicago Sun-Times* reported the following excerpts:

> Missbrenner testified during his trial that he wanted to return immediately, but was too busy avoiding Serbian mobsters, local police, and anti-American Serbs to surrender to U.S. officials until May. Prosecutors dismissed Missbrenner's claim as a story he concocted after he turned himself in.
>
> Family members declined to comment on the verdict, but Missbrenner's mother said before the verdict that her son had left the country only because he feared he couldn't receive a fair trial on the sexual assault charges he faces.

An attorney for the family of the girl allegedly assaulted during the 2002 party—which is pursuing a civil lawsuit against the Missbrenners—said they were satisfied with the verdict. "This is a victory for the rule of law," the attorney sad. Prosecutors said they were pleased with the guilty verdict.

Excerpts from the *Chicago Tribune* added:

On Wednesday, the jury of seven men and five women ordered lunch and began deliberations at noon. They reached a verdict at 1:30 p.m., before the food arrived. Supervising Assistant State's Atty. Peter Troy of the Bridgeview branch of the Cook County Circuit Court said, "We are satisfied and think it sends a message that the business of the court is preserved.

Since the trial was completed early in the afternoon on Wednesday, Dobrila and I still went to the jail to visit Adrian. We needed to express our continued support and assure him that this was only a temporary setback. Dobrila offered consolation by saying, "If it is a probation offense, then what better candidate to receive probation than a person who turned himself in? What message would it otherwise send to any fugitive who might consider turning himself in? Imposing a stern sentence would only deter any fugitive from such a decision.." Her logic made sense.

The remaining twenty-nine days leading up to the sentencing was a mixed bag of dreadful premonitions, futile expectations, and more foregone conclusions, sprinkled ever so lightly with the elusive prospect of a hopeful resolution involving only minimal punishment.

We talked to Adrian by phone twice every day, and visited him each Wednesday. We continued to advise and encourage him, and while we may have appeared convinced and strong, we nevertheless laughed and cried only in accordance with his feelings of pleasure and pain.

As the time drew closer to the day of reckoning, Patrick's resolve and opinions turned more cautious and ominous. "There isn't much of a choice for the judge," he cautioned. "It's a high-profile case for which the state's attorney's office has a hard-on," he continued. "And unless he wants to commit professional suicide, he's going to have to give them their pound of flesh."

Patrick was obviously preparing us for bad news. And while he continued to be optimistic and insistent that we remain positive, his own demeanor was clearly being influenced by the rhetoric and opinions of other attorneys and judges at that courthouse.

Again, it was the things that he did not say that presented us with the greatest concerns and fears. And yet he was saying them loud and clear. "During sentencing, we are allowed to present some character witnesses to speak favorably of Adrian, and whose testimony would support and encourage a lesser sentence . . . so prepare a list of individuals and let me talk to them."

Dobrila needed no further directions or encouragement, and immediately embarked on a vendetta for moral sustenance for this cause. She made a list, and checked it twice (as in a hundred times), and proceeded to contact each person.

Patrick had advised, "Friends and family members are fine, but they are expected to only say nice things about Adrian. You really need more independent individuals who could attest to his character." As a result, the first people on Dobrila's list were teachers who, from the beginning, had expressed their support to us. Sadly, of the dozen or so teachers, none of them was available to come to court. Apparently it was one thing to express support regarding such a sensitive subject in private, but totally another thing to publicly show such reinforcement. And in a way, I can understand the fallout that such public support might have entailed for these teachers. After all, Adrian had already been convicted in the media, and it seemed that the guilty verdict in the bail trial was only a prelude to bigger things to come. And no one wanted to support a brutal rapist.

Father Klees, on the other hand, immediately agreed to be a character witness. So did the parents of two of Adrian's friends, as well as a business associate of mine who had known Adrian since the boy was three. Surprisingly, a friend of our oldest son, a teacher herself, volunteered as well. This woman has since become a cherished, trusted, and close friend of ours (and not for the obvious reasons of lending her support in this regard, but for the person that she showed herself to be).

On September 9, 2005, the courthouse once again teemed with media crews and reporters to cover the sentencing of a notorious bail jumper and suspected rapist. We had mobilized our family members and friends and patiently waited in the gallery.

Once our case was called, Patrick advised Judge Smierciak of his wish to present testimony from several character witnesses. He first called the mother of a school friend of Adrian's to the stand.

Julia's clear and concise comments focused primarily on her experience with Adrian's relationship with her younger son, the brother of Tom (Adrian's friend). This boy had a slight mental handicap, which translated into the type or irrational behavior generally not appreciated by his older brother or his friends. Tom's pals, while visiting at Julia's home, would generally ignore and isolate the younger boy. But, said Julia, Adrian was different. "From virtually the first day we met Adrian, we noticed that unlike Tom's other friends, he did not ignore our younger son. In fact, it seemed as if he often spent more time with our younger son than with Tom, whether it was playing video games, tossing the ball in the yard, or even helping with homework. Tom's little brother always looked forward to Adrian's visits and even considered Adrian more his own friend than a friend of Tom's." Smiling in appreciation, Julia continued, "And this was not any single incident. It was a common occurrence every time Adrian would visit us. You just cannot teach a teenager such behavior. It's something within them that they either possess or they don't. It speaks volumes about the kind of person he is. And Adrian is a kind, considerate, and understanding individual, who was always welcome at our house. I simply cannot believe or accept that he could ever be guilty of the allegation he's accused of. It's simply not in his nature."

Julia's final heartfelt words of support touched us deeply. She pretty much set the tone for the other testimonials in support of Adrian.

Father Klees attested to Adrian's Christian beliefs and convictions, and that no matter what, he deserved the court's compassion and clemency. He argued that punishment by incarceration in prison would be grossly misguided. Such a vindictive measure served no useful purpose. I had come to understand and appreciate Father

Klees' pragmatic ability to underscore hidden values and virtues in every human being. It was more than simple forgiveness, one of the roots of Christian faith. It's that business of always turning the other cheek. Christianity, after all, will forgive anyone who truly repents, a wonderful value the law obviously cannot recognize or adopt.

David, my business associate, spoke of his experiences that began when Adrian was just a little boy. He commented that through the many years, and equally many hairstyles, he had only the best of memories of Adrian. While adjectives of kind, considerate, and understanding were once again the repeated, David extensively described Adrian's willingness to always lend a helping hand, and that it was in his nature to always lead by example rather than to follow out of necessity.

Anita, the schoolteacher, read from a prepared statement because she did not want to make a mistake or omit points she wanted to convey. She described him to be selfless and more concerned about the feelings of others than being worried about his own well-being. She confirmed that the accusations had been inconsistent to what her exposure with Adrian had been. "Please realize that Adrian is a kind soul and we must separate the person from the act . . .. We all make errors in judgment and no one wants to be judged or remembered because of a mistake. Please keep in mind Adrian should not be condemned and punished for an act of desperation. . . . The value of a person is measured in the love his friends and family have for him."

The last witness was Alice, the mother of another friend of Adrian's, who had flown in from out of town to speak in support of Adrian. She compared the association of her son, Danny, Adrian, and another boy named Kevin, to the friendship of the Three Musketeers, from Alexandre Dumas' classic novel (more like that of The Three Stooges, she later confided in private). She elaborated on the fact that since her house was close to the school that all three boys had attended, they had often congregated there. She explained that, while all three of them had been typical teenagers whose opinions on any matter varied according to the weather, Adrian had always stood out as someone whose moral barometer influenced the other two boys.

Alice explained how that friendship had been important to all three of them, and that she had dreaded the family move to a different state necessitated by her husband's job. She said that despite the distance, Adrian, Kevin, and Danny remained good friends, and that they had frequently communicated with one another.

A dramatic event in their lives, involving Danny, was singled out by Alice. Dobrila and I knew about it, and could not hold back the tears. We sobbed profusely, and I noticed that Adrian lowered his head as well and that he was shivering.

Only a handful of other friends in the courtroom had any knowledge of the events that had happened to Danny, and each of them tried unsuccessfully to keep from crying. It must have seemed strange and to anyone in the courtroom who had no knowledge of Danny's history. Obviously they couldn't know that the tears weren't due to the things being said, but instead in anticipation of the things that were going to be said.

Danny had been involved in a car accident, which affected his short-term reasoning ability. He would react to things in unexpected and unimaginable ways, only to remorsefully correct himself later on. Long before Adrian's arrest, but only shortly after his accident, Danny had visited Chicago and stayed at Kevin's house. Upon his return home a few days later, it was discovered that a significant amount of cash was missing from Kevin's house.

It turned out that Danny had taken the money. And while he denied it, Adrian talked to Danny and tried to convince him to return the cash. Adrian had even hinted that if Danny wouldn't do it, then he would. Adrian would repay it from his own money if necessary.

Alice made sure that everyone in the courtroom understood that this was not a threat by Adrian, but instead an attempt to do the right thing, to correct a situation which needed correction. To her, it exemplified Adrian's honesty and morality.

In the meantime, Alice and Danny's father had somehow been notified of this incident and confronted him. Danny finally admitted to taking the money, but confessed that he had already spent most of it. At this point, while continuously dabbing a handkerchief at my stream of tears, I noticed that even Patrick wore a sad expression. Alice continued her account of having instructed Danny to write a letter of apology to Kevin's mother, and to explain how he would repay the money he had already spent. He set to work on it in his bedroom. After a while, Alice decided to check on Danny's progress. Knowing that his attention span had been compromised by his accident, she assumed he might have fallen asleep. She slowly opened the door to his bedroom in order not to wake him.

Alice's description was calm and so matter-of-fact, that all of the crying and sobbing seemed inappropriate to observers. It must have appeared like an episode of Monty Python's Flying Circus to anyone outsider watching. Even Judge Smierciak seemed puzzled and even a little bit agitated by this spectacle.

Alice said, "I opened the door only a little bit and put my head through the opening so that I would not wake him, and as soon as I looked inside, I saw him suspended from the ceiling." Amazingly calm, she continued, "At first I didn't understand what I was seeing. But then it hit me, and all I wanted to do was close the door and have this vision go away. I hoped if I just closed the door and opened it again, I would not see . . ." She could not continue.

I was watching Judge Smierciak's face turn a dark shade of red, as he stared at Alice in astonishment. The courtroom had never been so quiet.

No further testimony was given.

The prosecution asked for the maximum fifteen years that were allowable under the statue for a Class 1 felony.

Patrick asked for probation. He pointed out that in situations like these throughout his career, almost all character witnesses would have elaborated on the progress of the accused and the improvements that they could speak about. He had never experienced a situation in which every witness consistently attested to the high moral standard of the accused and the inappropriateness of any incarceration. "Jail time is not going to change his life for the better. It's going to ruin it," Patrick pleaded. He was not suggesting or asking, he was begging.

In the end, Judge Smierciak's decision wasn't based on what had been said, even though it carried great weight. It wasn't the description of Adrian's character and moral aptitude which resulted in the sentence Judge Smierciak chose. It wasn't about the compassion of which Julia had spoken. It wasn't about his Christian morals to which Father Klees had attested. It wasn't about the willingness to help out which David had recalled. It wasn't about his friendly and thoughtful nature which Anita had described. And it wasn't about the tragic death of a boy which Alice had survived.

And yet it was.

It was the combined efforts of his family and friends, which could not be totally disregarded.

And in the end, after everything had been said and done, after everyone had a chance to do their best and do their worst, Judge Smierciak gave him six months in prison (which he knew had already been satisfied), and three years of probation.

So, I asked myself, what did this surprising ruling indicate? What can be learned from this?

Obviously, all of my fears had materialized. The prosecution's deliberate decision of selecting this trial first had resulted in the verdict they had been looking for. The fact that critical information relative to the reason for running could not be presented must certainly have played a major role in that guilty conclusion. The fact that he could not return within thirty days because of the kidnapping had been found unbelievable even though it had been truthful. And my reluctance to even proceed with the trial instead of just pleading guilty had proved intuitive and insightful.

Somehow I cannot shake the notion that Judge Smierciak had formulated his own conclusion long ago, and that the same instruments which had been used to unfairly solicit this verdict, had achieved the exact opposite, and might have actually nurtured his convictions. And one need to only look at his reference of "probational offense," which in retrospect had obviously been a signal for the prosecution. A sign which they had fortunately never picked up on.

I mentioned at the onset of this chapter that this trial has been about hope. But it has actually gone far beyond that, and has proven that no matter what the odds or obstacles one might face, determination, discipline, and a strong sense of convictions can beat even the million-to-one odds. And a little luck can't hurt, either. Or simply put, doing nothing will not work.

The next day, the following statements were made by Cook County State's Attorney Richard Devine (this would be the top chief) through the *Chicago Sun-Times*: "As prosecutors, we must accept the judge's sentence. But in this case, we are both disappointed and disturbed, especially in light of how the jury clearly found the defendant's testimony at trial to be incredible . . . .. I pledge to vigorously prosecute Missbrenner on the sexual-assault charges he still faces."

An editorial in the *Chicago Sun-Times* commented as follows: "What kind of justice is this? . . . The jury took only 90 minutes to decide Missbrenner was guilty of bail-jumping. The sentence for this is between four to 15 years. But Judge Smierciak said since Missbrenner had returned of his own volition to the U.S., since he had a clean record, he should get probation. What was the judge thinking?

"One has to wonder, if Missbrenner had been black or Hispanic, would probation have been in the cards? Fleeing the country after a charge of sexual assault in such a grave crime should warrant at least the minimum sentence. Letting Missbrenner off the hook sends a misguided message to others who may be charged with felonies. It was an injudicious decision."

Shortly after his ruling, Judge Smierciak was reassigned to a different courtroom (as in taken off this case). It was reported as a routine move.

In December of that year, Judge Smierciak retired (as in resigned his position as judge). Not a single member of the state attorney's office attended his retirement party.

CHAPTER 41

MADHOUSE MOTIONS

There was a new sheriff in town, and a new judge in the courtroom. Judge Smierciak, the judge who had heard all of the evidence over the past three years, who had witnessed all the drama, and who might have been the most qualified authority to reach the most unbiased conclusion, had been reassigned to a new courtroom by this time.

When court cases are first filed, a presiding official randomly assigns them to a judge without outside input or control. Judge Smierciak had been the initial recipient of our case based on such laconic lottery. This sudden change seemed anything but random, and unmistakably left a venomous residue of disbelief and surprise relative to the abilities of manipulation available to the State's Attorney's office.

But it must have been the "three strike" rule that had prompted such an unorthodox move. After all, Judge Smierciak had refused to modify the terms and conditions of Adrian's home confinement due to the DUI allegations, as petitioned. Second, he had been guilty of presiding over Anthony Robert's trial, which had resulted in a not-guilty verdict, and which had completely rendered the efforts of the State's Attorney's office as useless and ineffectual. Third, in some opinions, he obviously had made a grievous error in sentencing Adrian essentially to probation only, after a jury had finally delivered a guilty verdict after the trial for jumping bail.

I probably would have been upset too if I were in their shoes. But, then again, I was not being paid by the state to uphold the truth and the law, and my bias was justified. It was not my job to hold the scales of justice. That was the prosecution's obligation.

Kerry Kennedy, the new judge, had a reputation of not "rocking the boat" or "sticking his head out too far," and certainly was the perfect candidate to see things more clearly and to rule more favorably to the prosecution's interpretation of the law.

Colonial lawyer William Penn said, "Truth often suffers more by the heat of its defenders than from the arguments of its opposers."

In these proceedings, we had undoubtedly been the opposers, while the State's Attorney's office unquestionably had been the self-proclaimed defenders of this elusive truth.

Back in April 2004, Patrick had filed two motions to bring the questionable activities of the detectives to the court's attention. One motion addressed the evidence which had been illegally seized, and attempted to quash the actual arrest altogether on the basis that there had been no probable cause.

The other motion was intended to suppress all statements made by Adrian during his initial arrest.

A positive ruling in either one of these two motions would in essence default the prosecution's case because of improper procedures.

Apparently, it was too risky for the State's Attorney's office to allow Judge Smierciak's experience and prior knowledge relative to all the evidence to cloud his judgment and possibly induce him to make the wrong decision again. Interestingly enough, Judge Smierciak had presided over a similar motion in the Roberts trial, and had ruled in favor of the prosecution. However, we had witnessed those proceedings and had taken notice of the reasons for his decision. Essentially, we would have had a chance at a second bite of the apple, and could modify our motion in such a way that it would pacify and eliminate his previous reasons for ruling in the prosecution's favor.

Such a result would have been very embarrassing for the State's Attorney's office, and might have even compromised some career objectives or political aspirations.

While we recognized that this case had risen to such high notoriety, and that winning by default would be literally impossible, especially with the introduction of the new, hand picked judge, we nevertheless prepared to give it our best shot. Besides, we had to evaluate the new judge and the depth of his resolve and motivations. All the reasons which had encouraged us to go to trial in the bail-jumping case had again justified this course of action.

The trial for jumping bail was completed by September 11, 2005, and the motions related to the next trial had by then long been filed. Nevertheless, it took almost two months for the first motion to be heard. I am sure that it is probably redundant for me to even make this assertion, but the fact that Adrian had to remain in jail until his final trial must certainly have influenced the State's Attorney's office to slow down these proceedings. While we attempted to accelerate the entire process, and potentially be engaged in the final trial during the oncoming Christmas season, the prosecution was doing their part of prolonging these procedures as much as possible.

We had hoped that a "Christmas Jury" might be caught up in the joyous spirit of the holidays, and that a favorable verdict could be more easily obtained as a result. But the prosecutors, acting the part of Scrooge, must have had similar feelings as they routinely declined all suitable trial dates for hearing these motions, which might have accomplished our objective.

On November 7, 2005, we were finally able to argue the first motion. On the day of the hearing, Patrick unexpectedly asked to speak to Dobrila and me in the hallway. He informed us that Michael Deno, one of the prosecutors, had suggested to him that we should make an offer for a plea agreement, which might make this and any other trials unnecessary.

Patrick could not give us any compelling reasons why such a suggestion might have been made, and while he was reluctant to admit that this was a good omen relative to the strength of our ensuing motion and argument, he did encourage us to come up with an offer that he could present.

Adrian was delayed in transport from the prison, and the actual hearing was postponed until 2:00 p.m. This gave us enough time to ponder and second-guess the merits of the suggestion, as well as the terms and conditions of the offer that we might want to present.

I am an optimist who is always concerned about the bad things that can happen when you least expect them. And this inquiry regarding an offer certainly seemed to have the unmistakable makings of a trap baited by things too good to have been true. And while we were contemplating the tradeoffs that we might want to consider with a plea bargain, I kept reminding myself that it was always a lot easier to resist the temptation of the bait than to struggle on its hook. Besides, it was always a bad idea to bargain against yourself. In my mind, the reason for asking us to make an offer, rather than making the first offer themselves, was clearly an attempt to gauge our resolve rather than enter into an honest negotiation. And the more thought I gave this matter, the more I convinced myself that this was only a ruthless ploy, and that no matter what we would suggest, they would turn it down. Indirectly, they would be sending us a message on their opinion of the strength of their case, or more likely, the strength of their control over this new judge.

Dobrila had her own opinion. She scolded me for making things too complicated, saying, "This isn't a chess game."

Acquiescing to her criticism, I still retorted by quoting Sigmund Freud, "Well, sometimes a cigar is just a cigar."

So we formulated an offer, which under normal circumstances would have sparked some kind of counteroffer. It didn't surprise me that the prosecution responded with initial silence, then followed it with a resounding refusal of any further negotiations. This came from Peter Troy, the supervisor of the State's Attorney's office in Bridgeview. I remember thinking, "And sometimes a cigar is anything but a cigar."

This behavior, however strange it might have appeared to me then, held no real meaning for us back then, and its real significance would not be revealed until some time later.

Proceeding with the routine motion on November 7, we argued that Adrian's rights under the Fourth Amendment of the United States Constitution had been disregarded, and that his arrest, based on the lack of any probable cause, was illegal. Furthermore, since the arrest was illegal, then any information and evidence obtained as a result could not be used in his trial.

Specifically, the motion stated that "the stop, search and arrest of petitioner [Adrian] were made without authority of a valid search or arrest warrant.?" Furthermore, it asserted that "the conduct of the petitioner prior to being stopped, searched and arrested was such as it would not reasonably be interpreted by the arresting officers as constituting probable cause or reasonable grounds that petitioner had committed or was about to commit a crime, and that during the stop, arrest and subsequent detention, the police and prosecution became aware of the existence of witnesses and other evidence all of which were the direct and indirect fruits of the stop, arrest and detention, which connected petitioner with a crime." And, it continued that "during the stop, arrest and detention, verbal and written statements were elicited from petitioner, the detention having provided the police with the forum of interrogation."

Finally, it petitioned "this court to quash the stop and arrest of petitioner because of the absence of authority or probable cause to effect such arrest and to suppress from introduction into evidence all statements, utterances, reports of gestures and responses by petitioner during the detention and all other knowledge and the fruits thereof, witnesses, statements, whether written, oral or gestural, physical evidence, photographs and observations which are the direct and indirect product of the stop, search and arrest."

It was a well-thought-out plan of attacking the illegal behavior of the arresting detectives, and clearly identified the legal ramifications.

The prosecution, nevertheless, argued that the detectives, being reasonable and experienced officers of the law, had enough reason and probable cause to pursue an arrest. They pointed out that the detectives' insight, intuition, and experience with criminals could not be disregarded. In addition, they claimed that they had the testimony of the alleged victim, as well as the written statement of Jenny Weller, which had guided their actions.

Patrick countered by arguing that there were too many inconsistencies with the testimony of the alleged victim and Jenny Weller relative to the events which had occurred, and that as a result, the detectives' decisions and actions were not justifiable. As proof, he offered the claim that the alleged victim had insisted on only having had one or two gulps of a drink, while Jenny had testified that the accuser had at least five or six drinks before she had gotten ill.

The whole incident had been triggered by the alleged victim's claim, based on information she had heard from Jenny, that she had been raped. It had not been her own recollection, but instead the recollection of Jenny. But recollections have a tendency of being embellished and modified as they are passed from one person to another, and Patrick's point was that the detectives received all of the incriminating evidence based on embellished information, and that they modified that information afterward to actually match up with the actual events that had taken place.

Patrick told the judge, "We don't know what the alleged victim actually testified to, and we don't know if that testimony is properly and accurately reflected in the detective's report. So, before any decisions can be made relative to the correct information on which the detectives based their actions, we would need to verify the testimony of the alleged victim."

The judge was not persuaded and asked if there were any other points Patrick wanted to raise.

Frustrated, Patrick said, "Look, your honor, we don't know if the detectives lied, whether they made up any parts of their report, or whether the alleged victim was lying, or whether Jenny was lying. But based on all the evidence we have been able to collect, we know for certain that somebody was lying." He offered the bait, hoping to catch some kind of response.

The argument was obviously too reasonable and too convincing to turn down. The judge agreed to hear further substantiation of the argument. Patrick, in response, asked for the alleged victim, Conny Skinner, to take the stand in order to examine her testimony and to compare it with the written report of the detectives. This immediately caused a flurry of objections, all of which included the claim that ample evidence showed that the alleged victim did not remember any details, and that any further examination would only serve to re victimize her.

The reason for their argument against further interrogating the alleged victim seemed equivalent to the resounding "because" which my sons had often subjected me to as their compelling explanations during their early years.

Incredibly, the judge found that the highly technical answer of "because" was sufficient, and he ruled in favor of the prosecution. They would not be required to produce the alleged victim for examination. He also ruled in support of the prosecution's argument, that under the provisions of child pornography, the mere fact that sex had taken place, regardless of the circumstances, was sufficient for an accusation.

While this might have been a proper argument, I did not recall that any evidence regarding the alleged victim's actual age had ever been presented. It had been the "because" factor in, "because she was only 16 years old," which seemed to satisfy the judge once again.

Our motion was resoundingly denied.

While we lost this particular battle, the war had only started. And the judge's ruling had provided us with some valuable ammunition in case we needed to appeal the verdict of the final trial.

It took almost another full month to schedule the hearing of our second motion. This one addressed the fact that Adrian had asked for, but been denied, the counsel of an attorney during his arrest. The right to an attorney is one of the most highly regarded privileges of every American, and is outlined in the Fifth, Sixth, and Fourteenth Amendments to the United States Constitution. If they are denied, then statements made by the arrested suspect are not admissible in a court of law.

In essence, this was the same motion filed by Anthony Roberts' attorney, but had been ruled against by Judge Smierciak. The basis for his decision was that he accepted as truthful testimony by the detectives, but didn't believe Anthony. Patrick had carefully evaluated the transcripts of that trial in an effort to avoid presenting the same arguments made by Roberts' attorney. He also would not omit the damaging evidence—the handwritten, unsigned statement from Anthony Roberts in which he had requested an attorney. And even though Barrett had written that request himself, he never provided an attorney to Anthony. And what's even more amazing, Barrett had testified under oath that he was not aware of such a request.

The hearing took place on December 5, 2005, and like the previous court session, was attended by only a smattering of reporters. The first witnesses called to the stand were detectives Davis and Gleason. Their testimony was inconsistent regarding several events that had occurred, and appeared to conflict with statements they made as witnesses in the Roberts' trial. One clearly related to the time of the arrest. During Roberts' trial, the detectives maintained that the boys had not been taken into custody until they had been interrogated at the police station. Now, they claimed that the arrest had occurred at the house where the suspects had been first picked up. While this inconsistency might not have an impact on the case, it would strike me as unimaginable that such an important fact would not have been properly recorded.

The first matter Patrick addressed with them was the Miranda Statement all of the boys had signed. It is one of the most familiar of legal statements, and reads:

> You have the right to remain silent. If you give up that right, anything you say can and will be used against you in a court of law. You have the right to an attorney and to have an attorney present during questioning. If you cannot afford and attorney, one will be provided to you at no cost. During any questioning, you may decided at any time to exercise these rights, not answer any questions, or make any statements.

This advisory, which varies slightly from state to state, is firmly grounded in the law. Investigators are allowed to ask the suspect to sign a document acknowledging that they have been "Mirandized." Signing such a statement ordinarily does not mean the suspect is waiving the right to have an attorney present.

The prosecution offered the signed statements as positive proof that the rights to an attorney had been clearly made. And, they insisted, none of the boys, including Adrian, had requested an attorney. They pointed to his signature on the statement as proof.

The Miranda waiver that had been used indicated that, by signing the statement, the accused had understood those rights. By signing the statements, the boys had understood that they had those rights. Period. Nowhere did it say that they were giving up those rights.

Judge Kennedy carefully listened to the argument made by Patrick, but finally ruled that the intent of the Miranda Waiver was implied, and that a waiver was automatically understood to have been included.

"Come on, judge," Patrick's insisted. "How can anyone possibly argue with a written document. It is in writing so that nothing could be assumed as being implied."

The judge was not going to explain his decision, and simply instructed Patrick to move on. The anger was evident in Patrick's face. He couldn't believe that Judge Kennedy could sit there and say these things. Furious, Patrick made his feelings known by slamming his notepad on to the defense table.

The next witness was Assistant State Attorney Barrett, who had written the statements offered to the boys for signatures. Patrick attempted to prove that he was a lying bastard by introducing the corrected statement which Barrett had attempted to persuade Anthony Roberts to sign. It was the statement on which Barrett had added in his own handwriting that Anthony had requested an attorney. Yet, in the Roberts trial, Barrett had testified that he never heard Anthony request an attorney.

Judge Kennedy would not allow this into evidence, as that trial had long been over with, and Adrian's written statement had no correction with it.

While Patrick attempted to attack Barrett's credibility in general, the judge was only concerned about his actions as they applied to Adrian. In the end, our motion was again denied.

Judge Kennedy obviously seemed to understand the reason why he had been assigned to this case.

In the final status hearing before the actual trial, in January 2006, prosecutors Michael Deno and Cheryl Schroeder had another dispute with Patrick Campanelli. They could not agree which portions of the videotape should be shown to the jury in the trial. The prosecutors wanted to use only the second part of the tape, which showed Adrian. Patrick wanted the entire tape to be seen, as it showed the earlier behavior of the alleged victim, in which she was alert, responsive, and cooperative with the sexual antics.

Because no agreement could be reached, Judge Kennedy decided that it was finally time for him to see the tape. He, Campanelli, Deno, and Schroeder assembled in the judge's chambers to view it. Approximately twenty minutes later, all four of them returned to the courtroom. Patrick was grinning uncontrollably, unable to hide his excitement. Schroeder's and Deno's stern expressions betrayed their anger. The judge had decided to allow the whole tape into evidence.

But that was not the reason for the attorneys' variance in demeanor. It was based on a comment Judge Kennedy had made to the prosecutors after he watched the tape.

Patrick told us, "I can't believe that I actually heard what the judge said. He looked at Cheryl and Mike and asked them, point blank, what it was they were trying to accomplish with this case."

According to Patrick, Kennedy had said, "What I see on this tape is consent."

To us, Patrick expounded, "Kennedy thinks that the tape shows the girl was clearly cooperating." And before we could fully appreciate the impact of this, Patrick added, "I should have asked for a bench trial instead of a jury."

"My God!" was the only comment I could think of. This was too good to be true.

CHAPTER 42

THE BEST-LAID PLANS

"**B**ut it's the truth, even if it didn't happen," protested one of the unstable characters in the book, One Flew Over the Cuckoo's Nest.

Of the 140 counts which the Grand Jury had originally included in the indictment of Adrian, only four counts ultimately made it to court for the big trial. The other 136 counts, all represented as the truth at the time, now had apparently not happened after all.

Two of those four surviving counts consisted of criminal sexual assault, and the other two were child pornography. The penalty, if guilty could still be anywhere from six to thirty years in prison.

It had taken nearly five more months since the trial for jumping bail before the prosecution was ready to proceed with the main trial. And as time drew closer, we became increasingly more nervous. The prosecution's three-year pursuit of justice had, after all, broken our nerves just a little bit.

We also became increasingly angry. Somehow it would have been easier to accept the willful misrepresentations from a civil opponent, rather than from the government. Their obligation, after all, was to remain impartial and to simply uphold justice and protect the truth. Also, we had become more confused because of the conflicting information we had tried to process. The comments made by Judge Kennedy, when he had seen the tape, had obviously not made any impact on the prosecution's course of actions, as they continued to press forward, rather than resolve this issue through a plea bargain, which would avoid any potential embarrassments, such as another defeat. Unless, of course, they still felt confident that this judge was steering the case in accordance with their guidelines, and along their chosen path.

But we also still had hope, and we continued to believe in our cause and vindication. We believed that we had prepared ourselves as best as we possible could. Most important, we were able to rely on the knowledge that we had one very important witness on our side, who could attest to the events which actually took place on that December weekend in 2002. That witness was Anthony Roberts, who had already been acquitted of the same charges, despite the fact that his DNA had been found at the scene. He was in the room when all of the alleged incidents took place. His testimony could clarify exactly what took place and supersede all the speculation. An eyewitness account, from someone who no longer had any vested interest in the outcome, should carry substantial weight with the jury.

For the defense, Anthony could explain activities not shown on the tape. Things like the fact that the alleged victim had carefully folded her clothes after she took them off. Events such as her saucily picking the boys she wanted to have sex with, and occurrences during the actual sexual encounter, like her attempts at keeping Adrian's penis erect, which had obviously and purposely not been recorded. All the information he would have testified about if he had been called to the stand during his own trial. But he had been found innocent without testifying, and all this information had never been revealed.

And because he could not be retried and found guilty now, he could tell the whole truth and nothing but the truth without fear. And because of that very important reason, we had insurmountable hope.

Hope that justice would finally be served.

Hope that the lies would finally be swept aside.

Hope that Adrian could finally leave that hellhole of human despair and moral indifference.

We were desperate to reach the day that would provide vindication. And at the same time, we dreaded the possibility of a final outcome that might somehow and inexplicably be unfavorable. We knew that we held the winning lottery ticket, yet we feared that we might have mistakenly chosen the wrong numbers. Unlike anything I had experienced in my life, including my own dread of the medical test results for cancer, and what they finally revealed, nothing had caused me such a high concentration of mixed emotions. While I was still recovering from the unrelenting pain and insurmountable sorrow relative to my son's treatment, I was exposed to a new onslaught of anxiety, concern, and fear that rippled across every conscious thought. And yet I subconsciously experienced unimaginable jubilation that this dreadful day had finally arrived.

Anthony Roberts' trial had resulted in an acquittal of the two counts of aggravated criminal sexual assault. Because he was only briefly visible in the video recording, he was not charged with child pornography. His attorney had elected to keep the proceedings to a bare minimum, and had not presented any witnesses.

But that was then.

And if Judge Smierciak were still on the bench, we might have done the same thing.

But this was now.

The rules had changed and the scales of justice seemed tilted and unbalanced. We felt that we had to go all out. In accordance with this, we had issued subpoenas to every conceivable witness who could support our cause. Specifically, there were three more individuals, aside from Anthony Roberts, on whom we relied for favorable testimony. These three were Jenny Weller, Sal Begaj, and Jeff Brost.

Jenny Weller, the girl who had been only an acquaintance of the accuser and who had introduced her to Adrian, had been unavailable (as in declined to volunteer) for any of the other hearings. I am certain that she must have been intimidated and frightened by the detectives, the prosecutors, and the grand jury. The decision to stay out of this confrontation as much as possible must have appeared as the only logical solution for her. But she had to respond to the subpoena. In fact she did a lot more. She appeared to cooperate with us as much as she could. But while we were ecstatic about her help, Patrick was somewhat reserved, and cautioned us about negative things that might be revealed. Those items could include the fact that she would testify that the alleged victim had passed out, that she believed that Adrian had been in the spare bedroom during the third and insulting part of the evening, which might make him an accomplice in those activities, and that she had seen the tape, which might support the prosecution's assertion of "dissemination of child pornography." She would also state that she had been in our house on numerous occasions and during numerous parties that involved alcohol consumption.

We nevertheless insisted that the positive information she could provide would far outweigh any negative aspects. Information which included the fact that the alleged victim had told her, "I don't care who I meet, I just want to get laid." Also, that Jenny had seen Conny drink and flirt with several boys at the party, that Conny had walked into the spare room and voluntarily participated in the sex and the taping, and finally that she had confided in Jenny that, "I had a wonderful time," just before Jenny had left the party that early morning.

Throughout all this, Jenny firmly and consistently maintained a pure and simple fact: that the alleged victim had participated in sexual acts because she had wanted to do them, not because she was forced or because she might have been incapable of preventing them.

Sal, a cousin of Tarek, the other youth who had skipped bail, had been at the party for a short time only, and had left before the sexual activities commenced. He too would testify to the fact that the accuser was drinking and flirting with the boys there. In addition, he would repeat a startling comment he'd made to us. Sal had said, "I was sitting on Adrian's bed watching TV, when these two girls arrived. I knew Jenny, but I had never seen the other girl before. I immediately realized that she was out of my league, and that she was way too much maintenance to be interested in me." He added, "She was slamming vodka with Jimmy and bragged about the clubs that she liked going to, but I soon realized that I had no chance with her when I saw her pull out a package of condoms and hand one of them to my cousin, and the other one to Adrian." This was a bombshell, and could have an explosive effect on the jury.

Actually, we had talked to Sal on several occasions, but it wasn't until two days before the trial that he stunned us with this revelation about the condoms. He said he hadn't thought the information very important. Of course, to us it clearly indicated Conny's intentions. It could not possibly get any clearer that she had wanted to have sex.

In addition, I was also going to testify to the fact that I had called the police to file a complaint after the accuser returned to my house in an effort to get the videotape. She assured me that nothing had happened, that she had not been raped, and that this had all been a big misunderstanding. Because of these assurances, and because I had feared that her story might change over time, I decided to summon the police. And this would have been a perfect opportunity for her to file a complaint. It would have given her the chance to tell investigators what allegedly terrible things had happened to her. Instead, she ran away before the police arrived.

The third new witness we planned to bring in was the individual who had kept the videotape for a short time before handing it over to the police.

Finally, we were armed with the knowledge that a jury had already found Anthony Roberts not guilty of the charges, and while this information was not admissible as evidence, we knew that Patrick would somehow make that known to the jury. We felt that we had the means to repel the prosecution's assault. We had picked the winning horse (with all four legs), and while we watched it struggle and beat all of the odds and opponents, we still feared that the prosecution somehow had the power to make it stumble and fall before it crossed the finish line.

The more that we replayed this sum total of information in our minds, the more it seemed we had a chance to survive. Patrick continued to caution us, however, that all of our witnesses would be characterized by the prosecution as biased friends and relatives of the defendant. He feared they would challenge the integrity of the witnesses, and insist that the information being presented would be a far cry from the actual truth.

He also reminded us that all of the witnesses, and all of the information so far, had only addressed the assault charges.

The child pornography issues, he said, presented a completely different set of problems. First, these charges would be much harder to defend, because the law was set up to protect young victims, and did not give a lot of leeway for a defense. And, he explained, the prosecution could be selective in whom they would charge. Even though the alleged victim might have participated, in fact even if she had organized the whole party, they could elect not to charge her. Second, the fact that anyone had seen the recording, or that it was passed to any other person, could be grounds for a guilty verdict. And Jenny had admitted seeing the tape. Third, the tape was passed on to Jeff for safekeeping, which could be interpreted as dissemination, even though he had given the tape to the police in the end.

Patrick's strategy essentially involved clarification that child pornography laws were intended to protect children from being taken advantage of by mature adults. As such, the fact that Adrian was still a child himself as far as that law was concerned (under age eighteen) should not subject him to charges under this law. As far as viewing the tape, his defense would educate the jury that Adrian had not been involved in showing the tape, and thus could not be accused under this charge. Finally, regarding Jeff's involvement, the defense would rest on the fact that Jeff had been instructed to hold on to the tape so that it could be given to an attorney if the accusations were lodged against the boys. And Jeff was prepared to testify that he had never viewed the tape.

By way of further explanation, Patrick said, "They will attempt to simplify the charges, and claim that the jurors can only rule one way. Because it had happened was all that mattered. It was the "because" reasoning and rationale all over again. An effort will be made to persuade jurors that the authority vested in them means they have no alternative but to uphold the law and come back with a guilty verdict. This charge might be our Achilles heel."

Even though Patrick would not let on, we sensed that he, too, was satisfied with the strength of our defense as far as the assault charges were concerned. And he knew that the prosecution must have realized that their case by now had lost much of its momentum. They couldn't have totally disregarded Judge Kennedy's comment about his interpretation of the tape. Yet they had made no attempts at offering any kind of settlement.

This could only mean one thing. Their focus had shifted. It was an uphill battle to obtain a guilty verdict on the assault charges. After all, one jury had already found Anthony Roberts not guilty in that particular area, and their "scorched earth" approach of pursuing only one major charge in his case had backfired. They needed a powerful backup claim, and it was becoming clear that the child pornography charges were going to give them the leverage they needed.

The prosecution could live with a guilty verdict in this matter. It was the lesser of two evils, and the penalty was significantly less, so a jury could potentially be enticed to settle on a guilty verdict here. They were giving up the home run and instead hoped to score a guilty verdict with an infield hit. They just needed some kind of guilty verdict; any guilty verdict would do. And even though Judge Kennedy had made some disparaging and discouraging comments, those comments had applied to the assault charges only.

Their trust must have remained with the judge, and they were still relying on him to allow only evidence which would primarily benefit the prosecution. While the judge would not make the decision regarding guilt or innocence, he could starve our mission by not allowing critical evidence to be presented. We had experienced this with the exclusion of the Barrett evidence involving Roberts's case, during the pre trial motions.

It appeared that we had a fifty-fifty chance on the sex assault charges, but considerably worse odds in the child-pornography part of the trial.

CHAPTER 43

FINAL BATTLE

It took only two days starting Monday morning, February 27, 2006, to select twelve people who would decide the pivotal point of my son's life. By Tuesday afternoon, seven women and five men sat in the jury box, ready to perform their civic duty under Judge Kennedy's watchful eye. They were a cross section of ethnicity; two African American women, one Hispanic man, three white men, three white women, and three African American men including the foreperson, a school principal.

News reporters couldn't even get that information right.

According to the *Chicago Sun-Times* newspaper, the jury consisted of six men and six women.

According to *The Chicago Tribune* newspaper, the jury consisted of five men and seven women.

According to the *Suburban Life* newspaper, Judge Smierciak was still on the bench.

According to all of them, Adrian appeared guilty and had sought refuge from his guilt by fleeing to Serbia.

Testimony seemed to move along rapidly, or perhaps that just reflected our long experience and numerous weeks sitting in courtrooms. The prosecution called the same parade of witnesses we had seen before. Assistant State's Attorney Barrett once again testified to the accuracy and credibility of his actions during the initial arrest proceedings back in 2002. His answers were somewhat vague as to why no one had bothered to record various statements taken by investigators. It finally turned out that his department did not have the financial resources to record the activities which he had professed to be the complete and unadulterated truth. According to him, the Cook County State's Attorney's office did not have the budget to buy a tape recorder and a few tapes for a case that must have cost them millions of dollars in pursuing a guilty verdict.

Detective Davis testified to the accuracy and credibility of his actions, and appeared proud to inform everyone that he had since been promoted for the reliable and trustworthy work he had performed in the course of his duties.

FBI Agent Stover again told of his experience in Serbia and confirmed that it had been Adrian's surrender which resulted in his return to the U.S.

It amazed us when the prosecution did not call Jeremy Culp to testify in this trial. He had been their main witness in the Roberts's case. Perhaps his testimony hadn't met their expectations.

Conny Skinner, the alleged victim, repeated her claim that she was not able to remember anything that had happened that early morning in 2002. Appropriately dressed this time, she behaved more demurely, a drastic change from her appearance and demeanor while testifying in the Roberts trial.

But the Roberts case was then. It was a much simpler trial, almost like a rehearsal, which provided everyone with an opportunity to ready themselves for the big show, this trial. Adrian, after all, was the rich kid from Burr Ridge.

Patrick, too, had done some careful preparation, and saved his best for last. Because of the prosecution's overprotective nature during pre-trial motions in not producing the alleged victim, Conny, as a witness, he knew that he had to concentrate his focus on her, and to continue mining until he hit an artery. He could smell weakness in his prey, and recognized an opportunity to find a rich strike. He only had to look in the right places.

And gold he found.

First, Patrick requested of the accuser to verify the information on the videotape. He made a production of moving the TV monitor into position so that she could clearly see the screen.

Conny frowned, squirmed in the witness chair, and then refused to view the tape.

Stalking his prey, Patrick shrugged and pointed out that without such verification, there would be no legal basis to admit the video tape as evidence, as no one had testified to its authenticity or to the accuracy of the information on the tape. "Your honor," he said, "without the accuser's verification, no evidence exists to show that this is the tape which was allegedly made during the party." He explained, "I tried to have her testify in this regard during pre trial motions, but the court denied that opportunity, and there is absolutely no basis or foundation for its admission into evidence."

The tactic seemed to catch the prosecution with their pants down. Everyone had assumed that this was the correct tape, but no witness had ever identified it as the actual tape in question. Patrick elaborated. "In fact, your honor, the sixth amendment to the Constitution requires that the accused be granted the right to question the accuser and the evidence that is brought against him."

Judge Kennedy frowned. He had to agree with the defense attorney's simple and convincing argument.

Conny, though, felt no compunction to agree, and continued her refusal to view the tape.

Prosecutor Cheryl Schroeder leaped to her feet, almost screaming her objections. Her voice shook as she argued that forcing Conny to view the tape would re victimize her, and that only one tape had ever existed. "Mr. Campanelli only wants to humiliate and embarrass this woman . . .that's what this is all about," Schroeder insisted.

Patrick would not relent. He had cornered his prey and was moving in for the kill. "I take this as a personal insult," he shouted as he jumped up. "The witness has told us that she was unconscious," he reminded, while pointing to her. "The prosecution's argument is ridiculous. All the law I know says that the defendant's rights come before the victim's rights. And that's what we're having this trial for.

It's my contention that she hasn't been shown to be a victim yet. Those are rules that protect the innocent . . . If she refuses to abide by the regulations and requirements, judge, then I move to have this tape barred as evidence."

A low grumble rose from the spectators as both sides waged a key battle in this war. Judge Kennedy announced his decision. He ordered the witness to view the tape.

Conny again refused.

Judge Kennedy warned her that if she disobeyed his order, she could be charged with contempt of court.

Adamant, Conny still refused.

Turning to face her, Judge Kennedy threatened possible jail time until such time that she would view the tape.

Conny shook her head in the negative, and voiced yet another refusal.

Visibly agitated, Judge Kennedy sat silent, as if pondering his next move. Observers wondered if he had ever encountered such a stubborn witness, a 20-year-old woman totally rejecting his orders. Totally disobeying the sanctity that was the law. Making a complete mockery of his courtroom.

Patrick attempted to strike while the iron was hot, and immediately motioned the court that this case be dismissed.

But Judge Kennedy chose to let things cool off by giving the witness until ten o'clock the next morning to decide whether she would view the tape or risk the consequences, which would include the possibility of jail time. He informed Patrick that he would make a ruling on the motion for dismissal at the same time.

Nobody in the courtroom was prepared for this unusual turn of events. And I must admit that I was impressed by Conny's resolve and determination. Had I not been so convinced of my own righteousness and so firmly embedded in my own beliefs, I would have considered her as quite a courageous individual who was unwilling to compromise her own beliefs and stand up for her convictions. I'm not sure that I would have had the balls to do what she did.

But there was another possible side of the story. One of my other attorneys suggested that this whole thing might have been orchestrated by the prosecution as a ploy to prevent Conny from incriminating herself by impeaching her own prior testimony. She would have been caught red-handed through cross-examination by Patrick, which would have focused on her appearance of being fully awake and conscious on the tape. It would have been nearly impossible for her to avoid contradicting what she had previously said about passing out.

No doubt, the prosecution would prefer to shield her from getting caught red-handed, which would be much worse than mere speculations that she might have been lying.

The maelstrom of news unfolding that evening was something to behold. Every newspaper reported the unjust order imposed by the judge. Every newscast was outraged over the victim's treatment. Bill O'Reilly on his nightly show, "The O'Reilly Factor," spewed his vitriolic objections. A former judge, appearing as a legal analyst, defended Judge Kennedy's ruling, inspiring the host to call his guest a "pinhead."

Three separate advocacy groups, supporters of victims' rights, were widely interviewed, stating plans to file an appeal for the victim if the judge did not change his mind. I was amazed at the speed by which these groups had been mobilized, and had to wonder if the State's Attorney's office might not have had some role therein. Their assertion that the accuser had automatically been an innocent victim without the due process of the law certainly tarnished their image a little bit.

Illinois Governor Rod Blagojevic (you guessed it, a Serb) vowed legislative changes to prevent victims from being re victimized in this manner. This issue had arisen during the primary elections, and supporting popular opinions, even ones that had not been verified, always translated well at the polls. However, poetic justice would be done, when in 2009, on the eve of his impeachment proceedings stemming from his malfeasance involving the vacated Senate seat of now President Barak Obama, Governor Blagojevic pleaded on national TV that his constitutional rights had been violated because he was not allowed to present any evidence in support of his innocence. At the time of my son's trial, he was supporting the notion of withholding evidence if it adversely affected the alleged victim, while under more urgent circumstances (as in circumstances that affected him directly), he insisted that every individual was guaranteed that right (interestingly enough, he had quoted the same Amendments of the Constitution that we had raised ourselves). He must either have finally seen the errors of his ways, or he was simply still being a politician.

The *Chicago Tribune* newspaper ran a background check on Judge Kennedy and informed their readers that he had been accused of legal improprieties on five occasions during his tenure as an attorney.

The nation was in shock and its citizens were outraged. Everyone seemed to have forgotten a similar instance in 1995 during which a young woman had been jailed for refusing to testify against then U.S.-Representative Mel Reynolds, who was accused of raping her when she was sixteen years old. She decided to testify after seven days of incarceration. Reynolds was convicted based on her testimony. Might this not have set a precedent and be viewed as an appropriate guideline?

When we arrived Wednesday morning, Patrick appeared to be somewhat nervous. Before we entered the courtroom, he greeted us by saying, "There are at least twenty state's attorneys in there, including Dick Devine." I understood why our lawyer was shaken. Richard A. Devine was the Cook County State's Attorney, the alpha dog, chief of the 900-person State's Attorney's organization. His presence signaled the importance of the case to them. And the white-haired leader had brought a sizeable entourage with him. It was like the Chicago Bears taking on a high-school football team.

Our players consisted of Patrick, Robert Pervan, and Nicole Olovito. Robert was a friend of the family and had just passed his bar examination. His main purpose was to take notes and do any last-minute research in case unexpected issues popped up. Nicole was Patrick's secretary and in her early twenties. Her role was mainly a visual impact for the benefit of the jury. She was young and pretty, and sat next to Adrian. And Adrian, of course, was the dangerous rapist the prosecution had targeted for the past three years. We hoped that his rapist image might be smoothed a bit by the presence of young and pretty girl at his side.

The first order of business on this third day of trial was the issue regarding Conny's refusal to view the tape, which had abruptly ended on Tuesday afternoon. We felt really comfortable that she would finally be subjected to cross-examination regarding the video.

Judge Kennedy once again asked Conny if she would view the tape, and indicated that this would be his last such attempt.

Conny still refused.

Kennedy stunned everyone by his total capitulation. He muttered, "Well, I am not going to make you watch this tape then."

And he refused Patrick's motion to dismiss the case without bothering to explain his reasoning. Instead, he simply instructed Patrick to continue with his cross-examination.

There was nothing Patrick could do except plow ahead. He would certainly be entitled to file an appeal later, based on the unusual behavior and rulings of Judge Kennedy. That wouldn't help Adrian much, since he would have to remain in prison during the appeal, which could easily stretch into years.

Patrick continued where he had left off the previous day. He once again showed the value of experience and his abilities as a lone wolf, which had originally convinced me to hire him. He resumed stalking his prey in search of a weakness. This was his first opportunity for attacking Conny's testimony, and he did it with methodical, unrelenting precision. I could understand the other side's concern about him. In fact, had he been a prosecutor interrogating my own son, I would have found countless reasons to be offended by his tactics, methods, and perseverance. He combined crudeness with finesse, and by applying the undisputed principles of simple math, turned the product of two negatives into a positive.

Zeroing in on Conny, he asked, "If what you say is true, and if you cannot remember anything that happened during the party, then how can you testify that you could not have possibly given your consent?" He let her process that negative for a moment, then added, "In fact, isn't is possible that you could have given your consent, but just don't remember giving it?" To observers, it seemed to balance.

But Conny equivocated, speaking in halting jerks. "I could have given consent—I don't remember." This admission resounded throughout the courtroom. Patrick had drawn first blood. But it was only the beginning.

Richard Devine and his team stayed only that one day, but another official made his presence known regularly. Peter Troy, supervisor of the state's attorney's office in Bridgeview, would come in, talk to the prosecutors, scrutinize some documents, or just sit among the spectators. I know that his presence was not meant to educate him about the proceedings, as his visits were far too brief for him to make any sense of what was going on. Instead, he was clearly sending a message that he was interested in this case, and that he was monitoring its progress. While I don't know whom the message was intended for, I certainly wondered if it was publicity he sought.

Patrick called Jenny Weller to the stand as a defense witness. She told the jury that Adrian was one of her best friends. Other comments she made were not so helpful, but she said nothing of great harm.

Sal took the stand and announced, "Adrian, I love you, but I am not going to jail for you." He testified that Conny had brought condoms with her. His demonstration of how she handled them incited a few giggles in the audience. He lifted his right hand slightly, clasped his thumb, index finger, and middle finger, and moved them back and forth, in a gesture creating the impression of ringing a bell, as he described how Conny had lifted the wrapped condoms from her purse and waved them at the boys.

Jeff's testimony was short and simple. He stated that Adrian had given him the tape and instructed him, "Hold on to his. I may need it to show to my attorney." Jeff also said that he had not seen the video, nor had he shown it to anyone.

Finally, my chance to speak came. I testified about my son's state of mind prior to his flight to Serbia. I explained the news media's heavy impact on him, and told of our continuous fears that he might repeat the attempt to kill himself. I found it disingenuous that the judge allowed the information about Adrian's flight to Serbia to be presented. It obviously was meant as evidence in support of Adrian's guilt. While this had been evidence from another trial, he had previously not allowed such a crossover. He had refused to allow any information relative to Anthony's acquittal to be presented. Our fears that only selective evidence would be admitted had obviously come to fruition.

For reasons that I did not find altogether valid, Patrick did not want to call Anthony to the stand. I thought that he would have been our star witness who would silence all critics. Patrick felt that we needed to distance ourselves from everyone else involved in this case, and that Anthony's state of mind was such that he might not be convincing in his testimony. Patrick feared that he would appear hesitant, uncertain, and confused, which could cause jurors to find him unbelievable. Plus, in Patrick's mind, we had already won the assault case, and Anthony's testimony would have been part of only that part of the defense. He could have contributed nothing helpful in the child-pornography segment.

Everyone in the courtroom knew that certain seats were reserved for the family of the defendant. As a result, it was somewhat of a surprise when a white male took a seat where Dobrila had been sitting the previous three days. Her mother, who was sitting next to her, scolded that person by telling him, in her broken English, that the seat was taken. That man just looked at her and responded that no seats can be saved, and that he could sit anywhere he pleased. And he repeated that assertion to others in the courtroom who had expressed their displeasure over his actions.

It turns out that he was Judge Sterba, who had made the decision on Adrian's home confinement and who had refused to modify his ruling after he had seen the video recording. I was genuinely surprised to see that he was interested enough to witness the proceedings rather than to just read them in the papers. But then, maybe he didn't trust the papers to report the true story.

Later on that day, I recognized another familiar face in the gallery of the courtroom. That person was Judge Smierciak. He, too, seemed interested to hear the proceedings first hand. And he appeared a little shorter without the customary black robes. He also seemed a lot friendlier.

Patrick, too, was surprised to see both judges, and confided that this was unprecedented in his experience.

By the fifth day, Friday, March 3, we felt like we had been on a roller coaster of emotions the entire week of the trial. Our hope, faith, and confidence soared to new heights every time a positive point was made for our cause, and we descended to the lowest of gloomy valleys each time things did not seem to go in our favor. In between, we seesawed along with positive expectations and anticipations as well as hopeless desperation. We would swing from utter exhilaration to desolate despair. And in the process, we often did not have the time to stop at pain, or have the resolve to be slowed down by anger. Carl Jung said it best, "There is no change from darkness to light or from inertia to movement like consciousness that is fueled by emotions."

We were finally ready for the closing arguments, which would put all the testimony and evidence into some kind of logical perspective. The prosecution presented their case first, and offered that the woman, "Made two mistakes; she got drunk and placed herself in the hands of the wrong people." They argued that, "This defendant and his friends knew that she had no idea of what was going on. They took advantage of her."

Patrick responded that being intoxicated is no excuse for someone's actions, and he pointed out that a drunk driver is still held accountable despite his intoxication.

Next he advised the jury that he was going to isolate the actions of Adrian and Conny, so that their actions could be judged without the interference of the surrounding noise and activities. He had come up with that idea only two days earlier when, late in the evening, he was viewing the tape again while preparing the notes for his arguments. He was tired, and day's exhaustion had taken a toll on his eyesight and ability to focus properly. As a result, he turned up the brightness and contrast to its highest level. In the process, and by mistake, he also turned off the volume as well. To his astonishment, the imagery that he witnessed had suddenly transformed itself into a completely different presentation. There was now no audible interference, which had always distracted him, and there were no longer any dark and shadowy images which had previously made the whole episode grainy and ambiguous. With that, he commenced to watch the tape in slow motion as a wry smile crossed his lips. Not unlike a scientist who had finally stumbled onto the right formula after countless vain attempts, so too had he discovered the irrefutable evidence that had eluded him so far.

And he now played back a few minutes in front of the jury, showing Adrian with Conny, almost frame by frame, pushing the pause button to make explanatory comments.

"Here she is placing her hand on his head She is kissing him . . . that's consent."

"Here she is rubbing the back of his head. She is smiling . . . that's consent."

"These two people are in their own world . . . their own consensual world."

In his typical manner of staging and presenting his points, Patrick paced back and forth in front of the jurors, varying his emphasis and enunciation, declaring, "This was a moral issue and not a legal issue." He concluded by summarizing that the accuser "had been insulted but not assaulted."

Michael Deno, in rebuttal, was calm and subdued, almost to the point of indifferent disbelief. He said, "Good drugs are finally paying off." He paused to let his enigmatic remark sink in. Patrick looked at him in a clear gesture that he did not understand the meaning of his words. Deno smirked and continued in his low voice and methodical delivery, "This is what it's really all about. It's about drugs . . . and what drugs can accomplish."

There was total silence in the courtroom, as everyone tried to comprehend where Deno was going with this. Deno played back a certain portion of the video, with the volume set extremely high. At a specific moment, he stopped the tape, rewound it, and then replayed it again. Only the jury was able to see the screen, but the sounds were audible for everyone in the courtroom. It sounded as if someone on the tape could have been saying those words, "Good drugs are finally paying off?" The high volume setting, though, made most of it unintelligible. Every slight sound was over-amplified, and even the normally inaudible sound of sliding your hand across a pillow suddenly sounded like an avalanche of gravel. It distorted voices, making identification of the speakers improbable, if not impossible.

Yet Deno insisted that those were the words, and that they were spoken by Adrian. He could offer no proof of this at all. As an attorney, he knew that this tactic was highly unprofessional, and that such unsubstantiated claims would never have any effect on a judge. But a jury would make the decision in this case. And a jury was much more likely to allow emotions to play a role and to let unsupported claims be construed as evidence.

After all, they didn't do this for a living.

Patrick was visibly upset, rocking in his chair while he waited for his turn to address Deno's claims.

He finally jumped up, and standing halfway between the judge and the jury, he screamed at the top of his voice, "The government is getting sleazier every day. They're grasping at straws here!" His facial expression and body language equally radiated his fury. This type of outburst is not tolerated in any courtroom, and Campanelli's reaction would put to shame the most dramatic actor playing an attorney in a court drama.

Patrick was livid. He pounded his fist on the table, he stomped his foot, and he clenched his fists. He was the lone wolf who had been ambushed, and he was not going down without a fight.

The prosecution didn't dare object to his outburst.

The judge didn't dare reprimand him for his behavior.

The audience didn't dare make any noise.

"They know that I cannot bring in any witnesses to prove they are wrong," he continued. "They know this is improper procedure." Pivoting toward the jurors, he bellowed, "They know that they didn't prove their allegations and are now trying to bully you." Glaring at the world, he said, "They had already agreed that drugs were not an issue in this case, and they agreed that drugs would not be brought up." If they had kept their word, he explained, then he would have brought in experts to prove that drugs were not involved.

After what seemed about a half hour of ranting, raving, and shouting, Patrick finally calmed down. In the end, he offered a simple explanation for all of the legal ambiguities. "This is a case of consent, shame, and regret," he concluded.

Cheryl Schroeder, in the final round of summations, said, "They treated her worse than you would a dead dog in the street . . . He claims that the tape exonerated him, but then why did he flee the country . . . For once in his life, hold this kid . . . Mr. Burr Ridge . . . responsible . . ." She ended by saying, "The defendant just got what he was afraid of getting—a fair trial."

And with that the case was finally over.

CHAPTER 44

THE VERDICT

Because the best is usually saved for last, the comments surrounding the potential drug use, and Patrick's vehement response, impressed me as being the zenith of the entire trial. I had no idea what the jury would think of it. Did it put the puzzle together for them, or leave all the pieces scattered?

I did think that too many holes had been filled with the wrong pegs. I wondered if anyone had decided exactly what type of hole needed to be plugged before they tried to find the appropriate peg. The prosecution, it seemed to me, had done the exact opposite. When they found a peg they thought they could use, they tried to force it into a place it wouldn't fit.

It was the quintessential square peg into the round hole.

Their assertion that drugs had been involved just didn't fit the hole that needed to be filled, the one with strong potential to win their case. In fact, the tape had been scrutinized and evaluated by countless experts from the time it first surfaced. Every recognizable sound had been captioned into subtitles on the video footage. And at no time had that audible portion regarding the alleged drug reference been discovered. I would find it unimaginable that anyone had tried to dub the drug reference in at the last minute, but do find it possible that there was a fair amount of embellishment in its meaning and interpretation.

After the jury had deliberated almost two hours, we heard that the jurors had an issue not totally clear to them. They wanted to know whether they had to follow the strictest terms of the law, about which they admitted having some misunderstanding, or whether they could base their decision on how they interpreted the law.

To me, that meant the jurors wanted to know if they must use a legal basis to make their decision, or could they vote with their hearts. The judge answered by telling them that they needed to decide in a way that was consistent with the instructions that had already been given to them.

My interpretation of that meaning was that I had no interpretation.

About ninety minutes later, the jury sent notification that they had another question. They were not sure of Adrian's exact age at the time of the alleged incident.

This I interpreted as something favorable. The jurors were obviously considering his age as a rationale to their decision. As far as the assault case was concerned, they would find out that there was only an eight-months difference between the accuser and the accused. As far as the pornography case was concerned, Adrian was still a minor at the time of the video recording.

No more than another half hour passed before we were informed that the jury had reached a verdict. We took our customary seats in the courtroom. Tension resonated in the silent gallery and a somber mood showed on the face of every spectator.

All of our family members and our closest friends were there to express their support for us. I noticed that neither the alleged victim, nor anyone from her family, was present. Patrick whispered to us, "It is a good sign if the jurors look at you. It generally means that they have ruled in your favor."

When the jurors filed into the box and took their seats, I did notice that they were not looking at Adrian or Patrick. I saw Patrick snap a pencil, apparently distressed about their impassive demeanor.

Because of the silence, the noise of the breaking pencil seemed like a rifle shot. Patrick bowed his head, then turned to Adrian and whispered something to him.

My heart was pounding as my stomach wrenched in discomfort. Cold sweat was making me uncomfortably hot. I suddenly felt dizzy and light-headed.

Over the course of what could only have been a few seconds, I was reliving my life. I was suddenly back at Loyola Hospital in the disposable gown and mask required of all visitors to the Intensive Care Unit, stroking Adrian's lifeless arms with my gloved hands. He lay in the incubator, only hours after his birth, now close to death because his lungs had not properly inflated in those first few minutes out of the womb. And suddenly I was scolding him for the haircut he had given himself at age five, while I could not help from laughing, because of the haircut that he had just given himself. I saw the big tears rolling down his cheeks as he promised that he would never steal any more candy again, as he attempted to convince me that he didn't need to be taught a lesson by returning the candy to the store. I remembered holding him in my arms when he was almost ten years old. It was during a sailing vacation in the Caribbean as he vomited all over me, a victim of seasickness. I was so proud when, at age fourteen, he managed to say, "Ich liebe dich," as he had learned in a high-school German class. And I relived the shock when he told me in no uncertain terms, at age sixteen, that he hated me, and that he could not wait for the day when he would move out of my house, because I would not allow him to get his driver's license until age eighteen. I heard him assure me again that nothing bad had happened that early December weekend, as I questioned him about the presence of an unknown girl at our home.

I felt Dobrila's hands squeeze mine, as she buried her face into my chest, which brought me back from my painfully fond memories.

I knew that I would not be able to hold back my tears. They would be tears of unbridled joy. Or they would be tears of unimaginable pain.

Whispered words in my ear came from Dobrila's soft voice, "I have no more tears left to cry." And I felt her shiver in painful anticipation.

Judge Kennedy was handed the ballots. He looked at them for a few seconds. He seemed to be reacting to the realization of some foregone conclusion. I noticed that he could not help himself from smiling, before he handed the papers back to the bailiff. "Please read you verdict," he said to the jury foreperson.

It was a spectacle of constricting tension, increased exponentially with every second that ticked away.

"We, the jury, find the defendant, Adrian Missbrenner?."

Believing the best, dreading the worst, and not willing to accept any partial innocence, I could not believe the verdict when it was finally read.

And of course I cried.

I cried as we were giving our response to the media, because we were compelled to finally vent our frustrations.

I cried on our way home.

And I cried when Adrian finally came home after the prison doors were opened for him.

It was finally over.

He was innocent on all counts.

CHAPTER 45

LIFE BEGINS AGAIN

A drian's future finally arrived at approximately 4:00 p.m. on Friday, March 3, 2006. Judge Kennedy congratulated him on his vindication and seemed relieved and genuinely happy about the outcome. I had obviously and mistakenly identified his smile as a sign of some cruel gratification, when it now appeared to have been an acknowledgement of a more sincere satisfaction for the exact opposite reason. The DUI charges were inexplicably dropped by the state.

One of the two officers who had guarded Adrian waited until he was taken out of the spectators' sight, then playfully tousled his hair in an expression of joy. A second officer hugged him, and in the process, lifted him off the ground. Ten others, who had been assigned as additional protection when controversial issues raised public ire, offered congratulations and shook his hand. They seemed relieved to dispense with manacles and the bulletproof vest as they escorted him back to the jail to be officially released. News of the verdict had reached the cellblock, resulting in congratulations and embraces from smiling inmates and guards. No one could remember the last time an inmate from Division 1 had been allowed to go home. The great majority of inmates usually left en route to other prisons. At 10:30 p.m., on that same date, Adrian walked out of the Cook County Jail as a free man, and into the waiting arms of his mother.

In the aftermath, reactions to the acquittal varied widely. A few of the jurors helped the public understand, while reporters kept the controversy alive.

I don't see how you can second guess two juries who have seen and heard all of the evidence, including the damning fact that Missbrenner had fled the country . . . Even in a lurid case where we in the news media ascribe guilt to the accused from the day they are charged, there still has to be a presumption of innocence in court.
—**Mark Brown,** Eye Witness Reporter
   Chicago Sun-Times, March 5, 2006

It's very unfortunate that she [the alleged victim] or her mother didn't view the tape, so they could see what was on it . . . The tape was the linchpin in deciding for acquittal.

You couldn't see what we saw. If you did, there was reasonable doubt . . .

Women [on the jury] were especially troubled by the video and the testimony, which they felt raised doubts about her contention that she did not give consent.
—**James E. Patrick,** Jury Foreman
   Chicago Tribune, March 9, 2006

All we had to do was to see the tape to decide. From what we saw on the tape, it was consensual.
—**Meredith Marran,** Juror
   Chicago Tribune, March 9, 2006

The girl's parents said that they were told by prosecutors the case against Missbrenner was shaky, particularly if their daughter first didn't watch the videotape of the sexual activities.
—**Dan Rozek,** Eye Witness Reporter
   Chicago Sun-Times, March 9, 2006

Patrick Campanelli suggested if prosecutors had shown the girl the tape in the first place so that she could see for herself what it depicted, there might never have been a criminal prosecution. In light of the verdict, it makes you think.

It's one thing to say that a woman shouldn't have to watch a video of herself being raped, but what if it doesn't show her being raped?
—**Mark Brown**, Eye Witness Reporter
Chicago Sun-Times, March 5, 2006

Jurors were shocked when prosecutors alleged in closing arguments that Missbrenner could be heard on the tape saying, 'good drugs are paying off.' The jury watched the tape four times during the week long trial, but the audio was never strong enough for them to hear that.
—**James E. Patrick**, Jury Foreman
Chicago Tribune, March 9, 2006

If drugs had been used, then by her own admission she had vomited everything that she had drank, which must have included any possible drugs.
—**Patrick Campanelli**, Defense Attorney

During my trial, I purposely asked several times whether she had vomited up everything that she had drank at the party. I did this in order to eliminate any speculation about any drug use accusations.
—**Robert Kuzas**, Defense Attorney Anthony Roberts

This case was brought in good faith based on the evidence we had of a young girl being assaulted. We have no second thoughts about bringing this case . . . As for the acquittal, we don't agree with the verdict, but we respect it.
—**John Gorman**, State's Attorney Spokesman
Chicago Sun-Times, March 4, 2006

In their own closing, prosecutors turned up the sound, highlighting a snippet in which they said Missbrenner could be heard saying, 'Good drugs are paying off . . .' That drew an emotional outburst from Campanelli, who accused prosecutors of getting sleazier every day, because they had never previously suggested the girl was drugged. It struck me as desperate, too, the first sign they knew the case was weak.

—**Mark Brown**, Eye Witness Reporter
Chicago Sun-Times, March 5, 2006

We bent over backwards to work with the girl's family and to convict Missbrenner.

—**John Gorman**, State's Attorney Spokesman
Chicago Sun-Times, March 6, 2006

We had no evidence to support the use of drugs.

—**John Gorman**, State's Attorney Spokesman
Chicago Sun-Times, March 7, 2006

We turned that [the plea bargain for a misdemeanor] down. We thought the evidence was that this was a felony.

—**John Gorman**, State's Attorney Spokesman
Chicago Sun-Times, March 7, 2006

Before Missbrenner's trial, prosecutors rejected a proposed deal that would have seen Missbrenner agree to plead guilty to a misdemeanor charge . . . In return, prosecutors would have dropped the felony assault charge . . .

—**Dan Rozek**, Eye-Witness Reporter
Chicago Sun-Times, March 7, 2006

The fact that a plea deal was never accepted in this case continues to anger this family.

—**Accuser's Mother**
Chicago Sun-Times, March 7, 2006

They [the prosecution] told us many times they didn't think they could win in court.

—Accuser's mother
Chicago Sun-Times, March 7, 2006

ADDING INSULT TO INJURY

A popular proverb speaks fondly of a criminal's inability to escape the "long arm of the law", whose interpretation is meant to identify the fact that no matter how far a criminal runs (as in attempts to escape by any means), the law would sooner or later catch up with him and bring him to justice.

I have nearly lived through a three year period experiencing this very phenomenon, whereby this long arm had reached all the way to Europe. However, in my painful experience and humble opinion, it's really the "long *tentacles* of the law", which might be more applicable and which anyone might want to be concerned with instead.

And by "anyone" I don't mean just criminals or offenders of the law of any kind. I include every average citizen in that category who might never imagine to have any trouble with the law whatsoever.

Don't get me wrong. The mere fact that my son had been finally absolved of the crime that he had been accused of, speaks volumes in support of the fact that our judicial system does work in the end, and that people should have faith in our system of justice. In fact, it is quite amazing that this system had been enacted well over two centuries ago, and while there had been innovations and improvements in virtually all other areas of life since then, this system still works as it had been intended, and certainly is still the best system on the face of this planet today.

The fact that my son had been found guilty of trying to escape prosecution for running away was a condition which he had brought upon himself, and really cannot be considered a flaw of the system. At that point in time, he had chosen to disregard the law, which required him to remain at home in order to stand trial. The underlying premise of guilt or innocence rightfully did not matter in this equation. And while we have lost the money that had been posted for his bond, and while he had been incarcerated during the time that he had waited for his trial, it was really the price that was rightfully paid for that indiscretion. Now, I obviously still have major problems with the institution in which he had been placed, and the co-inhabitants with whom he had to live with, which I still believe to be a malignant flaw, but one which could be easily corrected if the proper incentives were provided (or maybe eliminated) for the individuals making these type of decisions.

And in the end, the flaws of our system can be attributed to individuals taking extraordinary steps, most of which involve the abuse of power which had been entrusted to them. And it's these incentives which certain individuals believe to be entitled to for just doing their jobs. It's the senators whose interests lie in national aspirations reflected in their benevolent gestures, rather than the recognition of repairing their own broken infrastructures. It's the governors who will jump on any bandwagon if it results in more votes, rather than neutrally evaluating the issues at hand. It's the local politicians who provide sought-after-jobs for their supporters in an attempt to strengthen their power base. And it is the prosecutors and detectives who believe that their careers are directly proportional to the number of convictions (or notches) highlighted on their resumes.

Of course, there are hundreds of thousands, if not millions, of public servants who properly perform their duties every day. These include our service men in the armed forces, fire fighters, and yes, even judges, prosecutors and police officers. Most of these individuals are not looking for incentives or rewards for simply doing their jobs. You need only look at the devotion and dedication exhibited by them during the 9-11 disaster.

With this preface in mind, allow me to elaborate on the sordid manipulations that had been attempted by a few individuals who have disguised themselves as public servants and who might not have been mentioned yet. But you be the judge . . .

On July 11, 2005, my 18 year old son Justin was charged with a misdemeanor charge of disorderly conduct, involving a fist fight with two other youths. His court hearing, which would normally be a routine dismissal of the charges after paying a slight fine and stern reprimand, was scheduled for early August of 2005. It was an incident which goes by unnoticed every day all over America.

Coincidentally (and by that I mean surprisingly), Adrian's first adjudication of his flight charges had been scheduled for August 8, 2005.

And it was during that period of time leading up to the August 8th trial date, that offers for a settlement had been actively solicited from the prosecution in Adrian's case.

In a clear interpretation of not recognizing the forest because of all the trees that were obstructing our view, we did not put two and two together, and did not consider the implications of Justin's case with the case involving Adrian.

We were steadfast and determined to prove Adrian's innocence and did not consider the impact our actions might have on Justin, as we had refused to really enter into any negotiations involving Adrian.

And this is where the interpretation of *tentacles* enters into the picture. Arms (as in the long arm of the law) will generally grab and hold you until such time that you are brought to justice. Tentacles, on the other hand, will grab you, encase you and immobilize you from directions, sources, and in manners, you might never expect.

But allow me to explain further.

The incident involving Justin took about all of 15 seconds on that July evening. He was leaving an end-of-school-year celebration attended by about 25 to 30 of his peers at a local forest preserve. As he was leaving to go home, he happened upon a confrontation with two individuals. One individual, who he did not recognize at the time, was about 6 foot tall and seemed well over 200 pounds in weight. The person who he did recognize, and who was a mere acquaintance, was about 5'6" and weighted 125 pound dripping wet. He remembered hearing a girl's cry for help in order to stop what appeared to quickly be escalating into a physical confrontation. Without really considering the consequences, Justin, who at the time was about 5'10 and 155 pounds, stepped in between the two individuals, and fearing that the more serious damage would be dealt by the 6 foot individual, attempted to push him away from the smaller individual. This taller individual didn't seem to appreciate the interference and was about to throw a punch at Justin. In a preemptive attempt to not get hit, Justin landed the first punch, which only served to slightly preoccupy that individual. As Justin was pushing the smaller individual away, the taller boy managed to grab Justin and throw him to the ground, while quickly engaging the smaller boy in a wrestling match. Justin quickly got up and managed to separate the two combatants by grabbing and throwing the smaller boy several feet from the taller boy. Worrying about his own safety at that point in time, Justin concentrated on the actions of the taller boy in case that he had to further defend himself. Luckily, both of the boys went into their respective cars and drove away. Believing this confrontation to have been terminated, Justin proceeded to continue on his way home, when several police cars and an ambulance arrived at the scene.

To make a long story less lengthy, Justin was arrested and taken to the police station where he was bailed out by his mother. Luckily (and by that I am being facetious), his mother had enough sense and experience to immediately involve an attorney. Further problems were alleviated by Campanelli's involvement once he arrived at the police station at about 2:00 AM. The police officers involved knew Campanelli and informed him that this had been merely a teenager skirmish which would neither involve nor entail any real consequences.

And this is what the situation was when we appeared in court for Justin in early August; only days away from Adrian's first trial. We (as well as Campanelli) were concentrating on defending Adrian's ill-advised actions, and really did not feel the need to pay a great deal of attention to the relatively minor inconvenience involving Justin's case. This scenario was equivalent to our defense of a full blown assault against one of our vital chess pieces while not worrying about the seemingly meaningless attack on the position of one of our less valuable pieces . . . chess wise speaking of course. Adrian could be sentenced to 60 years in prison while Justin might get a reprimand.

But this is where the tentacles started to take hold of us, and without noticing, started to encase us in their deadly strangle hold.

The hearing for Justin's misdemeanor charge went by without incident, and the prosecution surprisingly asked the presiding judge for a continuance. We thought that they were simply pre-occupied with more important cases and did not contest their request. A new date was set, and we proceeded to leave the courtroom. However, as soon as we stepped outside the doors, two detectives charged at Justin and arrested him again.

It turned out that his charges were elevated from one count of misdemeanor conduct to two felony charges involving "aggravated assault due to grievous bodily harm" and "aggravated assault on public domain."

This was no longer a teenager's skirmish which would be judged with a slap on the wrist. This now involved a permanent criminal record and possible jail time involving multiple years.

It turned out that the taller boy involved in the confrontation had accused Justin of initiating the confrontation. Furthermore, since the smaller boy had a baseball bat in his car, it was asserted that he had threatened the taller boy with a deadly weapon. Furthermore, the taller boy claimed to have suffered blows to the head and face and damage to his teeth. He had gone to the hospital where his mother worked as a nurse and accused Justin of punching him in the face several times. He further complained that Justin's actions had caused the smaller boy to hit him about five times, crack four of his teeth (even though he had never been hit in the mouth; but he did take the opportunity during his oral examination to have his teeth whitened in the process).

None of this had been known or apparent to Justin at the time of the incident.

The fact that the taller boy had been the middle linebacker on his school's football team as well as the star lacrosse player for the park district, who had played his most recent game that previous Saturday (with possible injuries of the nature described in his accusations ?), had not been mentioned to the police.

The other, more detrimental fact that was unknown at the time as well, was the fact that the taller boy's uncle was a state's attorney, who I assume, must have known Peter Troy's vigil involving my other son, to some degree.

But in the end, the jury realized the matter to have been exactly as it appeared to have been; simply a pushing match between high school students. He was found not guilty and all charges had been dropped.

FINAL RESOLUTION

O n Friday, the 13th of April, 2007, Tarek Ibrahimovic accepted a plea bargain. He received one year for inserting a cigarette into Conny's vagina. This was a misdemeanor charge. He also received four years for running away from justice. This was a felony charge.

He had turned himself in to authorities in December of 2006 after hiding out in Albania for nearly two and a half years, and was waiting for his trial while he was incarcerated in jail at Cook County.

Because of the success that Patrick Campanelli had with my son, Tarek's family had hired him to represent Tarek. It was Campanelli's opinion that the plea arrangements were an equitable resolution to Tarek's ordeal, as they gave a finality to his plight. He could be released after two years. At 3:00 AM on April 15, 2007, he was taken to Stateville Prison to start serving his time. Because of good behavior he was released in April 2008.

After the initial sentencing in 2007, Conny was quoted as being relieved that her ordeal was finally over and that some kind of wrong-doing had finally been admitted to; a sentiment heavily supported by her attorney who was pursuing a civil suit in the amount of $1,300,000 against us. In 2007, this suit was settled by our insurance company for $300,000 payable to the accuser. His fee for his services was a percentage of this award. Our insurance company elected to settle this claim without admitting any guilt, and did so based on disposing this matter in the most economical way. Further litigation, according to their experience, would have cost more than the settlement that had been reached. We had no voice in this matter.

A spokeswoman for one of the sexual violence support services automatically complaint that, "The system worked for the defendant, not the victim. A young woman went through a terrible ordeal. I'm disappointed there were no convictions on sex charges and no one had to register as a sex offender." She obviously had complained before verifying the facts, as she had not bothered to check Jimmy Brown's arrangement. And I wonder how familiar she really was about this case.

My family was attempting to encourage Tarek to not take a plea, as we were once again convinced that no jury would find him guilty of the rape allegations. Especially after two other defendants who had sex with Conny were acquitted, and everyone involved with the humiliating parts had received probation. Furthermore, the Duke University students, who had received national notoriety, had been pronounced innocent in a similar case. Their ordeal had ended because their prosecutor was found guilty of misconduct and falsifying key evidence. Clearly a situation that could have been examined more as it applied to this case. In addition, my son was given probation because he had fled, even though he had been convicted of that felony charge. We clearly felt that those rulings had to be taken into consideration as they applied to Tarek's charges. But that had been on Judge Smierciak's watch.

The prosecutors seemed satisfied as they had finally gotten their conviction. But what had been touted as, ". . . a brutal gang rape of an unconscious victim . . . ," and what had originally been a 140 count felony accusation, had been settled as a one count misdemeanor admission. They had asked for upwards of 60 years, but settled on one year . . . as long as they didn't have to prove their case. And Dick Devine, the head Cook County State's Attorney, was heralded on the front page of the *Chicago Tribune* as prosecuting his next big trial himself; the Brown's Chicken murders of seven victims in 1993 by Juan Luna Jr.. Luna was a fellow inmate of my son while he was held at Cook County. Ultimately, Luna would be sentenced to Life in prison for the murders. Other inmates from his block that had been sentenced by 2008 were, Carlos Magna (15 years for second degree murder), Rafael Belbonte (25 year plea for first degree murder), Cornell Milton (30 years for first degree murder), Antwon Hill (18 year plea for second degree murder), Stanley Garner (50 years for first degree murder), Robert Spurlik (25 years for child molestation), Wayne Willis (44 years for aggravated criminal sexual assault with bodily harm), James DeKalewe (15 years for kidnapping), Edward Leek (75 years for murder), Johnny Ruffin (21 years for murder and arson), Isaac DelRio (12 years for aggravated kidnapping of a child), and Paul Runge (death penalty for murder).

The final resolution occurred in June of 2008. The accuser had still pursued a second civil suit against the accused, the boys themselves. The $300,000 award had been paid on our behalf, the parents of Adrian, because the incident had taken place at our home. In this new suit she was seeking $20,000 from each of the four defendants as well as a personal apology from each of them. However, she quickly settled on $10,000 per person, as none of the boys had any traceable incomes themselves. Also any demands for an apology had been quickly dropped as well. Apparently she now no longer had any hesitation or remorse if she needed to testify and view the video recording, as giving her deposition and explaining the images on the recording would certainly have been the first course of business if no settlement were reached. At the risk of sounding insincere and perhaps even disingenuous, it would seem to me that money was able to sooth her pain and suffering, as she was prepared to relive this experience now. She was ready to scrutinize, analyze and dissect this harrowing ordeal that supposedly had changes her entire life forever. In the end, after deducting her attorney's share, her agony had a price tag of less than $30,000.

Because her name was not released during the criminal trial and because the civil trial was settled out of court, her identity, with a few exceptions, had remained preserved. Other than her friends and the people who had been involved in this matter, no one knew the name of the accuser. With the help of the monetary awards, she was able to move on with her life… words that I believe I had heard her attorney say to the media. And my words might still sound facetious and vindictive, but it is still my belief that she had come to our house that fateful early morning for the sole purpose of a sexual encounter. "...I don't care who I meet, I just want to get laid...," are incendiary words that I will never be able to forget.

Unlike the situation with the accuser, the names of the accused had been widely advertised. In fact, the case is still being adjudicated on the internet on a daily basis. The fallout thereto has been quite severe. In Adrian's case, the probation had restricted his activities, which he was able to mitigate for the most part. However, he could not escape the stigma that was forever attached to his name. He had interviewed with several dozen places for employment, whereby he had usually been informed that he was "as good as hired" after the initial interview, only to be fired as soon as a back-ground check had been obtained. His social life has been affected similarly. In this day and age of "googleing" anyone and anything, a seemingly endless barrage of adverse, ruthless and hostile information will forever soil his image. He will forever be identified as the individual who had "gotten away"... the "criminal" who had beaten the system. While I am tempted to disclose her name now, and I would be entitled to do so legally on account of the civil suit that she had filed, I nevertheless maintain that this injustice was not of her doing. This case, in the end, was not about her. It was the misuse of power by a select and privileged few which had allowed this matter to mushroom into what it had become.

But it is human nature to allow one's emotions to pass judgment. I certainly had been guilty thereof myself on countless occasions, of jumping to conclusions without verifying all the facts. For I too had painted the R & B singer R. Kelly as guilty of child molestation and pornography, for example, before he had his day in court. But in June of 2008 he was exonerated based on the very evidence that the prosecution had offered as undeniable proof, a video recording. But it did not show what the prosecutors had wanted everyone to see. But I still believe that he was found innocent based on poor evidence rather than for not being guilty. In fact, his situation was exactly the point that I was attempting to make all along. R. Kelly was in his 30's while the girl was 13 years of age. His actions were premeditated, and he knew that the girl was a minor. He knew the potential consequences of his actions. He chose to disregard the law. Somehow I fail to understand that a different set of rules would not have applied... should not have applied between his situation and the situation involving my son. And while our legal system is by far the best in the world, there obviously still are a few pot-holes that need to be repaired. Unless we strive and attempt to correct and improve on such inequities, then our judicial system will remain as a stoic court of law and not as a court of justice.

In September 2008, the imposed probation based on the flight charges had run its course. Adrian's probation officer was full of compliments and well wishes as Adrian prepared for his final court appearance in this matter. As he stepped up to Judge Kennedy that day, dressed in his best Sunday suit and an exceedingly sublime smile, the judge refused to acknowledge him by not raising his head or offering any advice normally bestowed by judges under these circumstances. No doubt, he didn't want any more publicity. No doubt, he too was glad that this case was finally over.

UNLAWFUL FLIGHT TO AVOID PROSECUTION - AGGRAVATED CRIMINAL SEXUAL ASSAULT

ADRIAN MISSBRENNER

DESCRIPTION

Date of Birth Used:	March 26, 1985	**Hair:**	Brown
Place of Birth:	Illinois	**Eyes:**	Brown
Height:	5'8"	**Sex:**	Male
Weight:	125 pounds	**Race:**	White
NCIC:	W726415150	**Nationality:**	American
Occupation:	Unknown		
Scars and Marks:	None known		
Remarks:	Missbrenner has ties to Yugoslavia, Croatia, Switzerland and Austria. He may have traveled to Yugoslavia or Mexico.		

CAUTION

Adrian Missbrenner and ▇▇▇▇▇▇▇ are wanted for their alleged involvement in the sexual assault of a 15-year-old female during a late night party on December 7, 2002, in Burr Ridge, Illinois. The assault was videotaped and then distributed among friends of the alleged assailants. Missbrenner and ▇▇▇ were each arrested and charged on December 12, 2002, with aggravated criminal sexual assault and then released on bond.

On September 9, 2004, a state arrest warrant was issued by the Circuit Court of Cook County, Illinois, after Missbrenner failed to appear for a scheduled court proceeding. On September 16, 2004, Missbrenner was charged with unlawful flight to avoid prosecution in a federal arrest warrant which was issued by the United States District Court, Northern District of Illinois, Eastern Division.

REWARD

The FBI is offering a reward for information leading to the arrest of Adrian Missbrenner.

SHOULD BE CONSIDERED ARMED AND DANGEROUS

IF YOU HAVE ANY INFORMATION CONCERNING THIS CASE, PLEASE CONTACT YOUR LOCAL FBI OFFICE OR THE NEAREST AMERICAN EMBASSY OR CONSULATE.

Robert S. Mueller III

ROBERT S. MUELLER, III
DIRECTOR
FEDERAL BUREAU OF INVESTIGATION
UNITED STATES DEPARTMENT OF JUSTICE
WASHINGTON, D.C. 20535
TELEPHONE: (202) 324-3000

FBI WANTED POSTER

REWARD

The FBI is offering a reward for information leading to the arrest of Adrian Missbrenner.

SHOULD BE CONSIDERED ARMED AND DANGEROUS

IF YOU HAVE ANY INFORMATION CONCERNING THIS CASE, PLEASE CONTACT YOUR LOCAL FBI OFFICE OR THE NEAREST AMERICAN EMBASSY OR CONSULATE.

Robert S. Mueller III

ROBERT S. MUELLER, III
DIRECTOR
FEDERAL BUREAU OF INVESTIGATION
UNITED STATES DEPARTMENT OF JUSTICE
WASHINGTON, D.C. 20535
TELEPHONE: (202) 324-3000

NEWSPAPER CLIPPINGS AND HEADLINES

COOK COUNTY SHERIFF'S POLICE

Case Number 02-15578

Statement of Miranda Rights

1. You have the right to remain silent. AM
2. Anything you say can and will be used against you in a court of law. AM
3. You have the right to talk to a lawyer and have him present with you while you are being questioned. AM
4. If you cannot afford to hire a lawyer, one will be appointed to represent you before any questioning, if you wish. AM
5. You can decide at any time to exercise these rights and not answer any questions or make any statements. AM

Waiver of Rights

I have read the above statement of my rights and I understand each of those rights.

12/12 5:34 pm

Witnessed by:

Date: 12 Dec 2002
Time: 5:34 P. M.

SIGNED MIRANDA DISCLAIMER STATEMENT

U. S. Department of Justice

United States Attorney
Northern District of Illinois

| Andrew C. Porter
Assistant United States Attorney | Dirk sen Federal Building
219 South Dearborn Street, 5th Floor
Chicago, Illinois 60604 | Direct Line: (312) 353-5358
Fax: (312) 353-4324 |

March 22, 2005

PATRICK M. CAMPANELLI, ESQ.
8855 South Roberts Road
Hickory Hills, IL 60457

      Re: _**Adrian Missbrenner**_

Dear Mr. Campanelli:

      I understand that you represent Adrian Missbrenner, who is currently facing federal unlawful flight charges and state aggravated criminal sexual assault charges. I further understand that you have made overtures to the Federal Bureau of Investigation about producing your client in exchange for the United States' agreement that the federal unlawful flight charges will be dropped. The United States will agree to dismiss its federal complaint dated September 16, 2004 charging Adrian Missbrenner with unlawful flight in violation of 18 U.S.C. sec. 1073 within 30 days of Mr. Missbrenner's custody on the aggravated criminal sexual assault charges pending in Cook County, Illinois.

      Should you have any questions, you can reach me at (312) 353-5358, or FBI Special Agent Michael Pavia at (312) 786-2652.

Very truly yours,

PATRICK J. FITZGERALD
United States Attorney

By: _____

ANDREW C. PORTER
Assistant United States Attorney

FBI LETTER

```
1-25-2006                    Visitor Pass                      12:13pm
                    COOK COUNTY DEPARTMENT OF CORRECTIONS

--------------------------- Inmate Information -----------------------------

CIMIS #: 2005-0041784 Name: MISSBRENNER, ADRIAN

Current Location: 01-H -01-05    Status: BOOK        Status Date:  5-28-2005

--------------------------- Visitor Information ----------------------------

        Name: MISSBRENNER, DAMIR I

     Address: 8335 COUNTY LINE RD       Apt/Suite:

        City: BURR RIDGE                 State: IL  Zip: 60527

      Status: ACTV  Date:  5-30-2005 Stop Reason:

Relationship: Father

--------------------------- Visit Information ------------------------------

Visit
  ID:2006-0125-1213-2908-26     Date: 1-25-2006 Time In:12:13 Time Out: 0:00

Type:General                               Property:N     Badge #:0000

----------------------------------------------------------------------------

Signature: _____

Issued By: _____
```

RELEASE OF ALL CLAIMS AGAINST ADRIAN MISSBRENNER ONLY

FOR AND IN CONSIDERATION of the payment to me at this time of the sum of Ten thousand dollars ($10,000.00), I, being of lawful age, do hereby release, acquit and forever discharge **ADRIAN MISSBRENNER**, of and from any and all actions, claims, demands, damages, costs, and expenses on account of bodily injuries and psychological damage resulting or to result from an incident that occurred on or about December 6, 2002 and December 7, 2002 at or near 8335 County Line Road, Burr Ridge, Illinois, which is the subject of a lawsuit titled ███████████████ *v. Adrian Missbrenner, et al,* 04 L 13663.

This Release specifically <u>does not</u> release Christopher Robbins, Sonny Smith or Burim Bezeri.

I hereby declare and represent that the injuries sustained may be permanent and progressive and that recovery there from is uncertain and indefinite, and in making this release and agreement it is understood and agreed that I rely wholly upon my judgment, belief and knowledge of the nature, extent and duration of said injuries, and that I have not been influenced to any extent whatever in making this release by any representations or statements regarding said injuries, or regarding any other matters, made by the person, hereby released, or by any person or persons representing him or them, or by any physician or surgeon by him.

It is understood and agreed that this settlement is a compromise of a disputed claim and that the payment is not to be construed as an admission of liability by the party or parties released.

It is further a condition of this settlement and release that the aforesaid ten thousand dollars ($10,000.00) payment be made and that it be received by my counsel within fourteen (14) days of my execution and delivery hereof. Said payment to be payable to "████████████ *and her attorneys, Acosta & Skawski, P.C.*" within the aforementioned fourteen (14) day period. This Agreement and Release is null and void if said payment is not received in compliance herewith.

This release contains the entire agreement between the parties hereto, and the terms of this release are contractual and not a mere recital.

I further state that I have carefully read the foregoing release and know the contents thereof, and I sign the same as my own free act.

WITNESS my hand and seal this ___8th___ day of ___May___, 2008.
Signed in the presence of

_____   ████████████████████

STATE OF _ILLINOIS_)
COUNTY OF _DuPage_)

On this __8th__ day of __May__, 2008, before me personally appeared ████████████ to me known to be the person described herein, and who executed the foregoing instrument and who acknowledged that ___She___ voluntarily executed the same.

_____
NOTARY PUBLIC

My term expire

```
        OFFICIAL SEAL
     MARY JEAN ROSELLI
NOTARY PUBLIC - STATE OF ILLINOIS
MY COMMISSION EXPIRES:05/02/11
```

```
        OFFICIAL SEAL
     MARY JEAN ROSELLI
NOTARY PUBLIC - STATE OF ILLINOIS
MY COMMISSION EXPIRES 05/02/11
```

FINAL SETTLEMENT AGREEMENT